Teaching Creatively

Teaching Creatively: Learning Through Discovery

by

BYRON G. MASSIALAS
and
JACK ZEVIN

ROBERT E. KRIEGER PUBLISHING COMPANY
MALABAR, FLORIDA
1983

Original Edition 1983
(Based upon "Creative Encounters in the Classroom")

Printed and Published by
ROBERT E. KRIEGER PUBLISHING COMPANY, INC.
KRIEGER DRIVE
MALABAR, FL 32950

Library of Congress Cataloging in Publication Data

Massialas, Byron G., 1929–
  Teaching Creatively

  Bibliograpy: p.
  Includes index.
  1. Creative thinking (Education) 2. Learning by
discovery.   I. Zevin, Jack.   II. Title.
LB1062.M35   1983   371.3   81-19375
ISBN 0-89874-437-7   AACR2

Preface to Revised Edition

When the first edition of *Creative Encounters in the Classroom* was issued in 1967 there were hardly any works in the field, works seeking to implement in the classroom the main ideas of the curriculum revolution of the late 50s and the 60s. In the fifteen-some years that followed the initial publication many of these ideas and practices found their way in schools, not only in the United States but in many other countries as well. *Creative Encounters* was issued into the native languages of Germany (1969); South Korea (1972); Japan (1973); and Greece (1975). The book gave some impetus to educators and curriculum writers worldwide to develop new programs of instruction and through them to introduce a new psychological climate for learning. The new climate was characterized by an emphasis on "springboards" which motivated students to advance their own creative ideas, by an encouragement of all, not just a few, students to participate in discussions; and by a stress on the need to justify one's own individual ideas in the open forum of the classroom. In this new environment the teacher assumed the role of a senior colleague who encouraged junior partners to learn by formulating, testing, and writing ideas, concepts and values about and toward people and their social and natural environments.

While the movement gained momentum and virtually all the new programs in the subjects taught in schools were based on the movement's educational philosophy, countermovements began to appear. The "back-to-basics" educational philosophy, for example, observed in the late 70s and early 80s sought to reintroduce learning based on memorization of ideas and facts and ground-covering techniques. This philosophy assumed that the number of pages covered and number of "facts" committed to memory constituted learning. Thus those who have followed this philosophy sought to bring back in the classroom such practices as drill, recitation, and strict discipline. Needless to say, in this environment there was no room for creativity and exploration of new ideas.

The new edition of *Creative Encounters* retitled *Teaching Creatively* seeks to explore and confirm further whether discovery teaching and learning works. To this end the work incorporates new lessons and classroom discussions which illustrate how this approach to learning and instruction is, in fact, being implemented. These lessons, which have been collected from a variety of schools, are placed in the context of an updated discussion of what is inquiry, creativity, conceptual learning, and analyze all the powerful ideas that made the curriculum reform reported here meaningful and appropriate for children and youth of our age. It is intended that the findings and classroom examples included in this volume be studied again by educators to determine whether or not *Creative Encounters* is a jusifiable approach to learning and a true antidote to the "back-to-basics" approach.

BGM
JZ

Preface

The curriculum and the instructional methods of the secondary school in the United States are currently undergoing extensive re-examination and revision. Although it is difficult to locate and isolate the main causes for this large-scale educational re-examination, it is apparent that the ideas resulting from the Woods Hole Conference of September 1959 have had considerable impact on subsequent curriculum change and development. These ideas were reported very competently by Jerome Bruner in *The Process of Education.*

Concepts that included "knowledge structure," "spiral curriculum," "analytic thinking," and "intuitive thinking," "the act of discovery," "learning how to learn," and "heuristic procedures" contained in the report became focal points in education circles and gave rise to nationwide debates on the role of the school in society. When the concepts were further developed and the relevant issues were reasonably clarified, it appeared that the main function of the school was to train children and youth to become rational citizens in pluralistic society. Rational citizens are the ones who can think for themselves, ones who can use the methods of disciplined inquiry to explore concepts in the various domains of knowledge and in the world around them.

The ideas presented by Bruner, and those of like persuasion, found a rather receptive audience in educators specializing in mathematics and the natural and biological sciences. The materials and curricula resulting from such group efforts as the School Mathematics Study Group, the Biological Sciences Curriculum Study, and the Physical Science Study Committee had already begun to emphasize the importance of the structure of organized knowledge or "how things are related," and they sought to develop a school program based on concepts, generalizations, and methods of research in the respective discipline. The social studies and the humanities soon followed this major curricular and instructional reorientation and "Project English" and "Project Social Studies," developed on a national scale, found support in the government and in private foundations and scholarly associations. Although the idea of structure was generally appealing to the latter groups, there was and is some scepticism as to how scientific procedures and discoveries, implicit in Bruner's report which stressed precise measurement, replication, public verification, and prediction, were to apply to topics and problems in the humanities and in the social studies. To put it differently, there was some concern as to how the concepts of inquiry and of structure, developed in the Woods Hole Conference and popularized by Bruner, could relate to ideals, human values, and social problems. Aesthetic, poetic, philosophic, historic, and social experiences or issues, the argument went, were not conducive to the kind of analysis and treatment that the "structure" group proposed. It was further argued that discourse in those areas was inextricably associated with emotions, feelings, appreciations, and nonreplicable human experiences which could not be easily discovered, neatly systematized, and subjected to rigorous scientific examination.

Because there is a lack of experimental evidence or application, many of the foregoing ideas and arguments about teaching and learning have not advanced beyond the conjectural level. The work reported in this book is an initial, hence exploratory, effort to make operational these provocative ideas and to apply them to classroom experiences. More specifically, the work carried on in two public high schools over a period of three years sought to explore ways in which students of secondary-school age may be stimulated by their teacher to order their own learning and to conduct inquiries into crucial problems of society and the world of nature. We have tried to reproduce for the reader the experiences we had in the classroom and to suggest appropriate intellectual climates that will give students the necessary tools to engage in productive thinking. By and large, our work corroborates the validity of the point of view on education expressed at the Woods Hole Conference, but it identifies many new areas and raises issues that need to be studied in the future. A new area explored in this book is inquiry into values and social policies. We hope that this area, which has been neglected perennially by educators, will be more thoroughly investigated by study groups and research centers.

We want to express our appreciation to Murray Hozinsky, Joann Podkul, and Louise Stanek, public school teachers in Chicago, who have aided the investigators in the pursuit of their research. To the hundreds of high school students who participated in this investigation in one way or another, we extend our gratitude.

Ann Arbor, Michigan   *Byron G. Massialas*
January 1967   *Jack Zevin*

Contents

Teaching Creatively

CHAPTER ONE

The Challenge of Ideas: Learning Through Inquiry

THE MANY FACES OF INQUIRY

One of the most important treatises on inquiry or "reflective thinking" is the work of John Dewey, published around the turn of the century. Although various authors since that time have referred to inquiry by using such terms as problem solving, inductive method, creative thinking, scientific method, or conceptual learning, the essential elements of the process in many studies are those identified and elaborated on by Dewey.

According to Dewey, inquiry is the "active, persistent, and careful consideration of any belief or supposed form of knowledge in the light of the grounds that support it and the further conclusions to which it tends."[1] Inquiry generally aims at the grounding of belief through the use of reason, evidence, inference, and generalization. Individuals are prompted to engage in reflective inquiry when faced with a "forked-road situation" or a perplexing problem that causes some discomfiture. Thus thinking moves from a state of doubt or confusion (the prereflective state) to a situation characterized by satisfaction and mastery over the initial conditions that gave rise to doubt and perplexity (the postreflective state). In between these two states of mind there are, according to Dewey, five phases of reflective thought which may be distinguished as follows: (a) suggestion, (b) intellectualization, (c) hypothesis, (d) reasoning, and (e) testing the hypothesis.[2]

[1] John Dewey, *How We Think: A Restatement of the Relation of Thinking to the Education Process*, Boston: D. C. Heath and Company, 1933 (revised edition), p. 9.

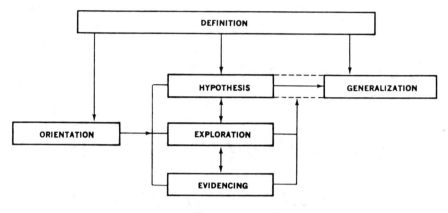

Figure 1

During the first phase, while the person is still under the immediate and direct influence of the felt difficulty, spontaneous suggestions (or wild guesses) are offered which may or may not lead to the solution of the problem. During this phase the mind makes leaps into possible solutions. The second phase which entails a more systematic and rational examination of the problem at hand, results in its location and definition. At this point the person begins to grasp the various aspects of the problem. A working hypothesis is formulated during the third phase of the thinking process (which may or may not derive from the original suggestion) that places subsequent intellectual operations under control and leads to the collection and selection of additional data. The working hypothesis, in other words, serves as the search model that guides the solution of the problem. The fourth phase is the time when the mind relates ideas to one another and traces the logical implication of hypotheses. Here the person tries to reason out what might happen if the proposed solution were acted on. The final phase brings about a confirmation, verification, or rejection of the idea or hypothesis based on direct observation or experimentation. If the hypothesis is confirmed the individual may generalize about its applicability to a category of problems, of which one is the problem that initiated the thought process to begin with; if the hypothesis is not confirmed, the individual may proceed to modify it in the light of this newly acquired experience. In sum, in inquiry intellectual activity is always purposeful, moves from problem to solution, and entails a series of related but operationally distinguishable cognitive tasks (e.g., hypothesizing and testing the hypotheses).

[2] *Ibid.*, pp. 106–118.

As Dewey himself admits, there is nothing sacred about the fore-going sequence of intellectual operations in thinking, nor does it make much difference how many discrete phases of thought we de-velop. It is possible that the elaboration of a hypothesis may take place before the careful clarification or definition of the problem or that a hunch or suggestion may lead without much interference to a valid conclusion. It is also possible that a task or phase may be given a disproportionate amount of time and energy because it met with un-foreseen circumstances and complicating factors. Similarly, there is nothing magic about number five; we can increase or decrease the number of operational categories of thinking to include all of the visi-ble basic elements in the process (e.g., we may add such operations as definition, observation, testing, generalization, or prediction to the list). But no matter how we perceive the order of the intellectual process and the number of phases composing it, there are certain intellectual traits necessary to reflective thinking. Thus Dewey, al-though keeping an open mind on the exact nature of reflective thought, purports to have identified in outline form "the indispensa-ble traits of reflective thinking."[3] It is at this point, perhaps, that Dewey becomes vulnerable to criticism. His critics contend that Dewey outlines the pattern thinking ought to take, using logically distinct steps or phases of the scientific method, but, they assert, he does not take into account how people really think from the psycho-logical viewpoint. Thinking, according to many psychologists, is not as orderly and sequential as Dewey suggests and it entails more complicated operations. As one psychologist put it, "Dewey's five steps . . . represent an idealized picture of logical thought rather than the more haphazard thinking in an ordinary situation, which is influ-enced by biases, needs, and habits."[4]

In addition to logic and science as a source of conceptualizing the process of thinking, we may turn to learning theory, developmental research on children, factor analytic concepts, or psychoanalysis. Al-though it is not the purpose of this book to elaborate on various com-plicated psychological theories relating to inquiry and problem-solving, it might be useful for gaining perspective to discuss briefly each of the foregoing sources.[5]

---

[3]*Ibid.*, p. 116.
[4]David H. Russell, *Children's Thinking*, Boston: Ginn and Company, 1956, pp. 16, 257.
[5]This discussion is based on an essay by J. W. Getzels, "Creative Thinking, Problem-solving, and Instruction," in *Theories of Learning and Instruction*, Ernest R. Hilgard, ed., The Sixty-third Yearbook of the National Society for the Study of Education, Part I, Distributed by the University of Chicago Press, Chicago, Illinois, 1964, pp. 240–267.

Learning theorists take different, often incompatible positions with regard to the process of thinking and learning. For Thorndike or Guthrie, learning, whether it is in the form of reproduction of nonsense words or of construction of high-level mathematical theory, is predicated on a stimulus and response principle. Individuals learn by selecting previous experiences and associations and trying them out in novel situations. For Wertheimer or Goldstein, thinking is distinguished into "ugly thinking" and "productive thinking" the first based on trial and error while the second is based on cognitive reorganization. The problem-solver engaged in productive thinking seeks to find the inner structure of the situation or to find the underlying concepts or principles of a problem. It is suggested that individuals seek to find the underlying structure of a situation naturally and spontaneously unless they are hindered by previous experiences that emphasize "blind association," "ugly trial and error," or ready-made solutions.[6]

Developmental studies of children as presented by the work of Jean Piaget suggests that thinking takes place in stages which are generally determined by the age of the child. From birth to two years of age the child performs only motor actions (the period of "sensory-motor intelligence"). From two to four years the child reasons from the particular to the particular rather than from the particular to the general (induction) or from the general to the particular (deduction)-(the period of "preconceptual" thought). During the next stage, from four to seven years, the child is "not yet freed from perception" (the "intuitive" period). The period between seven and eleven years is characterized by logical processes which are really not dissociated from concrete referents (the period of "concrete operations"). In the final state (i.e., from eleven to fifteen years), the child attains intellectual capability for deductive and inductive reasoning ("formal operations" stage). At this stage the child performs operations which we associate with scientists, logicians, or abstract thinkers. Children now develop the capability to solve all types of logical problems. Over this age span children develop the cognitive apparatus they will have for life. They can solve hypothetical problems and can use scientific reasoning. Piaget's notion of developmental stages in children is not entirely consistent with Bruner's claim that any idea or subject can be taught to any child at any stage of development in an intellectually honest form. It is Bruner's contention, based on research, that the intellectual development of young children can be facilitated and speeded up by introducing appropriate materials, instructional methods, and curricula; for

6*Ibid.*, p. 244.

example, a problems in physics may be presented to children in such a way that it will tempt them to explore and discover its underlying principles and thus move them into the higher stages of cognitive development.[7]

We advocate that the two philosophies are reconcilable. In this sense, the third stage, or operational stage is extremely significant for our model of teaching as introduced in this volume. It is evident, for example, that during this stage children and youth need to develop their cognitive strength, and the instructional program needs to focus on providing this strength. This is done effectively by combining theory with practice, i.e., formal logical operations with concrete problems facing children. Students are given a repertory of puzzling decision-making situations in their immediate environment and are asked to resolve them by applying various concepts and skills. Thus learning becomes a process of dealing with abstract ideas that become more meaningful as they are applied to concrete cases in which the learners themselves are involved.

Guilford represents the factor analytic approach to the study of intellectual behavior. According to him, intellectual performance may be divided into two principal categories: "memory factors and thinking factors." Under "thinking factors" we may distinguish between convergent thinking and divergent thinking, the former involving the generation of new ideas and facts from known information, the latter pertaining to new ideas or data which minimally depend on known information. Convergent thinking implies "a single already ascertained right response," whereas divergent thinking includes "a variety of responses involving 'fluency,' flexibility,' 'originality,' and 'elaboration.' "[8] It is claimed that society and schools generally stress the first kind of thinking, the formal-analytical or the conventional, and that they minimize the creative or imaginative type. Much more is said about formal-analytical or convergent thinking and imaginative-intuitive or divergent thinking later in the study. It suffices to say at this point that, although the process of inquiry is the main topic under consideration, the work focuses on the creative or divergent dimensions of inquiry, particularly as they apply to the teaching of secondary school subjects. For comparative purposes, however, both types of thinking are presented and illustrated.

Some insight into the thinking process is given by those who, like Sigmund Freud, specialize in psychoanalysis. It is suggested that creative thought results from conflict or interplay between "rational

---

[7]Jerome S. Bruner, *The Process of Education*, Cambridge, Mass.: Harvard University Press, 1960, pp. 33–54.
[8]Getzels, op. cit., p. 248.

primary" processes and "rational secondary" processes. The former is an unconscious process; the latter is conscious and controlled. Primary process fantasies, dreams, or plays are the major source of creative thought. In this respect there is an apparent discrepancy between those who emphasize the formal and cognitive aspects of problem solving (such as Dewey who minimized the role of fantasy and imaginative playfulness) and those who see arational or subconscious ("intuitive") elements performing a pivotal role in thinking. These positions, somewhat oversimplified here, and their underlying instructional implications create a real paradox to the education researcher as well as the teacher. This paradox is well summarized in the following statement:

"Despite the self-evident need for conscious effort and rationality in problem-solving, the development of reality-orientation and logic with age, and the required training in reflective forms of reasoning in school, mature creative thinking and innovative problem-solving entail, at least in some degree, a regression to playfulness, fantasy, and the arationality of primary process and childlike modes of thought."[9]

To sum up our discussion to this point, inquiry, as we define it, is behavior which is characterized by a careful exploration of alternatives in seeking a solution to a problem. Although such cognitive tasks as construction of hypotheses, definition of terms, and validation of propositions are critical to the intellectual process, creative ideas and conjectural thinking are essential ingredients as well. "Inquiry," as used in this study, includes both logical and psychological factors or, to use a different expression, both cognitive and affective behaviors. To these two factors we may add another—normative (i.e., inquiry aiming at examining, reconciling, clarifying, or justifying values). When certain judgments are made about what "ought" to be done in a situation or what is ethically good and bad about a behavior, act, or social policy, we operate basically in the normative or value domain. Although we recognize that thinking cannot be neatly categorized, for the purposes of this work we have recorded our classroom observations under three main headings: analytical thinking, creative thinking, and inquiry into values. We discuss these topics in that order.

ANALYTICAL THINKING

Often a distinction is made between analytical and intuitive thinking. Analytical thinking is generally sequential and it proceeds a step

[9]*Ibid.*, p. 251.

at a time. The persons involved in the process are more or less aware of the data, the concepts, and the operations employed; they may use deductive-logical processes in deriving certain conclusions from given premises or they may formulate and execute an experiment using inductive, laboratory, and statistical methods. Intuitive thinking, on the other hand, does not advance in well-defined and observable steps. The thought process does not usually move in any given order—it skips steps, takes short cuts, and makes leaps.

Analytical inquiry or reflection is guided by a purpose (the solution of a problem); it creates alternatives, and it sets controls to check the veracity of propositions and relate them to a more familiar body of theory. We have already referred to Dewey's phases in the complete act of reflective thought. For instructional purposes we may apply the following phases and procedures in fostering the analytical aspect of inquiry:[10]

1. *Orientation.* During this phase the person becomes sensitive to a problem, either by a question asked, an assignment, or an irresolution that is personal in nature.

2. *Hypothesis.* This is a statement of relationship between two or more events or phenomena. The hypothesis seeks to explain the problem or occurrence under consideration, but it escapes the particular by stating the nature of the relationship in general terms. The most important function of the hypothesis is to serve as a search model in collecting relevant information.

3. *Definition.* This task is associated with the meaning and clarification of terms and concepts in statements. We may use dictionary definitions or definitions by connotation, stipulation, or example. Definition does not necessarily follow hypothesis; it is a task that is important to all phases of the thinking process.

4. *Exploration.* Once a hypothesis has been stated in fairly clear terms, we may explore its implications; that is, the person will make certain deductions in the form of "if-then" statements. If the hypothesis is true, then certain consequences will follow. This task actually supplements and reinforces the quest for evidence to ground the hypothesis.

5. *Evidencing.* This is the process of collecting data relating to a hypothesis and to its logical implications. However, the evidence that

---

[10]Based on a model developed by Byron G. Massialas and C. Benjamin Cox in *Inquiry in Social Studies,* New York: McGraw-Hill Book Company, 1966. This model is placed in the "social family" of models in Bruce Joyce's and Marsha Weil's, *Models of Teaching, Second Edition,* Englewood Cliffs, N.J.: Prentice-Hall, Inc., 1980.

is brought to bear on the hypothesis may either confirm or refute the proposed relationship or explanation.

6. *Generalization.* A generalization is a statement or relationship universally applicable to a class of phenomena. Its main function is to explain reliably not only a given problem but a group of problems which share many characteristics. Usually if the original hypothesis passes the empirical and logical tests, it becomes the generalization or conclusion.

For purposes of convenience the six phases of critical inquiry were presented in a sequential order. It should be emphasized, however, that even tasks which are basically analytical entail many nonanalytical or "intuitive" acts. Furthermore, the intellectual operations as outlined here are not by any means performed in an orderly and sequential way in class. Often, many tasks are performed conjointly and, as a consequence, it is extremely difficult to isolate and define the elements inherent in a given task or to begin to establish priorities. Diagramatically the inquiry/analytical process is presented in Figure 1.

The model presented above belongs with other models of teaching to the "social family" or "social interaction family."[11] This family includes, in addition to the "social inquiry" model above, the following:

> Group Investigation; Herbert Thelen, John Dewey
> Laboratory Method; National Training Laboratory (NTL) Bethel, Maine
> Jurisprudential; Donald Oliver, James P. Shaver
> Role Playing; Fannie Shaftel, George Shaftel
> Social Simulation; Sarene Boocock, Harold Guetzkow

The reader interested in examining the key features of these models is directed to the volume by Joyce and Weil which pointedly summarizes all the works.

In discussing the aspects of inquiry that we have called analytical, many authors include a section on material, psychological, and logical fallacies which teachers and their students must guard against. Material fallacies are those that involve faulty classification or generalization. Jumping into conclusions or faulty analogy are examples of material fallacies. Psychological fallacies refer to the use of emotional language, appeals to tradition, authority, and prejudice, and the excessive employment of irrelevant argument. What is known as wishful thinking or rationalization is an illustration of this type of fallacy.

---

[11]Joyce and Weil, *Ibid.*, pp. 219–323.

Finally, logical fallacies refer to various flaws in deductive reasoning; for example, a non sequitur (when conclusions do not logically follow from given premises). Most commonly encountered logical fallacies are "begging the question" and the use of ambiguous terms. Teachers are certainly not expected to be master logicians or advanced laboratory researchers, but they should be cognizant of the major fallacies that may hinder inquiry in the classroom.[12]

Another way of looking at the analytical aspects of thinking is that presented by a committee of college and university examiners in a book entitled, *Taxonomy of Educational Objectives: Handbook I, Cognitive Domain.* The cognitive taxonomy generally deals with educational objectives which focus on knowledge and the development of intellectual skills and abilities. The main goals of the taxonomy are to classify educational objectives under defensible categories and to express these objectives in behaviorally or operationally measurable terms. The taxonomy as it moves from the lower mental processes (knowledge) to the higher mental processes (evaluation) employs six main categories in this order:

1.00 Knowledge
2.00 Comprehension
3.00 Application
4.00 Analysis
5.00 Synthesis
6.00 Evaluation[13]

By knowledge is generally meant the remembering of ideas, material, or phenomena. The student here is expected to store in mind certain information and retrieve it upon request. By comprehension is meant the ability to know what is being com ...unicated, although not necessarily relating it to a larger body of theory. Comprehension, according to the taxonomy, is the lowest level of understanding and it usually involves translation, interpretation, or extrapolation. Application refers to the ability to use abstract principles in concrete situations. The abstractions to be applied to a particular case may be presented in the form of ideas, rules of procedure, or methods. Analysis involves the breakdown of a given material or a communication into its constituent parts. Furthermore, analysis involves an explicit identification of the relationships of the parts. Generally, we may analyze

[12]A brief but good discussion of logical, psychological, and material fallacies in propositions is given by W. Ward Fearnside and William B. Halther, *Fallacy—The Counterfeit of Argument*, Englewood Cliffs, N.J.: Prentice-Hall, 1959.
[13]Benjamin S. Bloom, ed., *Taxonomy of Educational Objectives:* Handbook I, Cognitive Domain, New York: Longmans, Green and Co. (now Longman) 1956.

elements, relationships, or organizational principles. Synthesis aims at putting together the parts or elements of given material to form a coherent whole. Synthesis may entail a reorganization of the constituent elements into a pattern or structure not available before. It is claimed that this category "most clearly provides for creative behavior on the part of the learner."[14] Finally, by evaluation is meant the judging of a communication in terms of a set of criteria, quantitative or qualitative. The validity or accuracy of a theory may be judged by use of internal evidence (e.g., absence of logical fallacies, consistency) or external criteria (e.g., comparison of major theories or generalizations). At this level of behavior some affective considerations enter the picture, for evaluation necessarily implies values and judgments. Note, however, that even though affective behaviors are linked with the cognitive, the major emphasis of the sixth level of the taxonomy is largely intellectual rather than emotional.

As we mentioned earlier inquiry processes using the analytical mode have been applied successfully to teaching virtually every subject in the curriculum, e.g., geography, biology, art, geometry, reading, music, history or science, and involving in addition to regular students, urban and disadvantaged youth, educationally and mentally retarded, the gifted, and adults.[15]

Our discussion of the analytical process is certainly not exhaustive. Many more proposals are grounded in different interpretations of learning, logic, and education goals, but they are beyond the scope of this work.[16] By analytical we mean, for our purposes, the conscious process through which alternative hypotheses are tested and confirmed. The process is generally characterized by cautious, step-by-step methods of research and by conscious avoidance of logical, psychological, and material fallacies and pitfalls. The end product of analytical thinking is reliable explanation, prediction, and control of natural or social phenomena.

[14]*Ibid.*, p. 162.
[15]See for instance, Alice Legenza, "Inquiry Training for Reading and Learning Improvement," *Reading Improvement*, Vol. 15, No. 4 (Winter, 1978), 309–316. Richard D. Shepardson, "Simple Inquiry Games," *Science and Children*, Vol. 15, No. 2 (Oct., 1977), 34–36; L. A. Seymour et al., "A Successful Inquiry Methodology," *American Biology Teacher*, Vol. 36, No. 5 (September, 1974), 349–352; Marion Casey "History as Inquiry: Introducing Gifted Students to History," *Social Studies*, Vol. 70, No. 3 (May–June, 1979), 99–102; Emily F. Elefant "Deaf Children in an Inquiry Training Program," *Volta Review*, Vol. 82, No. 5 (September, 1980), 271–279.
[16]See Bibliography.

CREATIVE THINKING

We have mentioned before that creative thinking as contrasted with analytical thinking makes leaps and does not proceed in easily observable and definable phases. However, as in analytical and cognitive learning, the creative process or creativity is subject to different definitions and interpretations. Although a full-scale analysis and review of the literature on creative thinking is not the purpose here, we present a discussion of the topic so that subsequent illustrative material may be placed in its proper context.

Generally speaking, creativity may be defined in terms of personality, product, process, or environmental conditions. If personality is used as the focus, an examination of the traits that discriminate a creative from a noncreative person may provide possible clues. One author suggests that to some degree a creative person should possess the following traits: intelligence, awareness, fluency, flexibility, originality, elaboration, skepticism, persistence, intellectual "playfulness," humor, nonconformity, and self-confidence.[17] Although no one would argue against the suggested list of characteristics, a main difficulty would come about in their definition and evaluation; that is, we may contend that these categories are not specific enough to allow one to discriminate between a creative and a less creative person. Also, these general traits taken together do not seem to provide adequate grounds to separate the analytically oriented person (the "convergent" type of student, to use Guilford's term) from the creatively oriented person (the "divergent" type). We may, for example, claim the same traits for those whose main concern is to produce and validate ideas, using scientific processes and tools. Perhaps the difference between analytical and creative thinking is not of kind but degree. Many of the studies focusing on personality traits have examined in great detail the background and the life of highly creative people in various fields such as mathematics, music, literature, history, or architecture. By the study of the life patterns of creative individuals such as Einstein, Mozart, Tolstoy, Toynbee, or Frank Lloyd Wright, as presented in biographical or autobiographical sketches, we can identify and abstract certain qualities they shared in common.

There are those who define creativity in terms of producing something new or insightful. To some investigators creative thinking means the production of an idea (e.g., artistic, mechanical, or theoretical) that is new to its creator. To others creativity implies something novel, something that did not previously exist in the same form in the

[17]Kneller, George F., *The Art and Science of Creativity*, New York: Holt, Rinehart, & Winston, 1965, pp. 62–68.

culture. Margaret Mead takes the first position in the following statement:

"To the extent that a person makes, invents, thinks of something that is new to him, he may be said to have performed a creative act. From this point of view the child who rediscovers in the twentieth century that the sum of the square of the hypotenuse of a right-angled triangle equals the sum of the squares of the other two sides is performing as creative an act as did Archimedes, although the implications of the discovery for cultural tradition is zero, since this proposition is already a part of geometry."[18]

On the other hand, there are some writers who must insist that the creative product must make a contribution to the culture and thus "it must be an achievement in its own right."[19] The creative act may entail the rearrangement of existing items of knowledge in a new form or it may require the production of novel elements. In this book we have generally taken the first attitude that interprets creativity in terms of discovery of ideas, relationships, and concepts which are new to the learner but not necessarily new to the culture. We agree with Margaret Mead that the child or adolescent who is able to draw new relationships from limited data is performing an act which is as creative as that of the "great" thinkers and inventors of the past (e.g., Plato, Aristotle, da Vinci, Galileo, or Newton). Such contributions on the part of students should certainly be rewarded.

As we mentioned previously, one of the most original investigators of creativity as a mental process is J. P. Guilford. According to him the intellect consists of 120 different mental factors, of which approximatly 50 are known. These factors or mental abilities may be divided into two general categories—memory abilities and thinking abilities. The second category is further subdivided into three groups of abilities: the cognitive, the productive, and the evaluative. Cognitive abilities relate to recognizing information or being aware of something; productive factors apply to the use of information and the generation of new information; evaluative factors refer to abilities to judge the correctness or suitability of propositions. The productive abilities are of two types, convergent and divergent. Convergent thinking implies a right solution and moves in a conventional way to confirm and verify knowledge (entails a number of analytical tasks). Divergent thinking,

---

[18]"Creativity in Cross-Cultural Perspective," in Harold H. Anderson, ed., *Creativity and Its Cultivation*, New York: Harper and Row, © 1959, p. 223, Reprinted with permission.
[19]Kneller, op. cit., p. 18.

on the other hand, involves a variety of responses to a problem which is not well-defined and which has no established way of solving it. Divergent thinking involves such attributes as fluency, flexibility, and elaboration. For more adequate information on creativity as a mental process the reader is directed to the works of Guilford.

Other researchers operating under the assumption that there are convergent as well as divergent types of students proceeded to analyze creative thinking both as a process and a product. To support their hypothesis that at a high average level of intelligence or above we may clearly distinguish between a highly intelligent student (as measured by IQ tests) and a highly creative student, Getzels and Jackson offered a number of relevant illustrations. In one case students were presented with a picture stimulus depicting a businessman returning from a business trip and were asked to interpret it. The high IQ student gave this answer:

"Mr. Smith is on his way home from a successful business trip. He is very happy and he is thinking about his wonderful family and how glad he will be to see them again. He can picture it, about an hour from now, his plane landing at the airport and Mrs. Smith and their three children all there welcoming him home again."

The highly creative person, on the other hand, interpreted the picture differently:

"This man is flying back from Reno where he just won a divorce from his wife. He couldn't stand to live with her anymore, he told the judge, because she wore so much cold cream on her face at night that her head would skid across the pillow and hit him in the head. He is now contemplating a new skid-proof face cream."

In another situation the picture represented a high school boy doing his homework. The high IQ subject responded to the stimulus picture in the following manner:

"John is a college student who posed for the picture doing his homework. It is an average day with the usual amount of work to do. John took a short break from his studies to pose for the pictures, but he will get back to his work immediately after. He has been working for an hour already and he has an hour's work yet to do. After he finishes he will read a book and then go to bed. This work which he is doing is not especially hard but it has to be done."

The highly creative person responded to the same picture:

"The boy's name is Jack Evans and he is a senior in school who gets C's and B's, hates soccer, does not revolt against convention and has a girl friend named Lois who is a typical sorority fake. He is studying when someone entered the room whom he likes. He has a dull life in terms of anything that is not average. His parents are pleased because they have a red-blooded American boy. Actually, he is horribly average. He will go to college, take over his dad's business, marry a girl, and do absolutely nothing in the long run."[20]

Obviously there are basic differences in response between the highly intelligent and highly creative students as defined and classified by Getzels and Jackson. The response of the former is rather conventional and "typical," the response of the latter is quite original and idiosyncratic. The following differences between the two types may be identified:

1. The highly creative adolescents are more stimulus-free; they are less bound by the instructions given to them than the other group. They structure the task at hand in their own terms.

2. The highly creative members of the group are much more humorous and fanciful. They seem to "experience a special delight in playful intellectual activity for its own sake."

3. The high creative subjects seem to exhibit more violence and aggression. For highly creative students the pictures assume a personal meaning; among high IQ students the pictures have only "superficial representations." In general, the high IQ adolescents "tend to converge on stereotyped meanings, . . . to move toward the model provided by teachers." In contrast, the highly creative students "tend to diverge from stereotyped meanings, to move away from the model provided by teachers. . . ."[21]

So far we have been discussing creativity in terms of personality, process, and product, but creativity can also be examined in terms of environmental conditions or "press." We may identify certain features in the environment which relate to creative thinking either negatively or positively; they either inhibit or facilitate the process of imaginative thought. An example of "press" influences may be derived from this experiment: an audience is presented with four different sound effects from a tape recording, ranging from familiar sounds (with few "missing elements") to less familiar sounds. The listeners are asked to write down a word picture of what was generated by each sound effect in the recording. They are encouraged "to let the imagination swing free." Throughout the experiment the audience is not threatened by

[20]Jacob W. Getzels and Philip W. Jackson, *Creativity and Intelligence: Explorations with Gifted Students*, New York: John Wiley and Sons, 1962, pp. 39–41.
[21]*Ibid.*, pp. 51–52, 60.

evaluative criteria, and an attempt is made to produce the conditions for the audience to have fun and to break any preexisting "sets" between the different sound effects. In the end the audience is asked to identify its favorite image by drawing a new picture. Finally, the audience is asked to describe its experience and point to the elements in the environment that were helpful or restraining. The audience reports such things as "the warm-up process, going from the easy to the difficult, the legitimacy of thinking divergently, freedom from the threat of evaluation, and the like."[22]

As a result of new research findings on creativity, some of which have been reported here, educators sought to develop instructional approaches which would maximize the creative talents of students. Thus *discovery learning* methods have been introduced in a variety of classroom settings. While this book focuses on this method of teaching we make reference here to the works and findings of other investigators and educators utilizing the approach.

Discovery learning can be thought of situations in which students are presented with subject matter in an incomplete form and required to organize it by finding relationships among the facts or events presented through their own efforts rather than passively registering information supplied by the teacher.[23] The goal of teaching through discovery is to encourage students, through various stimuli (usually not standard textbooks) to advance ideas of their own (thus employing their creative talents) in the solution of problems confronting them personally. Some authors draw a distinction between "guided discovery" and "free discovery." Guided discovery usualy refers to formal inquiry processes, much like those discussed in our chapter on analytical thinking. Teacher direction is heavy. Free discovery, on the other hand, is the process where stuents find themselves in an open classroom environment and are motivated by various "springboards" to follow their hunches without necessarily paying much attention to the formal logical and scientific processes involved.[24] Discovery learning seems to have no comparative advantage over formal types of learning as far as attainment of knowledge is concerned. However, "it is superior in motivating students, in the learning of broad concepts and principles, and in developing social skills."[25] The point the

[22] E. Paul Torrance, *Rewarding Creative Behavior: Experiments in Classroom Creativity,* Englewood Cliffs, N.J.: Prentice-Hall, 1965, pp. 9–10.
[23] Derek C. Vidler and Jonathan Levine, "Discovery Learning and Motivation," *College Student Journal,* Vol. 13, No. 4 (Winter, 1979), p. 387.
[24] Kenneth T. Henson, "Discovery Learning," *Contemporary Education,* Vol. 51, No. 2 (Winter, 1980), pp. 101–103.
[25] *Ibid.,* p. 103.

reader should keep in mind when "knowledge" is made reference to, is the concept of "knowledge" that is used. For example, for many of the "back-to-basics" advocates knowledge consists of committing to memory myriads of information items. For those who propose discovery learning, on the other hand, as we do, knowledge is the ability to explain puzzling or perplexing events in one's environment utilizing broad ideas generated on location backed up by one's own personal insights and experiences as well as theorems and facts. More on this later.

Wadsworth, in trying to implement some of Piaget's ideas in the classroom, proposes the introduction of "surprising events" to encourage the acquisition of knowledge among school children. In order to promote cognitive growth "surprise must be surprise to the *individual child.* There is no assurance that what is surprising to one child or to an adult will be surprising to other children. Surprise occurs only when an individual child makes a prediction that *is not* confirmed."[26] Surprise, according to Wadsworth, brings about disequilibrium and provides spontaneous interest in students. All surprising events will not apply equally to all students, therefore the teacher needs to individualize classroom work to the extent possible. Teacher demonstrations are often boring and "fatal from a motivational point of view." Cognitive change can occur only when the student is active. "It is essential that children be given the opportunity to be active with the surprising objects rather than remain passive observers."[27] When examining the material of student exchanges in the classroom presented in this book, the reader should be able to get a better idea of how the concepts of surprising events and active involvement are implemented. In the authors' judgment these two elements are key to the successful implementation of discovery approaches to learning and instruction.

As was the case with the formal, analytical type learning mentioned earlier, discovery approaches have been used in connection with all subjects or courses included in the school curriculum. For example, discovery learning has been used in a calculus and in an algebra class, in history, in science, in landscape archaelogy, in geography, etc.[28]

---

[26] Barry J. Wadsworth, *Piaget for the Classroom Teacher*, New York: Longman, 1978, p. 93.

[27] *Ibid.*, p. 94.

[28] See for example, Thomas W. Shilgalis, "Using Discovery in the Calculus Class," *Mathematics Teacher*, Vol. 68, No. 2 (February, 1975), 144–147; Henry Borenson, "Promoting Discovery in Algebra," *Arithmetic Teacher*, Vol. 71, No. 9, (December, 1978), 751–752; Albert S. Anthony, "What Will George Washington Do? An Exercise in Discovery Learning," *Social Studies*, Vol. 64, No. 6 (November, 1973), 257–262;

Also, it has been used successfully with both gifted and mentally or physically handicapped, with ethnic, linguistic, and racial minorities, and with adults in nonformal education settings.[29]

In this work we are primarily concerned with the group process in class and with the instructional conditions which facilitate learning. Conversely, our work does not deal directly with individual students, their personality and their family background, nor does it try to advance a new theory of creativity. We are basically interested in reproducing as accurately as possible a classroom experience in which creative thought is encouraged and rewarded.

INQUIRY INTO VALUES

To inquire into values is to propose and explicitly or implicitly defend something that "should" or "ought" to be done in the sense that it is desirable. Whether the bone of contention is our policy in the Middle East or whether it is the issue of building a new community juvenile center rather than a new auditorium for musical performances, we inescapably take positions reflecting our personality and cultural setting and we make value judgments or normative statements. We may say, for example, that we ought not to continue our present policy of producing the B-1 bomber and deploying the MX missile because this action may lead to a deterioration of East-West relations, and possibly, war. We may reiterate that a community youth center should take priority over a center for the performing arts because the youth center is more relevant to present-day community problems (e.g., vandalism, juvenile delinquency, high rate of automobile accidents, and race riots). In both cases we are asserting that something (a policy in both of these examples) is worthy or not worthy of being valued, and we are stating the grounds for our assertion. We do not approve the policy of arms buildup because it can lead to a worsening of the cold war; we believe that the building of a new

Shirley M. DeShields, "The Traditional Approach versus the Process-Discovery Approach to the Teaching of Science to Urban Youth," *Journal of Negro Education*, Vol. 44, No. 1 (Winter, 1975), 1–5; Colm O'Brien and Hazel Wheeler, "Discovery Learning in Landscape Archaeology," *Adult Education* (London), Vol. 51, No. 6, (March, 1979), 352–357; H. Wells Singleton, "Mapping for Discovery: A Reflective Thought Exercise," Social Education, Vol. 43, No. 3 (March, 1979), 220–221; Clinton A. Erb, "What Do You See?—A Discovery Approach to Prime Numbers," *Arithmetic Teacher*, Vol. 22, No. 4, (April, 1975), 272–273.

[29]See, for example, Katherine Y. B. Yao, "Teaching Science to Bilingual Children," *Journal of the National Association for Bilingual Education*, Vol. 3, No. 3, (Spring, 1979), 71–76.

youth center may solve some of our youth problems. In other words, we are grounding our value preferences by giving reasons expressed here as consequences. However, the reasons or consequences may not be empirically sound and thus, although we may ground our value assertion in reason, we do not ground it in fact.

It is suggested that value assertions may fall into one of three different categories. The first category includes statements which assert that X is good because it leads to Y. The consequence provides sufficient grounds for valuing X. The assertions about our foreign policy and the new community center above are examples of this type of value statement. The second category includes propositions which assert that X is good because its meaning is entailed in another value, Z. Helping a man in distress is an action worthy of being valued because it is logically entailed in the Judaic-Christian concept of morality or the practice of trial by jury of one's peers is entailed in the Anglo-Saxon system of jurisprudence. Thus, as in geometry in which axioms and principles are logically related to one another, we may ground certain value judgments in the system to which they logically belong, notwithstanding the difficulty that Z might be a loose set of principles, maxims, or exhortations. To the extent, then, that X is systemically a part of Z or is entailed in Z, X is worthy of being valued. The last category includes statements which simply assert a personal preference, "X is good because I like it." If the assertion is merely an expression of personal taste or desire the value under consideration may present very few, if any, negotiable referents. On the other hand, the assertion may imply a host of reasons or warrants which the person may have seriously considered at one time or another. Thus the simple value expression may be the result of prolonged consideration and serious thought. Generally speaking, unless assertions, such as, "I hate blacks," or "I prefer redheads" are open to public negotiation, they remain private and often hinder the process of inquiry in the class.[30]

Controlled inquiry into values implies willingness to open up our personal beliefs to public scrutiny, an acceptance of the democratic process which encourages and legitimizes the expression of conflicting value positions, and a search to find the root base of a given judgment. Furthermore, inquiry into values and norms seeks to establish the warrant of justification of a value assertion. The extent to which value judgments are rationally examined is in part a function of

---

[30]For detailed statements of value judgments in instruction see Massialas and Cox, op. cit., Chapter 7; Hullfish and Smith, op. cit., Chapter 7; and Philip G. Smith, *Philosophy of Education*, New York: Harper and Row, 1964, Chapter 7.

the participants' willingness and ability to provide defensible reasons for the acceptance of such judgments.

It is certainly not the intent of this work to present a comprehensive treatment of all the philosophical aspects of a value assertion. Indeed, a series of volumes may be written on the role of values in the selection of problems, on the distinction between fact and value (the is-ought dichotomy), or on the meanings, grounds, or contexts of values. Nor is it our intent to engage in the intricacies of the current philosophical debate as to whether values are subject to validation or whether they are relative rather than absolute. For our purposes we accept the fact that all humans have biases and values which are inescapably brought to bear on their daily tasks. We recognize, also, that predispositions, appreciations, or values are developed in a given cultural setting, and all cultural agents—the family, the peer group, the ethnic community, the church, the school—play influential roles to varying degrees. We also know that the personality, age, sex, and inherent intelligence of the individual make some difference in the formation of beliefs and values. Most of these topics have now been undergoing careful investigation by anthropologists, sociologists, political scientists, philosophers, and psychologists,[31] who, without any question, will provide considerable assistance to the classroom teacher in dealing responsibly with current social problems and ethical questions. Our main concern in this area is to see how students react to emotionally charged and socially controversial issues in a classroom situation, and to explore various ways in which the teacher may encourage and promote the objective examination of such issues.

It may be helpful at this point to review briefly the second handbook of the *Taxonomy of Educational Objectives* which focuses on the affective domain. The affective domain includes the learning of skills which would enable the individual to take defensible positions on social issues, to apply ethical standards and rules in judging individual or group behavior, and to develop predispositions and orientations toward society within a positive and optimistic framework (increased self-concept). As we have already mentioned, the first handbook develops a scheme which classifies cognitive objectives and

---

[31]See, for example, the special issue of the *Comparative Education Review*, Vol. 21, No. 2 & 3 (June/October, 1977), pp. 151–419 dealing with the impact of socioeconomic factors on educational development, worldwide; Christopher Jencks et al., *Inequality: A Reassessment of the Effect of Family and Schooling in America*, New York: Basic Books, 1972; Otto Klineberg et al., *Students, Values, and Politics: A Cross-Cultural Comparison*, New York: The Free Press, 1979; Edith Blicksilver, ed., *The Ethnic American Woman*, Dubuque, Iowa: Kendall/Hunt Publishing Co., 1978; James M. Becker, ed., *Schooling for a Global Age*, New York: McGraw-Hill, 1979.

tasks under six categories; it begins with the lowest level which is knowledge of facts (remembering) and it ends with the highest level which is evaluation (judgments on the basis of internal evidence or external criteria). Similarly, the classification of educational objectives in the affective domain takes the following form:

1.0 Receiving
2.0 Responding
3.0 Valuing
4.0 Organization
5.0 Characterization by a value or value complex

Theoretically, the process of internalizing a value begins when the interest or attention of individuals is captured by a given stimulus. The individuals operate in the receiving category when they become aware of a phenomenon or a value. Awareness may be followed by a willingness to receive and by controlled or selected attention. At the next taxonomic level the individuals begin to respond to the affective stimuli either by mere compliance with expectations (acquiescence in responding) or by willingly responding to and getting a satisfaction from the stimuli in question. At the third level, valuing, the individuals are internalizing a value in that their behavior is increasingly consistent with that value. The process of valuing or internalization may range from acceptance of a value to preference for a value and to commitment or conviction. At the level of organization, the individuals arrange their values into a system. Two main tasks are involved here—the conceptualization of a value (ability to see how the given value relates to other acceptable values) and organization of a value system (the acceptance of the place of a given value in one's life as a dominant value). Here the individuals try to integrate a value complex of a high order. Characterization is the peak of the process of internalizing a value. At this level individuals have developed a philosophy of life or a view of the cosmos. They have a generalized set (a behavior which has reached such a high degree of internalization that it is displayed spontaneously), and they form a consistent philosophy of life. The classroom typescripts reproduced in this volume present the whole range of responses, thus illustrating for the reader virtually all the categories in the taxonomy.

The foregoing classification of objectives in the affective domain provides a useful tool to the teacher in measuring and explaining student behavior in the classroom. Juxtaposed against the classification of objectives in the cognitive domain, the taxonomy may be used to account for a good portion of all classroom learning activity. Also it should be noted that there is considerable overlap between the two taxonomies and there appears to be a close level-to-level correspondence, especially in steps 1, 4, and 5. For example, some knowledge is required before one is willing to receive a stimulus and respond to it, or, some skill in analysis and evaluation is needed before one can balance or organize one's values in an articulate manner.[32] Thus the complementarity of skills in the two systems becomes apparent.

During the decade of the 1970s, or the post-Vietnam and post-Nixon eras, moral development became a key concern among educators. Prominent among those who sought to explore the matter in depth was Lawrence Kohlberg. Patterned after Piaget's stages of intellectual development, Kohlberg has suggested three levels of moral development in individuals.[33] As Kohlberg explains, moral decisions involve "considerations of the rights of other people and of obligations to them."[34] The levels of moral decision making are the preconventional, the conventional, and the postconventional. The preconventional level is characteristic of children below the ages of nine to eleven (the age range varies with individuals). During this level, "the moral rules and values of society are understood only as 'do's' or 'don't's' associated with punishment." Individuals who function at the second (conventional) level of moral development understand, accept, and attempt "to uphold the values and rules of . . . society." Individuals at the postconventional level critically examine customs and social rules "in terms of universal human rights and duties and universal moral principles."[35]

During the preconventional, or premoral, period children are oriented toward obedience to power and avoidance of punishment. Children respect physical power. The concept of fairness is, "You do something for me; I'll do something for you." At the conventional level (roughly the ages between ten and fourteen), children develop a sense of "good motives" and a concern for others. Children consider it a moral value to maintain the conventional rules of society and satisfy the expectations of others. The postconventional level begins when the individual recognizes individual rights. There is a social contract (in the legalistic sense) between the individual and the society. Fi-

---

[32]David R. Krathwohl, Benjamin S. Bloom, and Bertram B. Masia, *Taxonomy of Educational Objectives: Handbook II, Affective Domain*, New York: David McKay Company, 1964, pp. 49–53.

[33]Lawrence Kohlberg et al., *The Just Community Approach to Corrections: A Manual, Part I* Cambridge, Mass: Moral Education Research Foundation, 1974). See also Lawrence Kohlberg, *Collected Papers on Moral Development and Moral Education II*, Fall 1975 (reprints of articles).

[34]Kohlberg, *The Just Community*, p. 5.

[35]*Ibid.*, p. 1.

nally, the individual reaches a stage where rights are defined as universal principles "of respect for human personality and justice and equality."

What Kohlberg has said about moral development corresponds to what Piaget reported with regard to cognitive and social development. Young children are generally egocentric, but as they grow older they become socialized into the norms and values of the culture and the groups to which they belong. Piaget's stage of concrete operations seems to correspond in part to Kohlberg's conventional level of moral development: Individuals seek to maintain and support the rules of society and its institutions—family, peer group, government, and so forth.

While identifiable stages of intellectual and moral development occur, no learning theorist would suggest that these stages are invariably fixed and limited to the corresponding chronological age of each individual. All factors concerning readiness to learn should be considered. The instructional program should encourage individuals to reach new levels and stages of intellectual and moral development. Bruner, more than anyone else, recognized this when he proposed that "any idea can be represented honestly and usefully in the thought forms of children of school age. . . ."[36]

Before we close this part of the discussion, we must point out that Kohlberg's theories of moral development have recently been challenged by some educators.[37] The challenge is based primarily on Kohlberg's universality and hierarchy of moral stages and on his assumptions of how children learn. One educator suggests that different cultures have different moral norms; thus it would be inappropriate to say that people in those cultures have a low sense of morality if, for example, their sense of justice differs from that found in the West. Another challenger to Kohlberg's theory criticizes his notion that the lower moral stages are not as "good" as the higher stages of moral reasoning. What, ask his critics, are the basic characteristics of Kohlberg's higher stages that make them "better"? Also challenged is Kohlberg's claim that the majority of people cannot go beyond certain moral stages and stay at the level of "conventional morality" (i.e., accepting and maintaining law and order), never developing their own rules based on individual principles of conscience. One educator, Jack Fraenkel, argues that the importance of conventional morality is not duly emphasized by Kohlberg, especially in view of the

---

[36]Bruner, *Process of Education*, p. 33.
[37]David Purpel and Kevin Ryan, eds., *Moral Education . . . It Comes with the Territory* (Berkeley: McCutchan, 1976) pp. 288–307.

fact that the majority of the people seem to remain at that level.[38] Many of these points require further elucidation by Kohlberg if they are to be successfully refuted.

From this analysis it follows that the process of inquiry has many facets and can be examined from several points of view—the logical, the psychological, and the normative. The logical perspective emphasizes the analytical, cognitive, rule-based and sequential processes of thought; it generally seeks to validate and confirm propositions through the use of deductive and inductive processes. The psychological viewpoint seeks to establish the role of creativity and imagination in inquiry as well as the way feelings, appreciations, interests, and values are formed.[39] The normative perspective emphasizes the process through which values and social problems are examined and defended; this perspective may also be called philosophical because it tries to deal responsibly with value judgments and controversial social issues. We know that these dimensions are interrelated and, at times, it becomes extremely difficult to differentiate among them. However, for purposes of study and analysis we have sought to distinguish them by carefully planning relevant instructional sessions (with appropriate materials for each domain) and by recording classroom transactions.

MOTIVATION IN LEARNING

In spite of some uncertainty about the exact relationship between motivation and learning, it cannot be denied that the concept of motivation is an important one in understanding children and their schoolwork. According to some authors, it is possible to classify motives under three main categories: social motives (warmth and nurturance), ego-integrative motives (achievement motives), and curiosity or other cognitive motives.[40] In the first category we may include the motivational dispositions that come about through familial relationships. In this context, warmth and nurture of the child are clearly associated with concept attainment, memory, and maze performance. The second group of motives is characterized by a disposition to achieve and excel, or by what are known as motives of self-actualization or competence. Finally, cognitive and curiosity motives (known in the litera-

---

[38]*Ibid.*, pp. 295–96.

[39]How a value is formed is a psychological question; what should be valued is a philosophical question.

[40]Pauline S. Sears and Ernest R. Hilgard, "The Teacher's Role in the Motivation of the Learner" in *Theories of Learning and Instruction*, op. cit., pp. 182–209.

ture as the "neglected drives") are concerned with knowing, understanding, and explaining the environment. The focus of these motivational dispositions is concepts, ideas, and relationships. Our work of classroom explorations does not ignore the first two categories, but it is concerned, directly or indirectly, with the relationship between ways of motivating students and intellectual performance.

It is commonly held that motivation for learning is partly a function of general social forces, family influences, peer influences, the school milieu, and of the personality of the teacher and the student participant. For example, unless teachers understand and anticipate how a child coming from a culturally deprived environment would react to ideas relating to some traditional academic topics (e.g., biological evolution, political development, or rules of grammar), they will not be very successful in their work. The peer culture also prescribes, implicitly or explicitly, certain behavioral norms which may, in some cases, run counter to teacher efforts and school expectations. Knowing the character, the personality, and the background of each student as well as being sensitive to the cultural context in which young people operate is certainly a basic requisite for any kind of teaching.

Given these factors that relate to classroom motivation, the teacher may use various strategies in order to enhance learning, especially the type of learning that stresses inquiry and the employment of the higher mental processes. In motivating students the teacher may capitalize on student interests, on figures serving as models of behavior, student self-concept, competition, or on a system of rewards or punishments.[41] Use of student personal interests and curiosity and application of a system of rewards and punishments have been fairly common practice among teachers. It is claimed, however, that teacher attempts to capitalize on interests and to provide a number of figures for emulation are necessary but not sufficient conditions for maximizing motivation among students. The most important influence on motivation is "the student's own appraisal of his ability to achieve goals that he considers worthwhile."[42] In other words, the image that students hold of themselves determines to a large extent their goals and their ability and willingness to inquire into matters of social importance. If the view of themselves is limited, then in a variety of ways their work in class will reflect this view—for example, passive listening, unwillingness to challenge knowledge-claims advanced by the

[41]William K. Durr, *The Gifted Student*, New York: Oxford University Press, 1964, pp. 202–211. Also see, J. S. Renzulli and C. H. Smith, "Two Approaches to Identification of Gifted Students," *Exceptional Children*, Vol. 43 (1977), 512–518.
[42]Durr, p. 207.

teacher or other class members, or psychological withdrawal. When students begin to clarify their goals, take appropriate measures to meet their goals, and evaluate their own performance, they actually begin to function as autonomous, self-motivating persons, capable of organizing their own learning experiences.

It is this conception of motivation that Jerome Bruner advances in making a case for the "autonomy of self-reward" and for maximizing the conditions for inquiry.[43] Citing psychological research, Bruner indicates that encouraging the students to develop an image of self-capability and of individual accomplishment leads to a quest for knowledge which is intrinsically rewarding. When students are directly engaged in the process of exploration and confirmation of propositions, when they develop their own learning objectives, and when they plan their own strategies and techniques of investigation, they have achieved a high level of autonomy. The motivation to reach this level through inquiry and exploration is intrinsic (comes from within) rather than extrinsic (enforced by the teacher). Thus, in the words of the Affective Taxonomy, one has reached a point at which the quest to know is incorporated into one's character and becomes a part of one's philosophy of life. The sustained search to explain the world becomes its own reward.

It is this image of the self-rewarding school experience that we had in mind when we designed and executed the experiences reported here. We generally assumed that student ability to reason and to explain natural and social phenomena is in part a function of motivation level. If students are sufficiently motivated they will go to great lengths in planning strategies to figure out things for themselves, and their efforts will persist over a period of time. This assumption was borne out by our work.

INQUIRY LEARNING AND THE CLASSROOM TEACHER

A class that is directed toward inquiry needs teachers who have internalized the value of inquiry at the highest level of the taxonomy. As in student motivation, teacher motivation should provide its own self-sustaining rewards. When teachers depend primarily on external rewards (e.g., from the school administration, from parents of students, or from community pressure groups), their dependency is very likely to be reflected in their students who in turn may rely on the teachers for the authoritative allocation of values. Teachers who see

[43] Jerome S. Bruner, "The Act of Discovery," *Harvard Educational Review* 31: 21–32, No. 1 (1961).

their classroom objectives from an inquiry vantage point are inspired and motivated from within—the reward of inquiry is the conduct of inquiry.

It is claimed that the classroom role of the teacher who is inquiry-oriented is ambiguous, and it does not lend itself to "the transmission of the accumulated knowledge and wisdom of a culture."[44] Although we do not want to go into the many-faceted philosophical question as to the proper role of the school approaching the year 2000, we certainly agree with several authors and national commissions that our culture has reached a point of crisis, that we need to look at our social problems critically and judiciously, and that we need to train citizens who, in the true Periclean spirit, are "sound judges of policy."[45]

The goal of providing the conditions to create this critical-mindedness among young people is certainly consistent with the inquiry orientation of this work. Also, we feel that the role of the inquiry- or discovery-centered teacher is no more ambiguous than that of a traditional class where the instructor emphasizes the importance of hypothesis, exploration, validation, generalization—and then turns around and tells the students without any apparent equivocation what is "right" or "wrong" with a policy or what is "true" or "false" in a knowledge claim. If "ambiguous" means inconsistent, it is obvious that many examples of inconsistency, as in the case just given, characterize the "traditional" classroom, in that often teachers do not practice what they preach. If by "ambiguous," however, is meant an attitude which encourages innovation and experimentation, which frees individual intelligence, which invites opinions, suggestions, and the exploration of alternatives, then we think that this attitude comes very close to the one we have taken in this volume.

We believe that this attitude is the only defensible one that an inquiry-directed teacher may assume. Finally, if by "ambiguous" it is meant that teachers do not conform to the image of the classroom instructors who give all the answers in a conclusive manner and that they are performing in entirely new roles, we think it is time that the new teacher roles become part of our culture and educational development. The introduction of new teacher roles does not create any more ambiguity than the introduction of any new idea or invention in

[44]B. F. Skinner, "Why Teachers Fail," *Saturday Review*, LXVIII, No. 42, October 16, 1965, p. 101.
[45]See, for example, *Education for Responsible Citizenship: The Report of the National Task Force on Citizenship Education*, New York: McGraw-Hill, 1977; *Youth, Transition to Adulthood: Report on the Panel on Youth of the President's Science Advisory Committee*, Chicago: University of Chicago Press, 1974.

society. To hold back any new technological or social invention or idea because it may create role ambiguity or social anomaly (requiring, perhaps, readjustment) is not a tenable position in our civilization. It is like saying that the ethnic minorities' full participation in the cultural and technological life of our society and the creation of new roles for them lead to role ambiguity, hence we should not encourage it. The same unwarranted indictment may be expressed against any people or institutions that are assuming new roles in society.

An inquiry-centered classroom requires certain changes in the role of the teacher as well as in the role of the student. We have already mentioned that in the new environment the student participates directly in the formation and testing of ideas. Teachers no longer exercise a monopoly over discussion and they are no longer the undisputed authority on all matters of importance. It is common to refer to the foregoing teacher roles as nondirective. Although the term "nondirective" may describe part of the new roles it does not embrace several new teacher functions. In our experience with inquiry-centered discourse, teachers generally perform the following major roles:

1. They plan very carefully the topics, ideas, and generalizations that the class may want to explore, and they organize and time the spacing and sequence of the materials. They make available a wide variety of resources and material for student use.

2. Often they introduce the initial material that will serve as a springboard for inquiry and discussion. The preparation that goes into the construction of this material can never be overestimated. The aim here is to create an environment where students react freely to the initial springboards which serve as "jumping off" points.

3. They challenge and continuously prod the students to explore and test new alternatives. Students talk more than the teachers. When the teachers talk, they question, not tell. Most discussions (at least 95 percent) are based on ideas generated by the students themselves.

4. They insist on the communication of beliefs in public, and they ask for the defensibility of statements. They try to develop the notion that an idea or knowledge-claim is as good as its evidential base presented in the open forum of ideas. Questions are directed toward encouraging students to test the validity of their ideas in a broad context of experience.

5. They summarize, recapitulate, and ask for clarification of points made by the students. They stress the use of ideas rather than clerical tasks, such as record keeping and busy work. They provide for flexible seating, student movement, and maximum student use of materials and resources.

6. During times of impasse they may raise additional questions regarding the problem at hand. These questions may help the class to see alternative ways of solving a problem. They may also encourage the more reticent students to take an active role in classroom activities.

7. They legitimize creative expression. In contradistinction to traditional teachers who frown upon ideas that are unorthodox, the inquiry-oriented teachers constantly encourage the students "to play their hunches" and to conjecture. They consider this activity to be the core of formal classroom instruction. They avoid judging or criticizing ideas offered by students.

8. They perform some managerial tasks such as recognizing students and making class announcements. Class dialogue is conducted in a fashion that emphasizes courtesy and willingness to listen to each person's ideas. This climate of classroom interaction emerges naturally. It is not superimposed through the use of external rewards and punishments.

9. They form an environment in which concepts, ethical principles, social issues, policy decisions, attitudes and values are legitimate areas for discussion. All topics are critically examined, not "taught" as closed issues with a single "right" solution. The use of unfounded, emotionally charged language is minimized in discussing attitudes and values.

10. They state their instructional objectives clearly so that they can ascertain whether they have achieved them. They use evaluation measures that relate directly to their stated objectives, and they share the results of evaluation with the students, identifying strengths as well as areas where both need to improve. They consider evaluation to be a means to improve instruction, not to judge people.

Many of the teacher roles above in relation to increasing student thinking are substantiated by research. Gallagher, for example, found that student expressive behavior in the classroom depends a great deal on "the teacher's style of question asking" and "the goals of the teacher in a given lesson."[46]

All in all, we may say that the new teacher role is dialectical rather than didactic in the sense that it assumes that students will learn more when they are given the opportunity to participate in discovering ideas and relationships for themselves. This role, briefly described

---

[46]James J. Gallagher, "Expressive Thought by Gifted Children in the Classroom," in James Raths, John R. Pancella, James S. Van Ness, eds., *Studying Teaching, Second Edition*, Englewood Cliffs, N.J.: Prentice-Hall, 1971, p. 306.

here, will become clearer as we present the case studies of our experiences.

THE AIMS AND PROCEDURES OF THIS BOOK

We should state at the outset that this work and the direction it has taken have been greatly influenced by Jerome Bruner's *The Process of Education* and his articles and monographs on the act of discovery. Several concepts which may be attributed to Bruner and his associates, such as "intuitive thinking," and "analytic thinking," "learning through discovery," and "the structure of a discipline" along with a number of related hypotheses, gave us the theoretical framework and the initial focus in carrying out this work.

In general, we sought to explore further the ideas generated by Bruner's proposal and to test several hypotheses on instruction in actual classroom practice. Although many claims advanced by Bruner were confirmed, there were some which gave rise to discussion and reconsideration. For example, on the conclusion of our experience we were not as sure as when we started out that each discipline has a discrete knowledge structure that can be learned. The concept of structure may be debated on three planes:

1. The fact that if there is a distinguishable structure separating sociology from anthropology or from any other social sciences it is at best invisible—the various fields of study within the social sciences, (and in the natural sciences or in the humanities as well) are not discrete since they basically deal with broad social concepts and employ similar methods of investigation. The relation of two or more disciplines is further indicated by looking at such college offerings as political sociology, economic history, social psychology, and historical geography. A case can also be made regarding the claimed separation between the humanities, the social sciences, and the natural sciences. Where do subjects such as these belong: environmental education, computer science, consumer education, women's studies, business math? Although there are concepts and tools of inquiry that are peculiar to a field of knowledge, there are as many that are shared by all.

2. The emphasis on the structure of knowledge leaves very little room for values, issues, and social policies which are essential for the survival of every society. We felt that concepts and skills relating to value inquiry should be developed with the same care and rigor as cognitive skills dealing with analytic and empirically testable ideas. Consequently, our experience includes a unit dealing with value judgments and controversial issues.

3. The concept of structure implies to a degree that knowledge can be separated from the knower. This assumption may be challenged because the learners incorporate their own personality into what is learned about a subject, they make different use of it, and they attach different meanings to objects in nature. They also vary in the manner and extent of creating new ideas. For the foregoing reasons, we do not want to identify ourselves with a narrow definition of structure. Rather, we aim ultimately at familiarizing students with the concepts and methods of several fields of study and making them relate these concepts and tools to their own personalities, experiences, and to their own ideas about resolving crucial problems and issues of mankind.

The series of case studies and dialogues reported here are some of the results of our wish to explore the various aspects of teaching through inquiry. In more specific terms the purposes of these materials are as follows:

1. To test some hypotheses about the degree of student ability to explore and confirm alternative solutions to problems encountered in the classroom and in their own life.
2. To test some ideas about the relationship between independent inquiry and motivation to learn.
3. To reproduce as accurately as possible the verbal transactions in live classrooms, so that the reader can get an insight into the creative process and how it can be fostered.
4. To identify and describe some of the logical operations performed by high school students.
5. To describe and analyze the role of the teacher and the student in a climate aiming at generating inquiry learning.
6. To examine the kinds of materials and classroom aids that may be used in the conduct of inquiry, and to present them as models to interested teachers.

To accomplish these somewhat ambitious goals we began to organize a series of studies in the Chicago public schools. One of the authors, Jack Zevin, taught most of the experimental courses in which the case studies narrated here were developed. During the course of our work, we utilized the services of several colleagues who expressed interest in this area of endeavor and who opened their own classes to similar types of exploration. Also, in one way or another we received considerable help from our own high school students—with the operation of tape recorders, with stenographic assistance, and with other important tasks in the classroom. Most of our case studies were conducted with "average" or "slightly above average" high school students. For comparative purposes, however, we have also included dialogues from "below average" groups. We indicate the specific characteristics of the group in each session. The material presented here goes beyond those classes taught in Chicago. For example, it incorporates new experiences provided by former graduate students and colleagues in other sites such as in New York City.

It should be stated explicitly that we have not sought to discover any foolproof formulas that will revolutionize curriculum and instruction. Nor did we seek to illustrate the range of student ability and quest for independence and to reach definite conclusions. Although we have confirmed some of the ideas about teaching and learning mentioned earlier, we have suggested new ones that may be explored in future studies. Our work is exploratory in nature. We hope that our explorations will be followed by others.

CHAPTER TWO

Analytical Episodes

We have divided examples of classroom exchanges into three general categories: analytical episodes, discovery episodes, and episodes focused principally upon the examination of values. As introduced previously, analytical types of lessons stress specific ideas or propositions which are either "given" by the material or offered by the teachers. These ideas are then examined in a careful and logical manner and later tested or cross-examined for reliability and accuracy against related documents, data, and authoritative references.

Analysis is basic to all reasoning in problem-solving situations, and is allied to the more open-ended processes of discovery and value examination. Typically, analytical discussions move from the recognition of a problem to the search for a solution incorporating along the way several important skills of critical thinking, for example, constructing a hypothesis, defining the terms of the hypothesis, probing the assumptions behind the main idea, tracing logical implications, testing against evidence, and generalizing.

An important result of the whole process is to formulate a statement of relationship about phenomena which is grounded in evidence. In other words, analysis is characterized by the conscious verbal expression of connection between interpretation or theories and the data which suggest these conclusions, however, tentative or solid. It is sometimes difficult to distinguish between discovery and analytical episodes since both share procedures and logical operations centered on a data base acting as the springboard of thought. Nevertheless, there are distinctions in the process itself and in the line of reasoning followed. Analytical thinking tends to move in sequential and orderly steps, and is often deductive for lengthy periods of time, whereas creative thinking tends to progress in leaps and swift turnings which may bring out unfamiliar and unusual relationships or develop full-blown hypotheses before the data seem thoroughly digested. Discovery or creative episodes tend also to emphasize inductive processes more than the deductive, although both remain rooted in evidence and require, at some point, a defensible logic to explain conclusions. Furthermore, analytical thought stresses more explicit and public expression while the creative tends to display only the peaks and flashes of the reasoning that are expressed in verbal insights. We would submit that truly powerful inferences can only occur if the student has somehow absorbed and critically reviewed a quantity of information related to a problem. Can any of us escape "doing our homework," whether completing a straight-line task or engaging in creative reasoning? Thus, analytical lessons may be viewed as those dominated by the processes of interpretation and inferences with a strong basis in data, whether art, music, literature, scientific experiment, historical document, or textual. The analytical episodes that follow are presented as examples of critical thinking in the classroom. Each example represents a different subject or way of building reasoning skills. All are attempts to deal creatively with topics commonly taught at the elementary and secondary levels.

In the lesson that follows, a passage from a popular history text about non-Western cultures was presented for discussion to a world history class composed of students of average to somewhat above-average intellectual ability. The social studies course was offered at the sophomore level in high school and included historical topics from the Renaissance to the present day. At the time of the transcription, this class had met for about five months and the students had become accustomed to the inquiry approach utilized by their teacher during this period.

THE NATURE OF THE NON-WESTERN WORLD

"The influx of immigrants from Yemen, Iraq, and other non-Western areas means that today 40 per cent of Israel's population is non-Western in origin. It is predicted that within a decade the population of the country will be 60 per cent non-Western. The more non-Western Israel becomes, the sooner and the more effectively it will fit into the Middle East—and we must remember that, whatever may be the intellectual and spiritual attachments of Israel's European-born population, the new state, for better or for worse, must live in the Middle East, and not in Europe or the United States,"[1]

[1]Vera Micheles Dean, *The Nature of the Non-Western World*, New York: New American Library of World Literature, 1960, p. 65. Reprinted by permission.

TEACHER.   Who would like to interpret the next passage? Look on page 65.

KATHY.   Well, it tells us about the immigration of non-Western Jews to Israel, and predicts that they will soon outnumber the European or Western Jews. I'm not sure of this, but the author seems to be saying that, as Israel's people become more Oriental so will Israel, and that this will help the country fit into the Middle East better.

STEVE.   I think this is a terrible passage.

TEACHER.   Why so?

STEVE.   Because it's wrong.

TEACHER.   Why?

STEVE.   Well, for one thing, how can Israel fit into the Middle East if the Arabs don't want it to happen? Maybe the author thinks they should become Arabs.

RANDY.   Also, as far as I know, the Arabs are having a great deal of trouble Westernizing. Why should Israel become like them? That would be a step backward for Israel.

HELEN.   Well, maybe the author means that Israel should develop its own special brand of life that combines Western life with that of its Arab neighbors.

STEVE.   That might be, but she doesn't really say so. She says that as Israel becomes less Western, the better it will become a part of the Middle Eastern way of life.

BOB.   I have something to add, (*pause*). How can Israel fit in with its neighbors if they are at war with her? That's pretty hard to do, isn't it?

MARY.   What is Israel supposed to fit in with? Since we've been studying something about the Middle East, I know that all those neighbors of Israel aren't the same at all. Lebanon, I think, is more Christian than Moslem; whereas most Arabs are supposed to be Moslem. What exactly is Israel going to fit in with?

BILL.   Furthermore, from what we read out of Dean's book, Israel is a nation with its own way of life, traditions, customs, and ideas. I thought nations generally try to set themselves apart from other nations. People in different countries feel different. If not, then why are they separated?

KAREN.   If we Americans felt like Canadians we could join them and call off the whole thing.

GEORGE.   I think Egypt, Israel's worst enemy, is trying to find its own special way of life. That speech by Nasser that we read points this out.

SHARON. Doesn't each person have the right to choose his own destiny? I think Israel has already chosen a Western democratic, industrial civilization like the U.S. or England. It has chosen its own national language, customs, and laws. If that's what the people over there want, why should they bother to become like their neighbors?

JOHN. Well, they could become a little like their neighbors. For instance, Israel's stamps are printed in Arabic, as well as in English and Hebrew.

SHARON. But that might be because of all the Arabs still in Israel, and anyway, if you learn your neigbor's language, that doesn't mean you like him or will imitate him.

JOHN. I guess you're right.

KAREN. Couldn't we also say that, since a country can choose to be whatever it likes, Vera Dean is wrong about the business of population?

TEACHER. Would you explain what you mean by that?

KAREN. I mean her statement that the more non-Western Israel's population becomes the more non-Western Israel becomes.

GEORGE. Why should it? The Japanese are not even of the white race and they have Westernized, at least to a great extent.

HELEN. Add to that *all* the underdeveloped countries that want to become rich and industrial like our country.

STEVE. I think the author is inconsistent. In one place in the book she talks about all the countries that are trying to Westernize and want to become nations, and now she seems to be saying that all this doesn't apply to Israel.

KAREN. Why does any country have to become like any other country near it? Or even far from it? Why should Israel fit in with Arab neighbors? Any country can make itself into whatever it likes if it has the will power.

GWEN. Saying that Israel should fit in with its neighbors means that Australia, Japan, Turkey, and other countries should give up being Western, or trying to Westernize.

BILL. Puerto Rico also ought to become more Latin American than American.

BOB. Hey! I just thought of something, even the U.S.A. should not even be Western. All our Southern Latin American neighbors are very different from us, and we're not like them.

KATHY. This whole thing has nothing to do with place, or where a country is located; it depends on choice and traditions.

GEORGE. Yes, the U.S.A. would be a good example. I think that the

United States is a country mostly of English traditions, yet probably a majority of people living here are the descendants of immigrants who were not of English descent and traditions.

JOHN.   My own parents had to take "Americanization" courses when they got here. They told me about it. This just goes to show that any country can become, by choice, what it wishes to become. Also, any country, like the United States, can help newcomers to believe in the traditions of their new home. This goes for Israel, too.

MARY.   Yes, and the author is wrong on both counts. Just because Israel's people are becoming non-Western in origin it doesn't mean that the country will become non-Western. They can try to make the newcomers more like themselves.

KATHY.   And no country has to fit in any particular place with any neighboring states if it doesn't want to. If a country is located in a certain place, it still doesn't have to be like its neighbors, or become like anyone. It can even become very different from its neighbors like Japan did.

This transcription demonstrates the manner in which a fairly sophisticated and knowledgeable high school world history class analyzed, criticized, and tested an idea extracted from a passage in a book. The students began their criticism of the passage in a very direct way; they brought information to bear on the situation of Israel, particularly in relation to some of its internal and external difficulties. As the class tested the author's claims about Israel against their own knowledge of it, they moved in the direction of identifying the broader generalizations underlying the quotation in question. These generalizations or relationships, as the students perceived them, might be paraphrased and stated as follows:

1. The more non-Western a country's population is in ethnic origin, the more non-Western that country will be.
2. Countries should develop in such a way as to fit in with the civilization and culture of their neighbors.

After these two generalizations had been more or less identified, the comments of the class moved away from the specific case of Israel to a search of the globe for examples to use as tests for these generalizations. Evidence was brought in to support or refute the individual interpretations of the ideas implicit in the passage. As the class considered the implication of the author's proposition, they became increasingly critical of them.

The foregoing episode illustrates the way in which students engage in inquiry. Among the inquiry tasks performed in this dialogue were (a) the identification of hypotheses implied in a statement, (b) the tracing of the logical consequence of the hypotheses, (c) the testing of the original hypotheses and their consequences against knowledge about similar experiences of other people, and (d) the conclusion that the ideas under scrutiny are not borne out by the evidence.

APPLYING AND TESTING PRINCIPLES ON EVOLUTION

Thirty-one students, almost all high school freshmen, were enrolled in a course entitled early world history. This particular class was not being taught through any of the traditional textbook approaches, but through a unit study of the evolution of man, developed by the Anthropology Curriculum Study Project. The group had already spent a good deal of time studying man from his earliest known beginnings to his present-day development. The teaching materials involved in this course generally represented a synthesis of many disciplines, especially archaeology, anthropology, and biology.

The classroom dialogue presented on the following pages constitutes somewhat of a digression from the main body of the unit, but it is offered as an example of the way in which a class may be prodded into understanding and applying basic scientific concepts—in this case the concept of evolution. The students had not only been studying the evolution of man (i.e., changes in the biological make-up of man), but had also been attempting to establish for themselves a clear idea of the meaning of evolution. They had spent a considerable amount of time reading literature describing primate fossils found throughout the world. The group had thus acquired a general notion of the types, ages, and distributions of a variety of mammalian fossils. The fact that there has been a complete absence to date of monkeys, apes, or the remains of ancient man in Australia aroused the curiosity of several members of the class who promptly requested that the teacher explain the peculiar lack of primates in this continent. The class knew that monkeys had been found in South America; monkeys, apes, and ancient man in Africa, Asia, and Europe; and modern man throughout the world. However, the instructor, rather than solving the students' problem, turned the entire question over to the group in order to encourage independent thinking. This task was accomplished mainly by (a) not giving direct answers to questions, and (b) developing a chain of interrelated questions that were put to the students to answer them as best they could. The discussion and response to the interrogation that ensued are given in their entirely in the following exchange:

BRUCE.   Why were no apes or monkeys or ancient men found in Australia?

TEACHER.   Why do you think they were not found there?

BRUCE.   I'm not sure . . .

TOM.   Maybe they died out there and the men that live there now came recently.

DIANE.   The men probably came recently, but if they died out you would have found some old bones in Australia, and they haven't. That means they never lived there.

TEACHER.   What can you say about Australia if no remains of any primates were found there?

RANDY.   They never got there.

TEACHER.   Is that all you can get out of this idea?

JOHN.   If they never got there at all, then they didn't evolve there.

BARBARA.   Then what animals live there? I know something lives there.

MYRON.   The animals that live there are not like any other animals anywhere on earth. All the animals that live, or almost all, are like the opossum—they have babies in pouches.

TOM.   Say! That's right. Kangaroos are like that, and so are koala bears. They look like teddy bears.

MYRON.   Duck-billed platypuses live there, too. I have a picture of one here in my science book.

TEACHER.   Why don't you pass it around?

(*Book is passed around.*)

DALE.   It says here that the platypus has fur, is warm-blooded, and lays eggs. What a peculiar animal.

TEACHER.   Well, what does all this information tell you about Australia?

RANDY.   Australian animals were there before other mammals evolved and before monkeys, apes, or men evolved.

TEACHER.   So? What about Australia?

BARBARA.   Australia must be the oldest continent, and probably broke away from the other continents a long time ago.

DANNY.   Then how did modern man get there?

MYRON.   He probably came by way of the islands that you can see on the map over there.

TEACHER.   Show us, Myron.

MYRON.   Here. (*traces the East Indies from Southeast Asia through New Guinea to Australia*)

(*several minutes pause*)

BRUCE.   Maybe it was North and South America.

TEACHER.   Why?

BRUCE.   Well, only modern men and monkeys are found in North and South America. There are no apes or ancient cave men like there are in Africa.

TEACHER.   What does that show us?

DENNIS.   It shows us that North and South America probably got separated from the other continents after Australia and apes and ancient men never got there. That means man did not evolve there and neither did apes. The modern men that came there were Indians.

DANNY.   Maybe South America was once attached to Africa the way Australia was attached to Asia.

TEACHER.   Why do you think that?

DANNY.   Because both Africa and South America have plenty of monkeys around. They broke off from each other while monkeys were evolving, but before apes.

CARY.   And Australia broke away from Asia before monkeys evolved, and before most other animals that we know evolved, like lions, deer, horses, pigs, and elephants.

TEACHER.   Does this interpretation sound reasonable to everyone?

(No further comments made or questions raised.)

TEACHER.   OK then, I have a problem for you. Listen closely. What if I told you that there is an island called Madagascar that separated from Africa a long time *after* Australia separated from Asia. However, it separated from Africa *before* South America became disconnected. Let's just suppose that this is correct, then what kind of animals would you find on Madagascar?

(Teacher repeats the supposition.)

GAYLE.   It would have to be some kind of in-between type animal.

DIANE.   If that island broke away from Africa a long time after Australia separated from Asia, but before South America, then cats, dogs, deer, and other common animals probably would live there.

TOM.   But not monkeys.

DENNIS.   Hmmm! Then the animals would have to be between the evolution of cats or dogs and monkeys since monkeys evolved after most other common mammals that we know about.

SANDY.   They'd probably look like half-monkey and half-dog. Or maybe half-cat and half-monkey. They must be pretty funny looking.

BRUCE.   We'd have to find in-between creatures on Madagascar.

BARBARA.   They might just be beginning to turn into monkeys.

TEACHER.   Does anyone here know what these animals are called, or what most of them are named?

SANDY.   You mean we were right?

TEACHER.   You've come very close.

DENNIS.   Tell us what they are called so we can,look them up. I want to see one.

MYRON.   I think I've seen some, but I don't remember what they are called.

GAYLE.   Show us a picture of one.

DIANE.   Yes, tell us the name!

TEACHER.   All right, the period is almost over so I will tell you by writing the name on the board.

(Teacher writes lemurs on the blackboard.)

Though students spoke in response to the instructor's questions in the dialogue, motivation was strong to solve the problem because the discussion developed rapidly and in a logical fashion without the flagging of group interest. The instructor did not ask leading questions, but confined himself to interrogation devoid for the most part of informational content. The learners were forced to draw evidence for their claims from their own pool of knowledge.

Many questions were put to the students in the form of problems about Australia. An adequate response called not only for additional evidence but also for logical explanation. The participants had to defend the validity of their statements rationally and with factual evidence. This task was accomplished by many students who offered bits and pieces of data which were eventually welded into a complete interpretation of the problem. The problem itself was metamorphosed from a particular question concerning the peculiar fauna of Australia to a much more general problem encompassing the unequal distribution of primates and primate fossils over the entire earth.

The class began its discussion by concentrating its attention on a satisfactory explanation of the unequal distribution of living and fossil primates throughout the continents. They pooled their informational resources in an attempt to clarify the problem and finally to resolve it. They concluded their inquiry by accomplishing much more than this; that is, in addition to employing the principle of evolution, the participants developed an additional idea of their own which helped them to arrive at a defensible conclusion. From knowledge of mammalian evolution a geologic timetable was pieced together giving the probable point in time that each of the earth's continents became separated from each other. In effect, the class probed the point at issue until a time sequence had been established that explained the existence of divergent types of fauna on the different continents, with Australia probably being the first area to become separated from the larger land mass. The discussants applied the principle of evolution to their investigation and produced the idea of continental separation over time, which was used to solve the initial problem. Thus two principles or conceptual tools were satisfactorily used to settle a question. However, the principles themselves had not been tested by any new evidence and had not been proven reliable. To encourage students to test the principles the instructor asked for a solution to a novel hypothetical question that required the use of both of these principles. Given an island that had separated from Africa at a time in between the separations of Australia and the Americas, the students were requested to *predict* what type of *special* fauna they would expect to find there. They reapplied their principles to the new problematic situation and predicted a fauna that was wholly in accord with the evidence later revealed by the instructor. In this case the instructor did not release the confirmational evidence until the students had proceeded with their predictions as far as they could go. This was done to heighten interest in the solution of the problem and to quicken and sharpen student response to questioning. As a result, not only did the participants utilize an anthropological principle but developed one of their own. They tested their ideas in the light of new evidence and found them reliable and worthy of further application.

It is interesting to note that although the instructor played a rather active role in the discussion as an interrogator the participants raised the initial question, a question that aroused enough class interest to serve as the basis for a lively and extended discussion. The discussion itself proceeded in an orderly and logical manner, starting with the statement of a problem and the collection of evidence, and concluding with the development, application, and testing of general explanatory principles. At the heart of the entire investigation was the students' desire to obtain a satisfactory and valid explanation of a problem perceived in a given set of data. They achieved their goal by searching out answers to their own and to the teacher's questions.

TESTING AN AUTONOMOUSLY DEVELOPED GENERALIZATION ABOUT SECRET SOCIETIES

A unit about imperialism, nationalism, and revolutionary activity in the nineteenth and twentieth centuries was being intensively studied by a group of high school sophomores of average ability. This elaborate unit formed part of a required course in modern world history, usually taken at the tenth-grade level. The unit was being taught almost entirely by the use of original source materials, particularly historical documents, literature, and paintings.

The students had spent a great deal of time studying a series of documents, each of which represented the oath or official position of a secret society. The various underground organizations investigated by the class were drawn from different countries and culture areas as follows:

1. The Serbian Black Hand
2. The Hung Society of China
3. The Italian Carbonari
4. The U.S. Ku Klux Klan
5. The Kenyan Mau Mau
6. The Pre-Revolutionary Russian Communists

The documents had been presented to the students *without* such identifying information as time, place, or authorship. The class was asked to discover the origin of each of the underground societies and to analyze each document for clues as carefully as possible. Thus each historical source had been debated and thoroughly scrutinized by the members of the class before they attempted to reach any general conclusions concerning their studies.

The conversation presented in the following pages is the culmination of several weeks of study about imperialism, nationalism, and revolutionary movements in the nineteenth and twentieth centuries. It is also the climax of an analysis of six secret societies, each selected from a different country. The students showed a desire for discussion that would help them to organize, order, and test their ideas about the large amount of evidence they had investigated. The general conclusions they developed about the causes and consequences of secret organization are illustrated in this dialogue:

RICHARD.   I think that all violent secret societies sprang up in countries where people were oppressed by their governments.

DEBBIE.   We could make up a rule for ourselves: If we hear of a violent secret society in a certain place or country, then we can say that there is an oppressive government there also.

ANNE.   Many of the societies we studied fit in very well with our rule.

TEACHER.   What if I asked you to prove your rule?

ANNE.   Well, I could get examples of secret societies that fit our rule.

TEACHER. Well?

ANNE.   For instance, the Serbian Black Hand was very violent, and helped bring about World War I. The Serbians and Yugo-slavians were being oppressed by the Austrian government which seemed to want to make these areas part of its own Empire. The Serbs wanted to unite their people and free themselves from Austrian rule and pressure, so many Serbs joined the Black Hand to hurt the Austrians.

JANET.   They even used bombs and all kinds of terrorist methods.

JAVIER.   The Carbonari in Italy also wanted to free their country from the rule of a foreign, oppressive government. I think it was Austria, too. They wanted to have Italy governed by Italians.

JOHN.   Italy for the Italians!

ALLEN.   When Israel fought for independence, many of them be-longed to underground groups to get the British out of Palestine.

DEBBIE.   They showed something about that in the movie "Exodus."

ALLEN.   They felt that the British were siding with the Arabs, and were just being oppressive. That's why they joined secret underground groups. If these groups hadn't been secret, all the members would probably have been arrested and exe-cuted.

DONALD.   The Mau Mau fought the British, too. They must have felt pretty much the same way as the Israelis did. They hated the British as foreigners and as oppressors, so they took matters into their own hands and organized a secret society to drive the British out of Kenya.

RUTH.   We forgot all about the oath of the secret society from China. I think they were called the Hung Society. They also wanted to free their country, China, from foreign op-pression. Their society was like a huge international under-ground, with members all over the world who were sup-posed to help and protect each other. In their oath they say that they will use force against their enemies if they think it is necessary.

JANET P. Cuba might be an example of what we are looking for. Cuba was ruled by a dictator who the Communists overthrew. I read that they might be part of the reason Castro was so popular. He threw out their dictator, but then he put him-self in the dictator's place.

STEVE.   Yea, Communists are actually a kind of secret organization and they are for overthrowing governments.

JOHN.   They were the ones that took Russia over. According to that speech we read by Lenin, they were secret, and they even thought that the Russian government was made up of foreigners and was rotten and oppressive.

RUTH.   Of course, in the United States the Communists are kind of quiet. They aren't openly violent here or even secretly violent. If they were, the F.B.I. would catch them all and put them in jail.

ANNE.   Our government isn't oppressive.

TEACHER.   How do you know that all the other goverments were oppressive?

ANNE.   Well, in those countries the people had to resort to violence to get what they wanted, while here the people can talk openly about it, even the communists, I think.

JAVIER.   Why aren't there any secret societies in Russia now? We think their present form of government is oppressive and the people are not free there. There should be secret societies there.

JANET.   We never hear of assassinations there, or street bombings like there are in Viet Nam. Maybe the Russians are peaceful because they have their *own* bad government and they are not being ruled by foreigners.

TEACHER.   That's assuming they were ruled by foreigners before. Aren't you taking Lenin's word for that?

JANET.   I suppose so.

STEVE.   If we reverse our rule. . . . Let me see. . . . It will read differently. Uh . . . It will read that we should find secret societies where there are oppressive governments. But we don't in Russia. We don't hear of bombings, assassinations, revolts, or trouble there.

ANNE.   Maybe they don't let you hear about it.

STEVE.   That could be, but how could they keep a big revolt quiet?

ALLEN.   There was revolt in Hungary . . . in, I think . . . 1956 or 1957 . . . anyway, they couldn't keep that quiet. I guess there was an underground in Hungary.

JOHN.   That time the Russians would be the oppressors.

SHARON.   Maybe you don't hear about these things in the newspapers, until one of the secret societies, or the underground, starts to act. You won't hear of these things because the bad government wants to keep it all quiet.

LAUREN.   When the United States was oppressed, I think that there

	were secret organizations here too, to fight the British during our Revolutionary War. The British would be our oppressors.
JAVIER.	They would sort of be foreigners, too. That seems to be important. Maybe people are less angry at being ruled, even badly, by their own countrymen, than by outsiders.
JANET.	Our rule seems to hold pretty good. If we reverse it, we do seem to have some trouble, but that's because the proof is so hard to find. It's easier to work after the fact, after something has already happened.
LAUREN.	I just thought of a new problem. Maybe we're all being too agreeable with our own rule. We didn't consider the Ku Klux Klan. We studied it, and we have their oath, but where do they fit into our rule?
TEACHER.	Ah! That is a very good question.
JANET P.	They thought that the American government in Washington was being oppressive to the white people of the South, so they formed their organization to protect their rights.
TEACHER.	I like your choice of words.
JANET.	What does that mean?
TEACHER.	What do you think it means?
STEVE.	Oh! I think I see what you're getting at. Janet said that the Ku Klux Klan *thought* the U.S. government was bad. But was it? For whom? It wasn't bad for the Negroes in the South.
DEBBIE.	No. It was giving the Negroes their rights for the first time. The KKK was oppressing the Negroes.
DONALD.	The KKK obviously thought that the U.S. government was interfering with their old way of life, and, since they couldn't get their old life back legally, they resorted to violence and formed a sort of secret club to frighten Negroes and Northerners who came South.
ALLEN.	They thought of Northerners as foreigners, and even called them all sorts of bad names.
DEBBIE.	But then they were twisting things. Northerners and Southerners are all Americans.
JOHN.	But they didn't feel that way. They had just fought a war over the problem of who was part of whose country, remember?
DEBBIE.	All right, don't be so smart!
LAUREN.	Maybe the important thing is that they *felt* the way they did.
JAVIER.	Yeh, but didn't anything have to be that way, really?

ANNE.   Maybe or maybe not. Can we tell?

TEACHER.   I don't know. Can we tell?

ANNE.   We'd have to do a lot of research, and even then I don't think we'd be sure everything we would read would represent someone's opinion. Everything might be partial. That's terrible.

RICHARD.   Of course, if there's trouble there, in some country, something must be wrong.

JAVIER.   Or people feel something is wrong. They must believe themselves to be oppressed.

DEBBIE.   Maybe we should change our rule to read that there are violent secret societies when people *feel* that they are being oppressed by their government or some foreign ruler.

ALLEN.   I just thought . . . what would we do with something like the John Birch Society? They keep their members secret.

JANET.   Yes, but are they using violence to gain control of the government? I haven't heard anything about it yet.

ALLEN.   Well, but they are sort of moving in, aren't they?

JANET.   But they are not causing revolts, or assassinations, are they?

ALLEN.   Well, no . . . but . . . they seemed to fit the pattern. I don't know.

SHARON.   Members of the Birch Society might feel oppressed for some reason. Maybe they feel the same way Klan members do. They don't really feel they belong to our society, unless it changes to something they desire.

JANET.   But so far, they aren't really violent towards our government. Maybe they aren't violent because our government is really not very oppressive.

JAVIER.   I guess it all really depends on what's in people's minds.

RICHARD.   But couldn't there be something definitely labeled a bad government allowing no freedom?

LAUREN.   But that's all according to the way we think. It really depends on what those people think. For instance, if most people in a country don't mind dictators, then you probably won't have any revolts or undergrounds. I don't think the French were so bad in Algeria or treated the Algerians so terribly, but the Algerian Moslems wanted to have their own country, so they formed secret terrorist groups and tried to force the French to leave.

RUTH.   They succeeded, too.

DEBBIE.   I guess we'll have to leave it that way—as feelings—and just keep looking for more proof.

ALLEN.   I'm going to keep my eye on Russia and China and see if any revolts break out.

STEVE. Something complicated must be happening in Viet Nam, because the Communists are there, and I think there are other secret fighting groups there, too. Is their government in South Viet Nam oppressive?

TEACHER. Don't look at me, you're deciding the question.

STEVE. Some people over there must think it is a bad government, or there wouldn't be any fighting.

ANNE. Oh no! Let's not start the whole thing over again.

TEACHER. Have you all had enough? Do you feel the question has been discussed thoroughly?

(general agreement that the discussion is ended)

The discussion progressed in a very orderly manner, beginning with the formulation of a guiding principle and developing into a review of pertinent evidence. Richard and Debbie jointly created a generalization which they hoped would explain the cause of all secret organizations. They both agreed that governmental oppression was a key factor contributing to the rise of violent secret societies. The instructor then challenged these students, and the other members of the class as well, to validate their contention. Various students reviewed the previous evidence in an effort to demonstrate that the specific cases they had studied were consistent with their over-all interpretation. Each review, in effect, constituted a test of the generalization in question.

The review continued throughout the conversation with new evidence being added from time to time. However, some of the data suggested by students for consideration raised problems with respect to the principle being tested. Javier and Janet argued that modern Russia does not fit the interpretation. Their comments led Steve to suggest that the principle be reversed and tested again as a predictive device; that is, ". . . we should find secret societies where there are oppressive governments." Several students attempted to deal with this idea, but discovered that a lack of evidence compounded the problem; for example, Sharon pointed out that, "You won't hear of these things because the bad government wants to keep it all quiet," and Janet's comment, ". . . proof is so hard to find." The difficulty of finding reliable evidence encouraged students to probe more deeply into the very complex problem of fact versus opinion. Whereas the causes of secret violent organizations formed the main line of inquiry at the beginning of the conversation, attention was turned to the motivational aspects of such secret groups. Students addressed themselves to the question: What caused people to join and support these organizations? The example of the Ku Klux Klan was especially responsible for prompting student inquiry into the problem of the psychological grounds for joining a secret association. The conflict between what is real and what is in peoples' minds was brought into the open during the discussion and caused participants to become suspicious of the evidence; for example, Anne's remark, "Everything might be partial." Debbie went so far as to offer a modification of the initial rule concerning the development of secret societies. She inserted the word "feel" into the generalization; thus she further emphasized the psychological roots of historical phenomena. The difficulty of determining "true" oppression caused the class to check this new idea against additional data, finally reaching a tentative consensus of opinion.

In summation, this class discussion represented an elaborate and well-organized evaluation of an interpretative framework designed to simplify and explain a large quantity of historical information. The discussion started out with a suggested interpretation which was tested against evidence gathered in the process; the idea was modified and tested again; then it was qualified, retested, and so on. The conversation closed when the students accepted their revised interpretation as a fairly reliable, but not absolute, guide to future studies. Thus, out of several cycles of generalization, testing, and modification, the students emerged with a new explanatory rule that may be validly applied to a given body of historical social phenomena. Their principle combined both a historical and a psychological perspective of human events. Finally, they seemed to achieve an understanding of some of the complexities of history, and of historical evidence. The students accomplished this with a minimum of teacher guidance and aid, and thus they developed their own framework for the interpretation and understanding of historical phenomena.

MAKING JUDGMENTS IN MATHEMATICS

Mathematics, a subject we all need in our daily lives, is conducive to a great variety of problem-solving modes and levels of inquiry. The subject of mathematics need not be one that is devoted to cut-and-dried calculation or the acquisition of techniques for manipulating numbers. Rather, calculations can be arranged to encourage both skill development and the analysis of the processes involved in solution-finding at the same time.

Creative lessons in mathematics may be developed with relative ease especially in an atmosphere where playfulness is accepted and questions rather than answers rewarded by the teacher. One example of this type of lesson is offered on the following pages. The lesson is excerpted from a fifth grade class discussion of a problem presented to them by their teacher.* The thirty-two students were generally of average ability, with mathematics scores on the standardized city test averaging out to 5.6 which is at or near grade level for that age group. Their teacher, as you will see, offered the material without previous comment and worked to foster a spirit of play with the numbers rather than direct discussion of a specific outcome. This instructional ploy of direct contact with problems in an atmosphere of "out-loud" thinking is vital to the development of independent problem-solving skills.

MATHEMATICS EXAMPLE

A)	B)	C)
24	16 × 24	24
24	8 × 48	16
24	4 × 96	144
24	2 × 192	24
24	1 × 384	384
24		
24		
24		
24		
24		
24		
24		
24		
24		
24		
24		
384		

> *While the other case studies deal with secondary school students this case study deals with elementary school students. This is done for comparative purposes.

TEACHER. Well, what do we have here? Can you describe the numbers to me?

RAOUL. These are problems all with the same answer.

SUSAN. They're the same answer, but each one is done in a different way.

JOHN. I don't understand the second way, B at all. I've never seen that before!

TEACHER. Why do you think people have reached the same answer in different ways?

SAL. Depends on what you know how to do. . .

NICOLE. Or like to do!

TEACHER. What do you mean by "what you know how to do"?

SAL.   I think that some people know their multiplication tables
              real well, and others don't so some have to do their figuring
              the hard way.

TEACHER.   Which do you think is the hard way? Which is easy?

SAL.   Well, I'm sure that C is the easy way if you know your
              multiplication, and A seems most difficult, longer, you
              know. . . .

TIM.   Yeah, there's so much work to do it like A. It's dumb!

TEACHER.   Why?

TIM.   Because A is really adding, not multiplying at all. So he has
              to add 24 sixteen times and that takes a long time.

NICOLE.   B is fairly long too and a little confusing to me.

SHARON.   And A is boring, too! You keep adding the same numbers
              up.

MARC.   Boring and a waste. I would only do it the way C did it.

TEACHER.   Is that the *only* way to do it?

MARC.   I don't think so, but it sure is shorter than the others. You
              can see that on the page!

SUSAN.   Well, then, the second way, B is pretty good but I don't
              think it's multiplication. They're borrowing from one side
              and adding to the other. That's pretty quick but I'm still not
              sure what's going on. Could you do any problem that way?

ROBERT.   Could you do odd numbers that way? Let me see.

TEACHER.   Why don't you try that. But what about our discussion about
              how to solve problems. Is there only one way? Is there only
              one best way?

TIM.   I think there is a best way here and that is still C because
              that's the shortest.

TEACHER.   Is shortest always best?

TIM.   Shortest takes less time and I think that's good in math.

TEACHER.   Very good answer. Does everyone agree?

SHARON.   Well, shortest is best if you understand how it was done.
              Otherwise it's better to go slower and know what you're
              doing, I think.

MELISSA.   Multiplication was invented to make it easier for us to fig-
              ure long problems, like it would take A forever to do a
              problem like 158×236, wouldn't it?

JEFF.   I don't think they could do it at all using method A—addi-
              tion—but maybe they could do it B's way and still avoid
              multiplication. But the bigger the number, the more com-
              plicated and crazy it would become.

APRIL.   Large numbers are easier to do using multiplication, but so
              are small numbers. These other methods are fine if you
              don't know any better.

JOHN. Speed isn't everything! You want the right answer, too. I think that the more numbers you have to handle, the worse it will be. You could make a mistake easy!

SHARON. So, I guess the shortest and quickest methods are best for getting the right answer. But B is pretty clever anyway.

SAL. Is that what math is all about: finding faster and faster ways of getting answers?

TEACHER. I would like to know what you think.

SAL. I think that *is* what it's all about.

MELISSA. Yeah, but it's good training for the mind, too, like working on a puzzle. I enjoy that.

TIM. Puzzles are fun.

TEACHER. Why?

TIM. Well, there is something you don't know that you want to find out, and there are lots of different ways of doing it to arrive at an answer.

TEACHER. Are there lots of ways of doing math problems?

TIM. Yeah, there are many!

SUSAN. But we usually think math is only done one way. There are probably many ways of working out answers, some we haven't invented yet.

RAOUL. I can do problems on my calculator many ways and still get the right answer. Calculators make math easy. We should use them in class all the time.

SHARON. Computers, too! Why not?

TEACHER. Computers, too! Won't that make things too easy?

JEFF. Well, we said shortest is best and fastest is best. So I think anything that helps us get the answer with the least trouble should be allowed.

JOHN. I think that's what this lesson was all about—to show us how to solve problems in more than one way, to compare ways of doing it.

MARC. Comparing the problems shows how it can be done. All the answers were the same, so we know that the same answer can be figured out in many different ways, some long, some short.

APRIL. And some fast and some slow, too!

ROBERT. Then, Mr. _____, why do you mark us wrong when we do the problem well but make an error in arithmetic and get a wrong answer.

The instructor of the fifth grade classroom whose collective reasoning we have shared has created a problem which stimulates mathematical reasoning through comparison and contrast between different methods of solution. The answers to the calculations are all identical thus changing the focus of the lesson from finding a solution to problem-solving strategies. Furthermore, the different methods for drawing conclusions encourage students to make judgments about the advantages or disadvantages of each solution style.

Both the comparison and judgmental aspects of the problem are utilized by the teacher to heighten and sustain the students' discussion of mathematical reasoning. Indeed, the teacher quickly changes the focus of the lesson from description and computation to reasoning by asking, "Why do you think people have reached the same answer in different ways?" This question poses a mystery and implies that nearly all problems are capable of a variety of approaches in seeking solutions. The students immediately pick up on the differences in approach and begin discussing which is "the easy way" and which is "shorter than the others." Speed and brevity are then developed as standards or criteria for judging mathematical methods throughout the entire conversation and lead to a number of insights into problem-solving and to several fairly high level judgments about the relative advantages of multiplication over simple addition and sophisticated addition.

It might be noted that several students were quite taken with the second system of calculation (B), often referred to as the Russian peasants' method. Students were intrigued by this method and at first unsure of its basis in either multiplication or addition. Many were impressed with the method's creativity, but still decided that it was ultimately, not as useful as multiplication particularly if large numbers were being manipulated.

IDENTIFYING AN OBJECT

A classroom exercise in observation was initiated when an unknown object was presented to a class studying ancient world history. Class members were encouraged to analyze, discuss, and defend their own perceptions of the object before them. All of the twenty-nine students, who were of average intelligence, were given the opportunity to examine the object thoroughly. The students were told nothing about the object's age, function, origin, or producer, thus creating an atmosphere of mystery. The main concern was to motivate the students to discover as much as possible about the artifact through their own power of perception and analysis.

The object shown to the class was a stone tool of American Indian origin. Photographs of the artifact appear below and in the next page. The tool was found in Southern Illinois, and it was probably the pro-

duct of an ancient Indian tribe, perhaps a group of mound builders. In shape and structure the implement was similar to European stone tools of the Mesolithic era and was most probably used to grind corn into meal. Because this grinding tool was most likely used for the preparation of meal, the Indians using it may have been engaged in some form of agricultural production. All of this information indicates that the tool was the product of an incipient farming community which was about a thousand years old. However, it should be emphasized that this description is largely guesswork, for no one could be absolutely certain of the age or function of the tool, much less the type of culture responsible for its production. The conversation in response to the unknown object follows:

JIM.   What is it? What is it?
TEACHER.   I'm not sure. What do you think it is?
JIM.   How should I know? You should know.
TEACHER.   But I want to know what you think.
ALEXA.   I think I know what is is. It looks like something made from stone . . . some kind of tool.
JEFF.   It looks like a weight.
DALE.   Yeah, it looks like a weight for lifting . . . a dumbbell.

MELISSA.   No, it can't be a dumbbell. The middle is too short and it doesn't look big enough.

HOWARD.   It's something man-made because of the definite shape. It's been smoothed down for some special purpose. I don't think it is an all-around tool because it seems specially designed.

RICHARD.   It's got to be a tool of some sort. Let me have it and I'll show you how it was used.

(Richard is handed the object and attempts to demonstrate its use. He holds it at the smaller end and engages in a mashing motion with it.)

LORRAINE.   I think it was used to grind with. Maybe these people ground grain or plants with tools like these.

DAVID.   Maybe it was a weapon. If someone were hit with it, they would certainly not get up.

RHONDA.   But it's not sharp at all. Why would people want to fight with something like this when they could make a weapon that had a sharp edge from stone, for instance, a point, or knife, or spearhead?

MIKE.   Let me see it. This thing is round at both ends and it looks as though it had been glued together. It just couldn't be a weapon, because there is nothing to hold it with except your hand. You can't attach it to another stick . . . you can't even make a club out of it.

EDWARD. It's just got to be a grinding tool. It fits perfectly for that purpose.

JANE. You could use it to grind with no matter which end you hold.

RHONDA. I think it would fit nicely into a stone bowl. I think they used this tool to grind with in a matching stone bowl . . . a round bowl just the right size for the grinder.

KARIN. You might also use it as a rolling pin or as something to flatten out dough.

RICHARD. Maybe you could use the tool for that, but I doubt it. A rolling pin should be long and round and this isn't. You can't hold this at both ends, and the middle is smaller than either end, and that's why I think it would make a bad roller.

LORRAINE. I think it was made as a grinder. It's been designed for that purpose. We haven't really been able to prove that it was built for anything else although it might have been used for other purposes.

WAYNE. These people might have been growing grain or other plants because they made special tools to grind the plants with to make flour or meal or something like that.

RHONDA. The people who used this were farmers . . . they grew their own food because if they only ate plants once in a while they would not need special tools to make food with.

JANE. They were growing crops to eat. This is not a hunting tool, but has to be connected to farming.

JEFF. The people who made this knew how to farm and plant crops so this must have been made in a village. These people were engaged in agriculture.

RICHARD. But can we tell that for sure?

LORRAINE. Well, what else could it be a sign of? Fishing? Hunting?

DALE. It's a grinder for grain. That's obvious. Maybe you could use it for pounding or crushing something, but certainly not for war or hunting. It's just too clumsy.

ALEXA. Maybe this was used to make other stone tools with. Maybe they struck other stones with this one to break off chips for new sharp tools. I think it might have worked well for that purpose.

HOWARD. But then why does it have two round knobs on it? Wouldn't one heavy round rock be enough to strike off a tool from

	another rock? This tool would be harder to control than a single stone hammer.
MELISSA.	Well, it still might be a stone hammer for making other tools.
DALE.	But that's not likely. Look at it. Doesn't it look like a grinder to you?
MELISSA.	Well, I'm not sure.
DAVID.	It might have been a tool-maker, but it still seems best suited to be a grinding instrument and not something else.
JIM.	All right, so it's a grinder. What do we know about it?
LORRAINE.	We know it was the product of a group of farmers who must have ground grain or corn with this. It's hard to tell how old it is, or where it came from, but it must be pretty old if they were using stone for their tools.
JANE.	We know people made it for a purpose.
KATHY.	We know that these people had invented, or had adopted, a farming way of life rather than a hunting life. That's why I think this couldn't be the product of cave men.
RHONDA.	This tool must come after hunting and after the invention of agriculture and village life.
WAYNE.	These people might not have been very advanced, but they knew enough to make special tools to fix up what they grew for eating. That's why I think they weren't real backward either.
DALE.	Do you have any of the other tools these people made? If we could see more of their tools we might be able to tell for certain what this one was for.
RICHARD.	What else was found with the tool? Where was it found? Who made it?
TEACHER.	Why would you want to know that?
RICHARD.	Then we could really know what the people who made this were like.
EDWARD.	Were there any animal or human bones found with this?
HOWARD.	We need to know more about how and where this was found.
RHONDA.	I'll bet this was found in some grave with other things. I don't think it was found alone.
TEACHER.	Let's calm down and I'll show you some more tools found in the same place as this one. Will that help you out?

(general agreement and nodding of heads to signify assent to the question)

Sight of the strange-looking artifact immediately aroused the participants' curiosity. They raised questions about the unfamiliar object, directing their queries to the instructor. The instructor, however, promptly supplemented their questions with other questions, forcing the students to seek answers by themselves. This technique apparently increased interest in the task of discovery since the students proceeded to examine the implement, raise questions, and develop and debate possible explanations of its function. Thus, because of their interest in the object, various members of the class raised pertinent questions concerning it. Since help from the teacher was not forthcoming, the group attempted to complete the task they had set for themselves by employing their own capabilities and resources.

The reward for participation was the solution of the problem—finding and putting some order into the unknown. The ultimate satisfaction of discovery was a function of the process itself and of the pursuit of reliable knowledge. Finding answers through their self-directed efforts created a feeling of pride and accomplishment, and it resulted in a better understanding of the problem. Being able to structure and master the learning situation independently led to a firmer control of evidence and to better self-control. The insructor interferred as little as possible in this situation in order to maximize the students' chances of reaching a conclusion on their own. He generally confined himself to keeping the controversy orderly and to posing questions that required students to defend their viewpoints rationally.

In addition to being motivated by a sense of discovery, the participants were also moved by the desire to develop a reliable idea of the object's function. To achieve this goal the group intensively analyzed the stone implement and attempted to study its qualities and properties down to the smallest details, such as its size, shape, texture, weight, and balance. The usual pattern of inquiry was in the form of proposals that were put forth and tested and then accepted or rejected.

The main goal of this class appeared to be the definition of the object and the clarification of its function. This aim included the categorization of the object according to its purpose, structure, and function. Several members of the group offered principles or ideas as guides for further inquiry. These ideas were utilized after being tested against evidence and logic; for example, the assumption that any stone given a special shape implies a human purpose in making it. The investigation concentrated on analysis of the stone tool rather than on gathering pertinent information from other sources. Ideas and interpretations were checked directly against the implement; very few comparative data were brought to bear on the problem until the latter part of the inquiry

CONCLUSION

Careful and perceptive observation is a skill closely akin to the ability to analyze ideas. Observation of an animal's motion, a stationary painting, or a stone artifact demands critical sight. Observation may be thought of as critical analysis that begins with sensory images. An object may be viewed, touched, weighed, or smelled as a preliminary step to the analysis of its function to form the basis for further inquiry and theorizing. In a sense observation leads to a definition of what is seen and to an understanding of the probable function or meaning of an object or artifact.

ANALYZING TWO DRAWINGS

Analytical skills may be evoked using a great many different types of data, particularly when these materials involve students in processes such as comparison and contrast, or developing criteria or standards for judgment. Art materials may be used to call forth the application of analytical skills in simple and direct ways. While the goals of art education often stress personal and esthetic development, artistic expression may also benefit from an awareness of the technique, form, design, function, and feeling that went into a painting, drawing, sculpture, or other product.

In the example that follows, the teacher used two drawings of a horse. Both of the drawings of a horse were done by Picasso as preliminary sketches for his painting, "Guernica." They were used to draw out comments about their differences and similarities in terms of both technique and quality from a group of average fifth graders in a New York City elementary school. These drawings were used on a recent test developed by the National Assessment for Educational Progress to assess students' knowledge, understanding, and appreciation of art.[2]

In the classroom dialogue that follows, the teacher did not indicate the origin or purpose of the drawings, nor give the name of the artist. The pictures were presented without comment and with very little direction. The contrasting nature of the drawings, one simple and childlike, the other complex and animated, and the teacher's questions rather than direction or background information structured and gave orientation to the lesson.

[2]*Art and Young Americans, 1974–79: Results from the Second National Art Assessment.* Report No. 10-A-01 by the National Assessment of Educational Progress. Education Commission of the States, Denver, Colorado 80295, December 1981.

TEACHER. Are these two drawings alike or different?

BRIAN. The same! Both are pictures of a horse. You can tell it's a horse.

FELICIA. Y'know, I don't think they're really alike. Both are horses, but they're different.

DEBBIE. One is not as good as the other one. I think B is better.

TEACHER. Why?

DEBBIE. 'Cause it looks more like a real horse.

JAN. Yeah, it's got a better face and head, but it's legs are funny looking, not right.

FRED. I don't think B is better. I think A is better because it's flatter and sharper with less swirly lines.

SUE. B is better because it's got more movement, more feeling.

TEACHER. Who thinks B has more feeling? What do you see in each drawing?

MARY. I see A as a kid's drawing.

TEACHER. Why?

MARY. Well, it's flat. It's just a line drawing. The legs are too straight and the neck is weird.

MIKE. I think so, too. It's a good kid's drawing, but still not like B. B is made up of many curved lines which make you feel the horse is angry or screaming or whatever.

PATRICIA. A shows feeling, too, I believe, I think it's a cute, friendly horse. See the little smile.

ELLIOT. I don't really see the smile. It's cute but I don't get much feeling out of it, but I'm sure the horse in B is upset or something.

SAL. B doesn't really look finished or else the artist doesn't care. Like there's a leg missing and the belly isn't drawn in.

ELLIOT. It doesn't look finished, but don't you still get more feelings from B than from A?

SAL. I guess so.

PATRICIA. I guess so, too, now but I still think A is cuter.

TEACHER. Is "cute" what we're talking about? What are we talking about? What do the two pictures mean to you?

HILARY. They show how the same thing can be drawn in different ways.

JOHN. They show that we can compare drawings. Some are better than others.

TEACHER. How do you tell what's better?

JOHN. By how it's drawn.

TEACHER. Can you give me a rule to follow so I can tell how to decide which is better?

JOHN.   Well, well. . . .

SANDRA.   I'll help John out! A rule would be use of lines.

TEACHER.   Explain.

SANDRA.   Whichever artists use more lines and shape them to be interesting are the better ones. A is pretty much straight and flat, but B has swirls and curves and you can feel the horse is moving.

CHUCK.   Movement is harder to do than something still, so I say movement makes drawings better and B has more movement than A.

TONY.   We're forgetting feelings. Feelings are very hard to draw in a picture. So I think the artist that can do this is better than one who can't.

BRIAN.   Unless you want to make a design—that doesn't have to have feelings, does it?

TEACHER.   No, I guess not, but what do you think?

BRIAN.   I don't think we do it that way.

TEACHER.   When do we want feeling in art?

BRIAN.   When we draw people.

CHEN.   Or animals, or plants, maybe, or tell a story!

JENNIFER.   Yep, this is a horse, an animal, and we usually like to have feelings for animals. Right?

MARY.   I think that's right! So B is better! Our rules say B is better, right, Ms. _____?

TEACHER.   I really want to hear what you think about this! So far, your rules are great!

CHEN.   You might not like our rules. I don't draw so good, you know.

TEACHER.   If you have reasons for your rules, for your opinions, that's what counts to me. We don't always have to agree on what we like, do we?

The transcribed excerpts from this class discussion about art clearly show that contrasting drawings can be used to promote analysis, synthesis, and judgment by relatively young students. The process of comparison and contrast engages most student minds upon contact with the data. If it is arranged in a thought-provoking manner, and presented with a minimum of background, the material itself induces commentary and invites judgment.

In this example, analysis and judgment were constantly intertwined in students' reaction to the drawings. As their viewing became increasingly critical, the judgments grew more sophisticated. Links were forged between such concepts as form, line, depth, design, and feeling, all ideas which can be applied to almost any work of art with productive results. These analytical concepts were used by the students to develop reasons in defense of judgments about which horse was drawn "better." Accuracy of representation and emotional content were used by students on the path toward evolving criteria for judgment. Although esthetic values were brought up to support evaluation of the drawings, we would argue that the dominant mode of inquiry was analytical. The orientation was very strongly in the direction of understanding and assessing the pictures, not on examining the values themselves.

With a bare minimum of teacher questioning (mostly clarification or redirection of ideas), the students moved toward a detailed comparison of the two pictures. The material itself, in this case drawings, invited students to reason and to form their own opinions about art. With the instructor acting as a guide, the students analyzed the drawings and probed their own reasoning to reach a series of tentative generalizations and to form rules about quality in art. These student-created standards were applauded and encouraged by the teacher who avoided imposing her own ideas on the class. Instead, the rules or criteria were portrayed by the teacher as conditional and open to argument (agreement or disagreement) but useful for future application to new cases and examples as they appeared in the classroom.

ANALYZING MUSIC: DEVELOPING CONCLUSIONS ABOUT SOCIETY THROUGH MUSICAL EVIDENCE

A recorded recital of classical Hindu music was played for a class enrolled in an early world history course. The group was composed of thirty first-year high school students (freshmen), whose IQs fell into the 90 to 110 range. This class had been studying the development of man and concentrating on the rise of the earliest civilizations.

The group as a whole had had a limited amount of musical and historical experience. Thus the Indian recital was likely to be a novel encounter. The Indian *raga* recording was selected for different reasons, the most important of which was that it would represent a dramatic and thought-provoking experience for this audience. It was valuable as a motivational device, for the students were not told anything about the piece of music or the performers—even the record jacket was covered so as not "to give away the show."

Indian classical music has an ancient heritage, and in the context of the history class provided the students with insights into a living culture's past and present musical traditions. Furthermore, the recital provided a base from which to begin the study of a society very different from that found in the United States. In a sense students were asked to develop ideas about a society through the nature of its music. That organized traditional sounds formed the evidence for analysis and the basis for generalization about society may be seen in the following classroom discussion:

Analyzing a Culture Through Its Music

TEACHER.   I'm going to play a piece of music for you. Please listen to it and then tell me what you think about it.

(Teacher starts record player. The recording lasts approximately twenty minutes, after which the discussion begins.)[3]

CYNTHIA.   There seem to be two instruments playing . . . a drum and some sort of guitar.

BOB.   There might be a third one, but I can't tell for sure.

GREGORY.   The music got faster and faster, and the beat was pretty wild.

MARC.   It didn't sound like anything I ever heard before. It was strange.

DANIEL.   It had a good, cool rhythm to it.

CYNTHIA.   It wasn't anything like anything.

RICHARD.   It wasn't anything like the Beatles.

TEACHER.   Where did you think it was from?

MICHELLE.   I think it was from some Eastern country, maybe Japan.

GREGORY.   It could have been from China.

MIKE.   Maybe it was from India.

TEACHER.   Why do you think it was from China, Japan, or India?

MIKE.   Well, because it was so peculiar sounding. It wasn't at all like our music.

CHARLES.   It had a sort of twang to it and the beat was so complicated that I thought of oriental music right away.

TEACHER.   What kind of music do you think it is?

ARTHUR.   It had to be something to listen to, and something special, but I'm not sure what.

PAUL.   It's hard to tell about it because it is so different from what we usually hear.

MIKE.   I don't think it was that different. It wasn't bad to listen to. I agree it was different, but we could tell something about the instruments and the way it was organized, so it wasn't so bad.

[3]The selection was drawn from a long-playing record entitled *Music of India,* Angel 35258. The particular piece being discussed was the morning *raga, Sind Bhairavi.*

CHARLES. It was music for a show . . . for entertainment. These men were putting on a duet. They probably were specially trained as musicians.

CYNTHIA. That's still music to listen to, and not to do anything with personally. We were supposed to hear it played by someone else, not participate in music or song or dance.

TEACHER. Just going by this music, what can you tell about the society from which the music comes?

JACKIE. They have expert musicians.

ARTHUR. They must have people who listen to these performances. They must like it.

DANIEL. They knew enough to make instruments.

FRANK. Of course, a guitar isn't very complicated. It sounded like it had three strings.

CYNTHIA. I think it sounded like it was being played with eight strings. I think it was a difficult instrument to play. The drums might have been simple to play, but the guitar wasn't.

MIKE. The society couldn't be too backward. They are able to make fairly advanced instruments and train musicians to play them. The musicians would be special, not ordinary.

BYNAM. You can't tell, though. The society might be primitive. After all, we weren't hearing an orchestra play, only two or three instruments. They were played well, but that doesn't mean the society is advanced.

MICHELLE. They weren't only playing drums or something like that, so these people must know more about music than primitive tribes. They planned their performance and might have had some sort of written music.

MARC. It might be their custom to have duets and not play in orchestras with lots of instruments. They might like fewer instruments played at one time. We don't always have orchestras playing when we hear music.

TEACHER. Have you reached any conclusions about the society from their music?

MICHELLE. I don't think it was popular because it was too long.

RICHARD. You couldn't beat your foot to it so I don't think it was dance music or folk music. It was just too long and complicated to be ordinary folk music.

CHARLES. Maybe it was classical music, but of another country.

MIKE. It certainly didn't sound like Beethoven.

CHARLES. That's exactly it. There might be other kinds of classical music. But I'm really not sure of it.

CYNTHIA.   It was planned-out music so maybe these people knew how to write musical notes.

PAUL.   Of course, they could have memorized these pieces and handed them down by practice from person to person.

DANIEL.   That's very possible, too.

CYNTHIA.   This music had to be planned because it sounded like the drummer and the guitar player—or whatever it was—knew each other's parts and were playing together.

JACKIE.   The musicians seemed to know what they were doing. They sounded expert at their jobs.

BYNAM.   The bongo drummer knew what he was doing. He could play them very fast and keep up with the other musician.

MIKE.   I'm not so sure those were bongo drums, but I think we can be certain that the musicians were trained for their jobs.

BOB.   Then this couldn't have been folk music because it was too well-planned. Folk music is simpler. So is Beatle music. I don't think I know what it is, but I do think I know what it isn't.

TEACHER.   What do you think was the purpose of the music?

RICHARD.   It couldn't have been dance music because you couldn't keep time with it and it was just too long for a dance.

MICHELLE.   I don't think it was ordinary popular music because pop music is usually sung or danced and there was no singing here.

DANIEL.   Maybe it was music for meditation. Man, that stuff was way out. It had to be for meditation.

MIKE.   It was music for listening because the players were experts and put on a good concert for us. You *must have had* to listen. You couldn't dance or sing to it because it got faster and faster.

ARTHUR.   It started out slow, and built up faster and faster with a few pauses here and there. That doesn't sound like the way popular pieces are usually organized.

BOB.   The society must be fairly civilized to produce expert musicians.

FRANK.   They knew how to make instruments something like our own; it sounded like a guitar and bongo drums to me.

CYNTHIA.   They have an advanced type of music, not just folk or popular music. I don't know about the rest of the society, but the musical part of it really must be well-trained and educated and studied a lot.

MIKE.   They have some sort of technology because they produced instruments with strings that had to be carefully put together according to rules if it would sound good.

GREGORY.   This music shows that this society had developed its own special kind of music. I mean they have their own traditions, not at all like ours. Their music sounded different from any I've ever heard.

MYRNA.   To develop such music must have taken a long time. This music must go way back in history. I wonder how old it is.

MIKE.   I think different musical traditions take a long time to build up and show us that we are studying a different society. Probably most societies develop their own kind of music to suit their own tastes and purposes.

BOB.   How old is this music?

CYNTHIA.   Where is it from? Let us have a peek at the record cover.

CHARLES.   Are we right about what we said?

TEACHER.   Think it over! Why don't you try again tomorrow? Then I'll show you the record jacket.

Throughout the episode the members of the class reacted positively to the music and to the teacher's questions. The teacher's questions were very direct and requested responses that were supported by analysis of the tonal evidence. Because the evidence was limited and other information was not available, the teacher assumed a more interrogatory and directive posture than usual to keep students' responses relevant to the question and linked to the musical data.

The class began its discussion by analyzing the music. They tried to ascertain its tempo, rhythm, type, and general complexity and the number of instruments involved. They even attempted to evaluate the quality and skill of the performers. Several participants compared the Indian music with their own musical experience in an effort to gain a better understanding of music per se. From this line of inquiry some interpretations were formed about music in general that helped the students to classify and identify the foreign sounds on a comparative basis.

After their discussion about music and the recording in question, the students attempted to discover the cultural origin of the selection; however, this phase of the inquiry did not last long because the class members felt they could not *definitely* ascertain the culture responsible for the immediate musical experience. Furthermore, the participants appeared to be more interested in analyzing the performance itself, and in deriving social implications from the sounds, than in determining its origin.

Many students tried to develop inferences about the society from the twenty-minute piece of music. This tendency implied an underlying assumption; namely, that music is a reliable clue to the unique culture of a people. This assumption served as a guiding principle, or tool, for further inquiry and was applied throughout the remainder of the dialogue. A large number of perceptive and pertinent conclusions were formed about the society that produced these sounds; for example, Mike's idea, "They have some sort of technology because they produced insruments with strings. . . ," or Gregory's comment, "This music shows that this society had developed its own special kind of music," or, finally, Myrna's statement, "To develop such music must have taken a long time. . . ." It was apparently assumed that a given society and its music are both unique and that the music faithfully reflects something of the culture's values and traditions rather than a collection of random sounds.

This particular episode included conversation aimed at both discovery learning and analytical thinking. It appears that analysis dominated the discussion, for students were more highly motivated to understand the performance and its cultural background than to discover the specific geographic origin of the music. During the act of discovery interest centered on finding the missing elements in the situation, the informational pieces that would complete the puzzle and resolve the problem. When analyzing the music, students tended to focus their attention on interpreting and meticulously scrutinizing the evidence. They probed the music for evidence from which they could form conclusions about the society that had created it. Analytical investigation centered on making sense out of the information at hand—placing it in a constructed framework of ideas that would give meaning to the musical experience. The two approaches to the problem, the analytical and the creative, were complementary processes and in many instances indistinguishable from one another.

CONCLUSIONS

The foregoing classroom episodes, although devoted to different topics, exhibited certain commonalities of organization, teacher behavior, and goals. Analytical discussion appeared to follow a logical and orderly pattern of development; that is, each conversation generally moved from point to point with few digressions or irrelevant considerations. Furthermore, when students analyzed something, whether it was an idea or a thing, they tended to relate their comments to the available evidence rather than to offer suppositions or suggest thoughts based on intuition.

The teacher tended to ask more questions of the participants when exploring analytical episodes compared with discovery episodes. Although he refrained from directly aiding the students with information or with solutions to problems, he often asked questions that channeled the discussion into a particular direction. Questions were usually stated in the form of a challenge, but requests for explanation were also quite frequent. Finally, the questions were often arranged into a sequence that forced students to face increasingly difficult and challenging problems. The questions usually culminated at a point at which students were led to test their explanatory principles against all available evidence. Thus, the participants in an analytical class session would ultimately be required to develop a rationally defensible interpretation of their materials.

Although it should be noted that students engaged in both acts of discovery and acts of analysis in the discussions presented in this chapter, these two processes are characterized by somewhat different elements. Though analysis and discovery may take place within the same conversational framework, they are not identical processes. Each process may occur independently of the other, although both types of thinking were found to some extent in each of the classroom episodes.

The major goal of analysis appeared to be the development of an intellectual framework through which problems, questions, data, and knowledge could be approached systematically. Analysis, as exhibited by our experimental evidence, seemed to be directed toward understanding of phenomena through a sequential patterning and organizing of the data. Through the process of analysis, students developed and tested general principles against available information.

Discovery, on the other hand, begins with the quest to attain a specific solution in reaction to a given set of materials. This solution involves the discovery of an unknown—a missing piece in a puzzle— involving anything from one bit of information to a whole set of facts. Once the needed information is found the act of discovery ends and its motivational source somewhat dissipates. For the student, discovery has a more immediate set of goals than analysis, though both operations necessitate a thoroughgoing study of the evidence and a careful testing of all ideas and suggestions. Certainly logical operations are involved in both processes.

In conclusion, if students are constantly required to think for themselves and inquire systematically into new materials, then analysis and related patterns of thought become valuable and extensively utilized classroom skills. In a sense analysis is a process by which an idea or a generalization is developed and thoroughly tested against relevant data by students, teachers, or both. To validate and analyze ideas is to bring order and meaning to information by applying consistently scientific skills—definition, classification, testing, logical inference, generalization, and so on. We may, perhaps, see the processes of discovery and of analysis as taking place, more or less, at different points in problem solving. Discovery, with all of its motivational and creative aspects, is primarily applicable to the initiatory phases of inquiry.

Discovery operates as a stimulus to further inquiry. Analytical thinking reaches its optimum point after the initial confrontation with the material has taken place, and generally it involves the application of scientific skills and methods to the solution of a problem. Needless to say, there is a great deal of overlapping between the two processes. More will be said about the two processes in the chapters that follow.

CHAPTER THREE

Discovery Episodes

The examples of creative teaching reported in this chapter are grounded in several of the hypotheses advanced by Jerome Bruner in his work on instruction.[1] According to this distinguished psychologist, the highest state of human autonomy and cognitive development is achieved when the child begins to discover regularities or irregularities in the physical, social, and esthetic environment. Although no earth shaking scientific discoveries should be expected, the person who is engaged in this learning process is given the opportunity to develop insights into a previously unknown and/or incomprehensible world. Through this procedure, a major element in creative thinking, the learner comes to understand the value of formulating and testing plausible hypotheses about the way life on earth interacts and develops. Bruner and other advocates of discovery and inquiry teaching maintain that facts and details which are part of a structured pattern, or which fit into or test a concept, are retained much longer than unconnected data and can be more easily retrieved and applied to new situations—as needed.[2]

The classroom examples which follow were the results of field demonstrations in public schools in Chicago, Ann Arbor, Michigan, and New York City collected over the last decade or so. Each lesson was created to explore the dimensions and implications of teaching creatively in a number of subject matter fields including the social sciences, science, mathematics, language arts, and the humanities. All

[1]Jerome S. Bruner. *Toward A Theory of Instruction.* Cambridge, Mass.: Harvard University Press, 1966.
[2]Kenneth A. Strike. "The Logic of Learning by Discovery." *Review of Educational Research.* Summer 1975. Vol. 45, No. 3, pp. 461–483.

are designed to stimulate the act of discovery and creativity, or what Bruner refers to as the process of "figuring out."

While the examples are meant to be experimental and exploratory in nature, they are also offered as exemplars for teachers who would like to develop strategies for fostering creative thinking in their classrooms. Each episode or example is meant to throw light on the following questions.

1. To what extent are students capable of participating in the discovery and inquiry process?
2. In what ways can material be presented to offer clues which invite solution, but do not give the "story" away?
3. How can teacher method and curriculum design be joined to encourage independent and self-directed production of questions and validated conclusions?
4. How might classroom atmosphere, materials, and teacher style cumulatively contribute to motivate learning and induce high level, quality insight into the underlying principles that explain patterns of nature?

Given these assumptions and queries, we have tried to experiment with a wide range of materials serving as springboards for discussion in a variety of subjects and classroom levels. The episodes which follow are presented as illustrations of discovery in action.

Our first case (reproduced below) is a poetry lesson that incorporates both literary and social analysis, while leading to discoveries about both the nature of language and the social context from which it springs.

HAIKU POEMS AS THE SPRINGBOARD

The class was composed of 35 students, most of whom were about 15 years old, with an IQ range of 100 to 120, enrolled in a required modern world history course offered at the sophomore level. The course began with the Reformation, and it generally followed the sequence of historical topics; selected social events were chosen to be investigated in some depth. All the aesthetic products of culture including art, music, literature, and architecture were drawn upon for classroom material; however, the study emphasized the use of historical documents in developing the students' ability to discover and explain their political and social environment. Secondary sources (e.g., textbooks, excerpts from monographs, magazine articles) were used only insofar as they related to the problem under attack, and they were introduced after the initial encounter with the discovery episode. On the average, a new discovery episode was introduced every two weeks, and, in the main, it consisted of a historical document, the origin, referent, and author of which were carefully deleted. The students were challenged to gather all the missing information. Although a discovery episode presupposed some general knowledge, it was not necessary for the student to have had special training or familiarity with the problem under consideration. In a situation such as this the instructor performs a nondirective role by explicitly refusing to answer any of the students' questions. The task in the classroom is twofold: (a) to instigate and challenge the students, and (b) to moderate the discussion.

In order to illustrate the flow of classroom discussion during a discovery session, parts of the student dialogue are reproduced here. In this particular case the students were given ten brief poems[3] and were asked to read them carefully. When the poems in question were introduced, the class had had limited experience with other discovery episodes. The participants were encouraged to discover a plausible choice for the cultural origin of the following poems:

1.

My Thoughts turn to the Ancient Capital
  Long life and peace during your reign
O, Emperor.

2.

The beginning of all art
  A song when planting a rice field
in the country's inmost part.

3.

Is there, I wonder
  A man without a pen in hand—
The moon tonight!

4.

On the temple bell
  Resting, sleeping
a firefly.

---

[3]The selection of material was based primarily on two criteria: (a) availability of data pertaining to a central or common theme, for example, the feudal system of Japan, and (b) careful avoidance of clues that would "give away" the puzzle. These poems were taken from *An Introduction to Japanese Haiku* by Harold G. Henderson, copyright © 1958 by Harold G. Henderson. Reprinted by permission of Doubleday & Company, Inc.

5.

A Great Lord—And Who
   makes *Him* get off his horse?
—cherry blossoms do!

6.

Snow yet remaining
   The mountain slopes are hazy—
It is evening.

7.

A crossroad sermon! True,
It's rigamarole—but then
It's tranquil too!

8.

So brilliant a moonshine
   When I am born again—
A hilltop pine!

9.

To the Great Lord's hall
   Five or six horsemen hurry hard—
A storm wind of fall.

10.

As he snoozes, the mountain stream he uses
   To wash his rice,
No simple peasant, this!

The discussion that ensued was tape-recorded and transcribed. Selected parts of the transcription are given.

First Day

TEACHER. Please read this. (*five minutes of silence*) Well now, everyone finished? What do you think of this reading? What are these?

TIM. This must be a collection of poems.

TEACHER. Why?

TIM. Because each of these little pieces is in verse. Some rhyme.

GEORGE. But they're so vague. What are we supposed to do with them?

TEACHER. Whatever you like. Are they really vague?

GWEN.   I don't think so. Some of the poems are very interesting,
            maybe difficult to interpret, but interesting.

SYLVIA.   Yes, I think we can find clues if we try.

GEORGE.   Clues for what? All this is still vague.

BILL S.   Yes, what are we supposed to find out? What do these
            mean? Where are they from? Who wrote them? When were
            they written?

TEACHER.   All of you should be able to supply your own answers to
            these questions. Who would like to make the first attempt?
            (*a moment of silence*)

CAROLYN.   Well, they're all poems, so they must have been written by
            a poet.

BILL S.   That's some help! How do you know they're not written by
            one and the same poet? They all look the same to me, same
            three lines, same style, all short and vague.

CAROLYN.   But they're on different subjects and they give different
            feelings. Each one gives me a different feeling.

BILL S.   Does that mean they can't be by one poet expressing him-
            self on different subjects?

SYLVIA.   I have a different idea. Maybe these poems are all by dif-
            ferent poets, but may seem to be the same because of the
            style. What I mean is that maybe these are the usual kind of
            poem for this country.

GWEN.   Or, it could just be the style of a particular poet.

JOHN.   I think this is getting us nowhere. Let's forget about the
            poet and try to find out where it's from.

BOB.   But these poems are too vague.

DIANE.   We're back to that again.

TEACHER.   Well, does everyone agree with this, or can someone offer
            advice or evidence to help us out? Where are these from?

SHARON.   They are from Europe because an Emperor is mentioned,
            and lords are also mentiond a couple of times. This means
            that there must have been an autocracy in this country.
            Many countries of Europe had monarchs and lords.

BERNARD.   At one time almost every European country had this kind of
            government. Maybe these poems are from Russia. Russia
            had an Emperor and nobles running it for a long, long time.

DIANE.   I think that this is from France or Germany, or Austria dur-
            ing the Middle Ages, because the lords seem to be more
            powerful; they are able to command cavalrymen and to own
            large halls. Maybe the emperor referred to is Charlemagne.

GWEN.   I think you're getting on the wrong track. This is no Euro-
            pean set of poems, certainly not American!

TEACHER. Why?

GWEN. Well, you're missing a lot of important parts of the poems that seem not to be European at all. What about the mention of a temple? Since when are Medieval churches called Temples? And what about the reference to rice in one of the poems? Rice wasn't one of the European's main dishes, at least as far as I know.

EDDIE. Rice is from the Orient, from China. The Chinese eat lots of rice. The poems must be translated from Chinese.

STEVE. They could also be from Japan or India. I've read somewhere that these two countries produce and eat rice as their main dish.

MARY. I read recently that Southeast Asia produced a lot of rice. Viet Nam exports rice, and eats some of it.

HELEN. I have a suggestion, but not of another country. I think we should try to get the meaning and message of each poem and then find out where they're from. Let's start with poem 1 and work our way down.

It is apparent that the first day is spent on orientation and organization of the materials at hand. During the introductory phases of the discovery episode the students are encouraged to come to grips with the responsibility of exercising independent judgment in pursuing a course of action. The teacher and the material, which includes only limited clues, create a sense of puzzlement. The students begin to suggest modes of attack and try to capitalize on the available springboards. For example, John proposes that the focal point of investigation should change from a quest to identify the poet to an inquiry into the national origin of the poems. This suggestion is taken up by several members of the class—for example, Gwen, who, in her first reaction to the poem, offers a hypothesis which harmonizes several problematic bits of data and refutes previous conjectures. At this point other students attempt to validate and to narrow down the proposition that the poems are of non-Western source. Helen, following up this line of investigation, concludes the deliberations of the first day by suggesting that each poem be thoroughly scrutinized and analyzed before returning to the main source of perplexity.

Second Day

Here the students are considering Helen's suggestion and studying each poem in depth. Only discussion relating to three of these poems (8, 9, and 10) is reproduced here.

HELEN. This poem (Number 8) is written by a Buddhist or a Hindu because it contains a belief in rebirth. As far as I know, only these two religions teach this belief.

GEORGE. I think it's called reincarnation. That means that you are born over and over again into new bodies or forms, although your soul remains the same.

HELEN. Well, I think this poet is a Buddhist or Hindu because he believes this idea. He wants to be born again as a pine tree on a hilltop so he can enjoy beautiful moonlight nights. Does anyone disagree?

MARY. I don't. Now we have a better idea of where these poems are from. They have to be from the Orient, and they have to be from a country with Buddhists or Hindus living in it. They can't be from anywhere else.

GWEN. Yes, and according to the ninth poem, these would have to be from a country in which great lords are important people. The ninth poem repeats the fourth poem, and the great lord is said to own a hall. This must be like a castle.

STEVE. The lord seems to have soldiers or cavalry working for him. Then the poem changes subject and tells of a storm wind of the fall.

GWEN. Maybe the poet is trying to tell us in a roundabout way that a war or fight is brewing. That's why the cavalry is reporting to the great lord. I don't think his poem is peaceful like the others at all. It's a poem that tells us of troubles in the country. People were fighting each other and each great lord probably had soldiers working for him.

SHARON. That's called a feudalistic system. These poems have to be from a feudalistic country. We have to find out which Oriental countries were feudalistic—or still are.

GEORGE. That might be a help. Find out which Oriental countries had feuding societies and feudal lords.

SHARON. I agree about the wars, but I don't think your suggestions will help because all those feudal societies used to have little wars.

STEVE. Like England during the War of the Roses and France during the tenth and eleventh centuries?

TIM. I think you are right. You have also missed something important. If there are great lords in this country, there are most likely other lords, lesser ones in the setup as well. This sounds very close to feudalism. Usually, however, feudalism is a system of many powerful nobles and a weak king.

SHARON. Well, that fits pretty well. We definitely know that the lords of this country are powerful, armed, and have castles of some kind, while the emperor is spoken of as being in his ancient capital. It seems to me that he's out of the picture.

BILL. But we really can't tell for sure.

SHARON. Well, at least we know that the nobility is powerful, and if that's true, then the emperor must have that much less power or say-so on everything.

TEACHER. Good point. Now what about a volunteer for the last poem?

BERNARD. The last one is about a lazy peasant. I guess it's a kind of joke because the peasant is taking a nap while the water washes his rice, which I guess is in some sort of sack hanging in the water. Say! That's pretty clever.

DIANE. Some people, including the poet, must have thought peasants were simple-minded, and the poet is showing us that this isn't so, because here's a peasant who can get his work done and sleep at the same time.

BERNARD. By the way, I think this poem and the second one about rice prove that rice is very important in the life of the people of this country, and it also shows that these two poems are by different people.

MARY. Why do you say that? We decided before that we couldn't be sure of that.

BERNARD. Well, in the second poem those who plant the rice are praised and in the last poem peasants are made fun of.

KAREN. That could still be that same poet in a different place or mood.

In this discussion the students are subjecting the poems to a detailed examination. All shades of meaning and location clues are explored. In part, they seem to be working in sequential steps or plateaus; once they have determined that the poems are of Buddhist or of Hindu origin then they strike out to reach a new plateau which would incorporate more data and eliminate fruitless speculations. In their attempt to explain the existence of "great lords" they begin to draw certain logical inferences; for example, if powerful lords are in control, the monarch must be correspondingly weak. It should also be noted that in the process of "figuring out" the puzzle the participants draw from personal accumulated knowledge which, on several occasions, provides the missing parts and clarifies certain ambiguities and vagueness in the material. For example, they are trying to interpret the poems in terms of a theory of feudalism. The discussion pertaining to the last poem is a clear illustration of an attempt to reconcile contradictory information and place it in the famework of a more inclusive and warranted hypothesis.

Third Day

TEACHER.   Now that you've analyzed all of the poems, where do you think they're from?

GEORGE.   We've ruled out the West, and this has to be from countries under the influence of Buddhism or Hinduism, the only religions preaching reincarnation.

EDDIE.   That limits our choices to India, China, or Japan.

EILEEN.   Or Southeast Asia. The question is which one?

STEVE.   It seems as though each of these places fills the bill. All are countries that are literate, religious, feudalistic at one time or another, and dependent on rice for a main part of their diet.

EDDIE.   Well, wait a minute. Now that I think of it, China may not be a good choice. It doesn't fit in with what we've been saying about these poems. China had a very powerful emperor who ruled through a civil service. As far as I know there was no nobility in China except for the emperor's household.

BILL V.   But wasn't there an earlier period in Chinese history in which feudalism was the form of government?

MARY.   Well, at least we can eliminate most of the Chinese history.

TIM.   I think it's India. Great Lord could be a translation for Maharaja, but I'm not sure if India has had emperors. Did it?

TEACHER.   You can find out, can't you?

BILL S.   Oh, please tell us where it's from. I can't wait any longer.

TEACHER.   But why should I when you can find out for yourself? Doesn't someone have any helpful suggestions?

DIANE.   I think it's from India, too. The mention of rice, temples, peasants, and the religious tone to several of the poems make me think of India.

GWEN.   But what you've said could apply to almost all of Asia, India, and the East.

TIM.   I think we can rule out China altogether because I remember reading that Buddhism and the idea of rebirth were introduced into China after China already had a system of absolute emperors who ruled through a civil service, and I think there were no powerful nobles.

BOB.   If all of that is correct, then China is ruled out, but that still leaves us with Japan, India, and Southeast Asia.

MARY.   These poems must be from a mountainous country because of the mention of mountains in several of them.

GWEN.   Northern India is very mountainous, so are parts of Southeast Asia, and all of Japan is that way.

RANDY.   Maybe it's Japan. Up until very recently Japan was a feudal country with lords, barons, and soldiers called Samurai, including a very shy, weak emperor. It is also a Buddhist country filled with ancient temples and preachers of religion. Japan sounds like a very good choice.

BILL S.   It could still be Northern India or Southeast Asia some time long ago.

BERNARD.   I believe there were emperors in India rather recently, called Moguls, or something like that.

KAREN.   What about the style of these poems? They seem pretty unusual. Maybe we can check into this by looking at sample poems from all over Asia until we hit on the same type. Maybe that will help us find a definite answer.

(Bell rings.)

During the third day of class deliberations the students begin to limit the range of alternative choices or hypotheses; on the basis of their previous analysis, they assert that the country in question will have to be Oriental and that it will have to be under the cultural influence of Buddhism and/or Hinduism. Once this has been determined, a search for specific countries within the given cultural region takes place. Here they attempt to match alternative countries with the criteria that they have established. They further delimit the field of choice by rejecting those Oriental nations that deviate from the image they have constructed on the basis of their interpretation of the poems. Throughout this process they draw inferences to aid them in the defensible elimination of unwarranted hypotheses; for example, the rejection of China as a possible choice by Tim and Bob, which takes the form of what Hunt and Metcalf call an "if-then generalization."[4] The primary goal of the group is the discovery of an answer that harmonizes all the evidence and integrates the ten poems. However, they soon realize that whatever data are at their command, they are not sufficient to support conclusively any of the proposed solutions. The realization of this difficulty motivates them to seek additional sources, especially those that include more detailed and authoritative information.

[4]Maurice P. Hunt and Lawrence E. Metcalf. *Teaching High School Social Studies.* New York: Harper and Brothers, 1955.

Fourth Day

BILL W.   We have final proof. We found it.

STEVE.

TIM.

KAREN.

KAREN.   We checked these poems against Indian, Chinese, Japanese, and any other Oriental types of poems we could find, and we found out that this type of poem is Japanese only, and is called a *haiku*.

During the last phase of the discussion the students offer concluding suggestions that are based on newly obtained evidence. For the most part the additional proof was the result of the collation of the poems under investigation with all other relevant material which was accessible in the library. This line of inquiry was in part instigated by Karen's suggestion at the conclusion of the third day that directed attention to the form and style in addition to the content of the poems.

SUMMARY

The following four points provide the major results of this case study:

1. Without exception, the students were able to participate directly in the process of discovery and inquiry. This process entailed a number of related tasks—identifying and defining the problems at hand, devising alternative plans of attack, formulating working hypotheses from the given data and their previous learning experiences, testing the hypotheses by drawing logical inferences and by gathering relevant information, and arriving at a theory or "grand generalization" which draws together all bits of data and supporting hypotheses. It is interesting to note that the process of discovery moves from a stage of hunch and intuition to a stage of in-depth analysis and, finally, to the point at which knowledge-claims are based on concrete documentary evidence. Although this is the general direction followed in the discovery episode, speculative or "intuitive" thinking may be found, to a great or lesser degree, in all of the phases; when there is a gap in knowledge, the student reaches out into uncharted and largely unknown realms of interpretation and thinking. From this observation the complementary nature of intuitive and analytic thinking may be seen.

2. Historical materials are used as raw data or as archeological remains from which students may reconstruct a society at a given place

and period. The historical document furnishes the springboards for inquiry into human thought and action and the evolution of social institutions. In the process of reconstructing the event, historical hypotheses are often checked against contemporary phenomena; the students employ both historical and social science concepts, research techniques, and methods of analysis.

3. The way material is presented, coupled with the nondirective behavior of the teacher, leads to the creation of a new psychological climate. The students now become increasingly independent and they begin to question the authority of secondary material. They generally adopt an attitude of intelligent doubt, and they tend to propose new ideas and explanations that must be carefully defended. The class is given the opportunity to exchange ideas and analyze different views and interpretations.

4. The method of discovery has a highly motivating effect on students. Almost without exception, the students, directly or indirectly, demonstrate a great deal of personal involvement with the material under discussion. During the duration of the study there was wide classroom participation and intensive utilization of library resources. The motivating effect of the discovery episode is due, in large part, to the gamelike situation which reinforces the element of perplexity and incentive to explore. The teacher indirectly encourages student exploration by stubbornly refusing to provide ready-made answers.

INQUIRY INTO THE CULTURAL ORIGIN
OF AN UNFAMILIAR ARTIFACT

How do students respond to a strange-looking statuette that is a representative product of a culture separated from their own in time and space? To what extent does the confrontation with this object induce and motivate students to identify problems and seek reasonable solutions? These were some general questions raised by the authors in an investigation of the process of discovery as defined by Jerome Bruner.[5]

This particular study was conducted in a class of thirty students (juniors) of above-average intelligence who were studying topics primarily relating to American history and culture. A discovery episode was introduced at different intervals and, in the main, it attempted to sharpen the skills of problem solving and to encourage the development of creative ability.

[5] According to Bruner the highest state of human autonomy and perfection is reached when the individual discovers for himself relationships in his social and physical environment. See Jerome S. Bruner, "The Act of Discovery," *Harvard Educational Review* 31:21–32 (1961).

The teacher generated discussion by providing the object of inquiry and by presenting it in a gamelike atmosphere. His role was mainly nondirective and it consisted of such tasks as recognizing students, rephrasing questions, insisting on the defensibility of assertions, and creating a climate conducive to a free exchange of ideas. The teacher consistently refrained from giving additional information or assistance in developing a plan of attack. In our illustration the teacher opened up a discovery session by casually presenting to his class a statuette, an unusual aratifact that provided a novel experience and elicited the following response.[6]

[6]Because of space limitations only selected parts of the dialogue are reproduced; the dialogue was recorded by stenographers in the classroom. The object presented to the class was an exact reproduction of a Sumerian statuette. The statuette is a full-length sculpture in the round, about eight inches tall, of an adult Sumerian male. It is purported to be a portrait of a public official or priest and dates from approximately 3000 B.C.

First Day

SEVERAL
STUDENTS. What is it?

TEACHER. I don't really know. What do you think it is?

(*rapid succession of comments by different students*)

> How should we know?
> We can't tell!
> Where did you get it?
> Where's it from?
> It's funny looking!
> Tell us about the statue!

TEACHER. Why don't you try to think this through by yourselves? I'm not telling you.

JIM. Let's have a closer look at it.

TEACHER. All right, but *be careful!*

(*Teacher passes the object around the room. As the artifact circulates, the discussion resumes.*)

SUSAN. It looks like a voodoo doll to me.

LARRY. I think it looks like Mrs. Doe in a nightgown.

(*General laughter. Mrs. Doe apparently is not a very popular teacher!*)

MARC. I definitely think it is not a Mrs.

(*more laughter*)

DAVE. It's a statue.

JOHN. That sounds safe.

(*more laughter*)

MARC. It's of African origin.

MIKE. No, it's a statue of an Egyptian priest.

EDWARD. I think it's a priest, but I'm not sure it's Egyptian.

PAM. It looks Middle Eastern to me,

MARC. Maybe it's Aztec or something like that?

LOIS. Yes, I think it's American Indian because of the dress—the dress looks like it's made of feathers.

EDWARD. Maybe he's a ruler?

EUGENE. I wonder why he is bald. That must be some kind of sign of someone special.

NANCY. Perhaps it's an idol of some sort.

JIM. It looks strange—maybe it's a Chinese lord.

JOHN.   No, he has a Jewish nose, can't you see? Looks just like Mike.

(laughter)

LOIS.   Just tell us what it is, please.

TEACHER.   Why should I when you're all making such good guesses about it? Maybe no one knows what this is.

LOIS.   I'm sure you know, but just won't tell us because you want us to think about it.

TEACHER.   Well, what *do* you think about it?

(pause)

BARBARA.   I think we could try to eliminate some of the suggestions.

JOHN.   Mrs. Doe, for instance.

RONNA.   I think we should try to establish where it's from.

EUGENE.   Yes, I think we can definitely say that it's not African or a voodoo doll, or anything like that.

TEACHER.   Why? Do you have a reason for saying that?

EUGENE.   From the sculpture, we can see that this person would be of the Caucasian race. His features are definitely not Negroid.

BERNIE.   Then we can rule out that he is an Asiatic on the same grounds. He is not slanty-eyed or particularly Oriental-looking.

BARBARA.   That narrows down our choice. Now we only have to find out what white society this statute is from. I think this figure represents a person of the Caucasian race.

EDWARD.   Maybe so, but it's still a strange-looking statue—nothing like an American or European.

PAM.   It's not anything from any society I'm familiar with. It must be an ancient object.

DAVE.   Yes, yes. I agree, too.

TEACHER.   Does everyone agree with this? Why? Because of the smashed hands, for instance.

JOHN.   It doesn't seem to be anything from European or American culture—modern or medieval—so, it must be ancient.

EILEEN.   Yes, yes, we all agree.

(Heads nod agreement: general agreement is expressed.)

LOIS.   I don't know exactly why, but I have a feeling that it has got to be ancient.

SUSAN.   It may be a person of the Caucasian race, but it seems to be the product of a very peculiar culture, distant in time from us.

MARC.   It doesn't even seem to be Greek or Roman.

PAM.   The dress is what bothers me—that strange dress. We ruled out the possibility that this man is from an Asian society, which means that Indians, who are supposed to be related racially to the Chinese would also be ruled out—but the gown still looks like it's made of feathers. I don't know!

As we can see from the foregoing dialogue, the first day is spent on the following general activities:

1. A careful look at and a close examination of the object in an attempt to become thoroughly familiar with it.

2. A series of questions (e.g., "Where's it from?", or "Where did you get it?"), each of which structures a problem and suggests possible modes of investigation.

3. Creation of a range of alternative choices some of which relate to a previous experience.

Actually, the initial student response to the object is unorganized and haphazard. However, as they proceed with their analysis they search for specific clues that will enable them to determine the cultural origin of the art object. For example, most of the discussion is focused on the dress and the physical features of the person depicted by the statuette. These elements are incorporated into a generalizable theory of racial differences which is used as a tool in interpreting the object. Also, the newly constructed theory allows them to delimit the field of choice by rejecting inconsistent assertions; for example, that the statue represents a person of a Negroid or Mongoloid background. Once they have accepted the proposition that the person in the statue has Caucasian characteristics (thus narrowing the range of possibilities at this level), they broaden their frame of reference by adding the dimension of time to geographical region. They seem to operate on the assumption that the less familiar an object is the greater the chance it is part of a culture remote from our own both in time and space. The drawing of logical inferences and the construction of a theoretical framework enabled the students to go beyond the information given.

Second Day

TEACHER.   Well, who would like to start us off today by summarizing what we have accomplished?

EUGENE.   As I remember it, we decided that the statue is very ancient and that the man is a Caucasian.

MARC.   That doesn't sound as though we have gotten very far.

LARRY.   All we have to look for is an ancient Caucasian society.

DAVE.   Yes, but where? And what is this guy?

MIKE.   I still think he looks like an Egyptian priest. He looks priestly to me.

TEACHER.   Why do you think so? Why?

MIKE.   Because of the pose and the bare head. He seems stately and important.

RONNA.   He must be someone of importance. Why should they make a statue of someone unimportant?

BARBARA.   The sculpture must have served some purpose. This is the true size of it, isn't it?

TEACHER.   Yes, it is.

BARBARA.   Well then, a small statue like this must be from a household or a tomb. It can't be for public view. It's not big enough.

MARC.   Maybe the person was an official or political leader in his community.

SUSAN.   A poor person probably couldn't afford such a delicately carved statue—and probably wouldn't be very interested in having one made.

NANCY.   Then, this must be from a pretty advanced culture—it must have been done by someone skilled. It looks to me as though the artist was trying to make a likeness of the person represented by the statue.

SUSAN.   That sounds like a good idea. In art, all the primitive groups that we studied made things that were symbolic or magical or decorative, not representational like this.

CHUCK.   This must be the product of a fairly advanced group who knew advanced ways of civilization.

(*pause of about a minute*)

JOHN.   I don't think it's an Egyptian. What I remember of the Egyptians doesn't compare with this.

MIKE.   But look, the way he's dressed shows that he must be from a warm climate. He's barefoot.

JOHN.   Maybe that's just his indoor dress.

MIKE.   Well, even for indoors that's a springy way of dressing.

JOHN.   Yes, they couldn't dress that way if they lived in a cold, wet climate.

LOIS.   It just must come from a warm, dry region.

JOHN.   Well, but we still cannot be sure of that!

RONNA.   Maybe we can't tell, but we know that this statue is a representation of a man of some importance, maybe a priest from an advanced group of ancient Caucasian peoples.

TEACHER.   That's quite a bit of knowledge. Where can you go from here?

MIKE.   This society must have forced important men to shave their heads. This character is too bald to be bald naturally. I think Egyptian priests shave their heads.

MARC.   Yes, that would explain a lot of details. Egyptians were mostly Caucasian and were also quite advanced at an early date.

BARBARA.   But the clothing doesn't look Egyptian and I thought the Egyptian statues were idols, half man and half animal type idols.

SHELDON.   I think this is too life-like and realistic and simple to be something else and must have served some special private purpose.

DAVE.   But Egyptians did make some statues that were life-like. I remember seeing Queen Neferti's head or something like that.

TEACHER.   Queen Nefertiti's head?

DAVE.   Yes, that's it.

ILYSE.   Well, I think that if we agree that this is very old or the reproduction of something very old and that this man is from an advanced Caucasian culture, then it can only be from one place—the Middle East or ancient Greece.

JIM.   That's the "cradle of civilization" area. All of the earliest advanced groups that were of the white race lived there as far as I know.

DAN.   That's about what I remember too. It's got to be from that area.

LOIS.   Now all we have to do is figure out which one it is.

MARK.   Maybe it's of the Hebrew origin.

ROBERTA.   Maybe it's Babylonian or Persian.

MIKE.   I still think it's Egyptian.

JIM.   It could be from the Mediterranean islands. Some advanced peoples lived there, but I don't remember their names.

JOHN.   Wait a minute, it couldn't be Hebrew because they were forbidden to make idols or images of any kind by the Bible.

MARC.   But it still looks like Mike—maybe someone sinned.

(laughter)

DAN.   I'm not sure whether I like the idea that this was someone important. Perhaps he was a commoner. My reasons for saying this are the fact that our friend doesn't seem to be wearing any jewelry or ornament of any kind. I thought that important Egyptians—priests, nobles, Pharoahs, or Gods wore some kind of insignia or precious stones.

LOIS. That is rather strange.

EDWARD. Maybe this just isn't an Egyptian. How can we explain the shaven head if this is the figure of a commoner?

EUGENE. Maybe that was the custom for all men.

EDWARD. Maybe, but it seems unlikely to me.

EUGENE. Oh! Good grief—tell us—I can't wait.

TEACHER. You're all doing very well as it is—try to finish by yourselves.

ROBERTA. We can't decide. We're stuck.

SEVERAL STUDENTS. Yes, give us some hints.

The quest to interpret the statue now moves from a detailed examination of its features to a consideration of its functional significance; that is, the central question is what function the statue performed in that particular society. Actually, there are two lines of inquiry that are closely related to one another: (a) The making of the statue itself implies that the person being represented is important; and (b) the posture and apparel of the figure implies high status. Comments at this point (e.g., by Mark and Susan) further bolster these two hypotheses, but since there are some students who are in doubt about the validity of the hypotheses they are not systematically confirmed. It appears that at this stage a number of strategies operate simultaneously. Nancy, for instance, building on Susan's description of the object, "delicately carved statue," suggests that the culture must have been pretty advanced. This assertion is later reinforced by Chuck. Nancy opens up an entirely new way of looking at the object by introducing an artistic-stylistic dimension. Susan, in an attempt to view the object from this perspective points out the possibility of a symbolic image but accepts the theory that the statute represents a real person. This generalization strengthens the previous implication that a personal representation is a sign of a fairly advanced society with a high level of artistic sophistication and it further delimits the possible place of origin. The dialogue on the second day in comparison with the first day is characterized by frequent use of cognitive skills such as hypothesizing, drawing inferences, and furnishing relevant facts to support given interpretations. While there is some overlapping of skills and behaviors, in general terms the first day may be described as mainly exploratory behavior with a great deal of random hunch-playing, and the second as explanation-oriented with constant attempts to clarify and support a variety of rational propositions. At the end of the second day failure to reach any reasonably acceptable explanation of the origin and function of the statue produced impatience and a feeling of frustration. The teacher, while not responding to student requests for an answer, contributed to their motivation and gave them some kind of assurance that they were doing well. Apparently, this session raised their level of interest so that they actively sought outside evidence to solve their problem.

Third Day

ILYSE.   Susie has found the answer.

SUSIE.   Yes—I found it!

TEACHER. Well, before we hear Susie, are there any other suggestions?

PAM.   Yes, I believe he is a Middle Easterner because Egyptians did not dress that way, although their priests did in fact shave their heads. I checked this by looking at Egyptian styles in history books.

JIM.   He is probably a Babylonian or Assyrian of some sort. If we get too far before them, then we would probably not be able to find any life-like sculptures, just symbolic or decorative objects.

ILYSE.   I checked on ancient Greek and Cretan styles and they don't compare at all. They wore clothes that were either cut differently, like a tunic or a short skirt, or they wore brightly patterned cloth, not this feathery or fringy looking stuff.

DAVE.   What is that stuff made of anyway? I still can't decide from the statue.

SUSIE.   Please let me tell! The man's clothing is made of fringe, like a flapper's dress from the 20s and he's a Sumerian official according to the reference book I found. Furthermore, I found an identical statue in the Oriental Institute at the University of Chicago.

LOIS.   What's a Sumerian?

SUSIE.   The Sumerians are the forerunners of the Babylonians and other Middle Eastern cultures. They were the earliest civilization in the area and the statue must be about 5,000 years old.

(*Susie passes a book around showing a Sumerian and explaining their origin and culture.*)

During the third day of deliberations the students clearly demonstrated that they were so moved to look up a variety of relevant sources. In checking these sources they were trying to confirm or reject the hypotheses formulated in class by collating the object under scrutiny with related artifacts or photographs. For example, Pam checked history books, Ilyse referred to sources dealing with Greek and Cretan styles, and Susie paid a visit to the Oriental Institute. At this phase of inquiry, several members of the class produced concrete evidence to pinpoint the precise culture responsible for the object. Furthermore, the students made an effort to present a more complete picture of the cultural and geographic setting of the artifact.

DISCUSSION

During the three-day period, the participants showed an increasing degree of involvement with the problems and ideas generated through their encounter with the object. This involvement was prompted by the initial perplexing material, teacher's indirect role, and a climate conducive to speculation. The high level of student motivation was manifested in their classroom behavior—for example, wide participation in discussion, a continuous exchange of ideas, searching questions addressed to each other and to the teacher, and intensive utilization of library and community resources. It appears that genuine interest in investigating the problem served to produce self-sustaining activity.

Intellectually, the dialogue moved from a random examination of the object (guesses, claims, intuitions, and feelings) to an analytical stage in which in-depth inquiry was emphasized. This stage was characterized by an increasing awareness of the complexities of the problem at hand and by the development of more sophisticated strategies of searching for a solution. A number of intellectual operations were performed throughout the session: identifying problems, formulating alternative theories, drawing inferences, examining relevant data, and arriving at a satisfactory solution. Thus the pattern of thought is characterized by an interplay of creative and analytical elements. This type of intellectual exercise seems to be valuable because it *forces* the student to explore and to become familiar with various research strategies and procedures.

It has been suggested that a discovery situation strips teachers of their most important classroom functions. Although it is true that the traditional concept of the teacher as the main purveyor of information is not lived up to, the conditions of discovery create novel yet crucial teacher roles. In general terms, the teacher operates under the assumption that students are capable of thinking for themselves. To facilitate independent inquiry, the teacher provides the initial springboard carefully prepared to cause perplexity. These materials may be chosen from a variety of sources such as objects of art, primary historical documents, statistical data, literary materials, paintings, and music. In our illustration with the statuette, the teacher spent considerable time in selecting an appropriate object and planning its introduction into the classroom. In addition to this task, teachers perform the following important classroom functions:

1. They may offer helpful hints or clues at points of impasse or stalemate (but they must be careful not to give away the story).

2. They prod students by redirecting their original questions.

3. They insist on the evidential or rational support of student assertions.

4. They create a classroom atmosphere which invites the free flow of views and comments.

5. They legitimize and reward creative thought.

At times it may appear as if the class were spending too much time on one discovery episode. Certainly, the teacher can give the answer to a problem and thus terminate the discussion in two or three minutes. The point is that if students are to engage directly in the conduct of inquiry they have to spend sufficient time to develop and refine relevant strategies and techniques. Reliance on drill and student-teacher question and answer sessions will not do the job.

COMPARATIVE ANALYSIS

For comparative purposes the same Sumerian statuette was used again to activate exploration. In this particular case we were experimenting with younger students (referred to as Group B) who were generally of lower intellectual ability. Although the students in Group A were juniors and averaged an IQ of 125, in the present experiment the students were sophomores and had an average IQ of 91. The class had been in session for only a few months and was not too familiar with the discovery approach. Two teachers, one of whom had had previous experience with this instructional strategy, cooperated in conducting this session. The general idea was to observe the pattern of thought and personal involvement of students, holding under control as many factors as possible, with the exception of age and intelligence.

In order to illustrate similarities and differences between the two groups, excerpts from the transcribed dialogue of the second group will be analyzed in the following pages.

First Day

(*Statuette is passed around among the students, who take about fifteen minutes to examine it.*)

TEACHER. What do you think this is?
GARY. A Buddha.
IVAN. A girl who lost her hair!
KEN. It's not a girl, but a man. Have a closer look.
GARY. A Buddhist monk.
IVAN. Is it Chinese? Aztec? Mayan?
MICHAEL. The Rolling Stones!
CYNTHIA. His ears don't match.
MARY ANN. And his head is lopsided.
CARLA. One eye is lower than the other.
IVAN. It's a Chinese god.
MICHAEL. It's an Egyptian god.
GARY. Some guy struck his father and they cut his hands off.
MARY ANN. It's some kind of priest.
NELL. Does it say anything on the bottom?
BILL. Made in Japan!
MICHAEL. It looks like a god.
BILL. It's a slave from Egypt.
GARY. It looks like a monk.
PAULETTE. It's a surgeon who got his hands cut off.
CAROL. But his hands look like they were broken off.
IVAN. Is it Chinese? Tibetan? Laos?
NELL. It's from a museum. Someone reproduced it in a museum. The hands were destroyed some time ago.
IVAN. Is it Greek?
MICHAEL. Guy's got a big nose.
GARY. I still say it's a Buddhist monk.
CARLA. There does seem to be something religious about the statue.
BILL (*to teacher*). Do you know what it is?
TEACHER. What would you do if I didn't tell you what it was?
BILL. Forget about it.
KAREN. I'd be so curious . . .
TEACHER. You'd do what?
NELL. I wouldn't be able to sleep if you didn't tell us.
KEN. If I thought it was something—like a Hindu—I'd look it up in an encyclopedia.

Generally speaking, Group B reacted to the object-stimulus in the same manner as Group A. In both cases the students touched and looked carefully at the artifact in order to get a complete picture of its facets. In both cases the statuette created a sense of puzzlement. Members of both groups offered observations about the features of the figure and simultaneously raised questions suggesting possible alternatives for investigation. The major difference between the two groups during the first day of discussion was the range of "intuitive" response. Group A seemed to be more restrained and systematic in volunteering hypotheses; Group B, on the other hand, was much more spontaneous in its response and rather uninhibited in providing a wide variety of imaginative ideas. For example, such statements as "The Rolling Stones," "Some guy struck his father and they cut his hands off," "Made in Japan!" are unusual hunches, yet are indicative of a high degree of creative talent.[7] As a result of this "wild" guessing by several participants, Group B does not advance much beyond the stage of "first reaction"; Group A, however, goes easily beyond this stage to develop plans for approaching the problem. It appears that without knowing it, Group A is more "economy" oriented, to use Bruner's term,[8] than Group B; that is, Group A poses for itself a limited number of questions which in turn suggest a limited range of alternatives for reaching a well-grounded solution. Group B, by suggesting a rather formidable list of possibilities, creates a situation in which the task of systematic examination becomes much more difficult. It should be noted, however, that what Group B lacks in systematic and analytic procedures it makes up in originality of thought; Group B exhibits a more "free-wheeling" stance in responding to the stimulus and less concern with logical implication and strategies. Although both groups are involved with exploration, Group B seems to be more caught up in the experience itself without paying much attention to the long-range consequences.

Second day

TEACHER.   Have you been able to figure out what this is?
BILL.   It looks like it's from Egypt.
PAULETTE.   It's a surgeon.
BILL.   But from what country.

---

[7] This is an example which corroborates to some extent the assertion by Getzels and Jackson that the highly creative students are not necessarily the highly intelligent.
[8] Jerome S. Bruner, "Some Theorems on Instruction Illustrated with Reference to Mathematics," in *Theories of Learning and Instruction*, The Sixty-third Yearbook of the National Society for the Study of Education, ed., Ernest R. Hilgard, Chicago: University of Chicago Press, 1964, pp. 306–335.

IVAN.   He's an Aztec.

GARY.   It's Mr. Smith.

(*These possibilities were put on the board: Egyptian, Hindu, Buddhist, surgeon, Aztec, etc.*)

TEACHER.   Let's approach this scientifically. If you dug this up somewhere, how would you go about finding out what it was?

BILL.   I'd know what it was from where I found it.

TEACHER.   Suppose you found it in a trunk at home and no one around you knew what it was.

CAROL.   I'd take it to a geologist because they know about different regions.

TEACHER.   But what does a geologist study?

CAROL.   Rocks and such.

TEACHER.   But you know more than a geologist just by looking at this figure, don't you? Yesterday we had a problem. Some of you said the hands were cut off, some said they were broken off. How can we come to a conclusion about this?

MARY ANN.   It would have been smooth if it had been made that way, but that's rough.

TEACHER.   Anything else?

CAROL.   There's an imprint (on the body) where the hand would have been.

KEN.   I still think that the hands weren't on it—that they were chopped off. That was made by a sloppy artist. It's an Egyptian priest.

MICHAEL.   It's an Egyptian slave.

BILL.   It's an Egyptian king holding those two things—flags?—emblems? and he has his hands crossed.

CAROL.   It doesn't look like a slave because he wouldn't have such a fancy dress. It's not a king because he would have a better dress.

BILL.   All Egyptian kings were bald.

MARY ANN.   No, those were the priests who were bald!

TEACHER.   Can you prove it? . . .

MARY ANN.   Look it up.

GARY.   Maybe it is an Aztec?

NELL.   No. If it were, he would have hair.

MICHAEL.   Indians had dark skin.

IVAN.   Aztecs had long hair.

CARL.   The Aztecs would not be dressed in leaves. They would have had cloth.

MICHAEL.   It's no priest. They always wore all kinds of fancy clothes and long capes.

TEACHER.   Can you prove it?

GARY.   Is it Chinese?

BILL.   It doesn't have slanted eyes.

CAROL.   We can eliminate the Egyptian. Page 53 in our book gives a picture of an Egyptian. They wore head pieces, and different clothing. The *World Book* has pictures of Aztecs. He doesn't look like them.

MICHAEL.   Whoever made that must have been intelligent. You can't just sit down and make something like that.

BILL.   The Egyptians were intelligent.

CAROL.   It doesn't have an Egyptian wardrobe on. It's not dressed for Egyptian weather. They wore headpieces like scarves to protect themselves from the sun.

BILL.   Kings dressed like that, but did the peasants?

MICHAEL.   I think he looks like a slave because he doesn't have a shirt on.

MARY ANN.   But that [outfit] took a lot of work to make.

MICHAEL.   He has to be in the lower class.

BILL.   He's Babylonian, or maybe he's Assyrian.

NELL.   I think he's a Sumerian. Page 61 looks just like him.

CAROL.   But there's a Sumerian woman on page 66 and the eyes and such are completely different.

BILL.   Is it King Hammurabi?

TEACHER.   How could you find out absolutely, for sure?

CAROL.   Take it to a geologist and find out what it is made of. Then find out what different people used to make figures out of.

TEACHER.   What else could you do?

CARLA.   Find the styles of the ancient times. Look up Egyptian styles—

MICHAEL.   Who's going to go through all that trouble?

BILL.   Page 43 looks like him.

CAROL F.   Would you give us more clues?

MARY ANN.   On page 40, there's an Egyptian wearing cloth.

BILL.   Maybe the cloth on the figure is overlapping.

CAROL.   But there are grooves in the cloth.

TEACHER.   Can we eliminate any of the possibilities?

CAROL.   Cross out Aztecs. It's not a Hindu. But maybe before we cross out the civilization, we should find out what class he was in.

MICHAEL.   He's no priest. They just didn't wear that. They wore capes and all that.

CAROL.   Cross out "king." He would have worn more than that. And he's not a god. Looks too lifelike.

During the deliberations of the second day the flow of discussion became strategy-oriented, much resembling what Group A did toward the conclusion of the first day and in the beginning of the second. However, at many crucial points the teacher led members of Group B into formulating plans of action. In contrast to Group A, Group B appeared to engage in random and disorganized conjectures, and it was not so quick to capitalize on whatever clues it had at its disposal to draw logical inferences. Its difficulty stemmed primarily from its inability to focus on a limited range of warranted possibilities. On the other hand, many intellectual operations observed in the performance of Group A were present in the exchanges of Group B as well. For instance, Carol refuted both Michael's and Bill's proposition by suggesting that the clothing worn by the figure is too elaborate for a slave yet not fancy enough for a king. This comment stemmed from an implicit generalization that high status is associated with style and quality of clothing. This assumption was further elaborated by Carol, Bill, Michael, Mary Ann and others who introduced additional pieces of information, generally in support of the assertions. Nell, going a step further, was able to find in the textbook a photograph of figures somewhat similar to the statuette. These figures were identified as Sumerian. Carol, however, challenged Nell's evidence by pointing out that certain features of the figures in the photograph were different, thus prompting a search for even more conclusive evidence. The deliberations of the second day were concluded by collating the statuette with pictorial material in the text and by eliminating what they considered to be unlikely possibilties.

Third Day

TEACHER. Have you found out what the figure is?

CARLA. It's not Egyptian. I looked it up in a book and they didn't dress that way. Will he tell us what it is?

TEACHER. What if he doesn't?

CARLA. I'd look it up again.

IVAN. Is what's-his-name coming back today? Nobody guessed and he'll have to tell us the answer. I'm not saying anything.

GARY. It's a Buddhist monk. I found it in my encyclopedia—the *World Book*—and it was just like that but had a gold dress on.

TEACHER. Would you bring the book in so that we can compare it with the figure?

GARY. I'll bring it tomorrow.

NELL. I'm almost convinced it's Sumerian.

TEACHER.   Prove it.
CAROL.   Maybe it's a Buddhist. The Aztecs had long robes and used feathers, so that's not an Aztec.
HOWARD.   Maybe his skirt was made of metal or wood.
KEN.   It could be an Egyptian servant. The picture in our book only shows a high-class person.
TEACHER.   If you think it's a lower-class Egyptian, what should you do?
KEN.   Find an example.

Fourth Day

TEACHER.   Have you found out what this is yet?
GARY.   I forgot to bring the book. But it's a Sumerian. We have evidence thanks to Ken.
KEN.   This book has pictures of Sumerian figures that look like that.
TEACHER.   How does this figure match the pictures?
MARY ANN.   The hands are the same.
CARLA.   The skirt is made the same way and so are the feet.
TEACHER.   What about the supporting column?
MARY ANN.   That's the same, too.
TEACHER.   Do you all agree that the figure matches the pictures enough to be Sumerian?
CLASS.   Yes.
CAROL.   I don't agree with it. Let me have another look at the picture. Well, I guess it does look that way.

The third and fourth days were mostly spent on other school work; the discovery episodes were given only limited time. During these sessions activity evolved around attempts to collate material in various textbooks and reference books in the library. Although not stated explicitly, the main thrust of independent study was to find indispensable proof in photographs of archeological remains. It appears that the major consideration underlying student exploration is related to the cultural style and artistic idiosyncrasies of selected artifacts. It is assumed that stylistically similar objects are the products of one culture. Although there was some anxiety, real or feigned, throughout the course of the dialogue, there was also a high sense of achievement and personal gratification. All in all, the students considered their efforts successful in the sense that they obtained a defensible explanation and they experienced the excitement of learning.

SUMMARY OF CASES INVOLVING SUMERIAN ARTIFACT

It may be said that the differences in response patterns between the two groups are of degree rather than kind. It is evident from the flow of discussion presented here that both groups generally move through the same phases of inquiry, and that the differences involve primarily levels of sophistication and organization. For instance, the response of Group B is characterized by a higher incidence of speculation and guesswork and a less systematic plan of investigation. Students in Group A are much more cautious in selecting a strategy of intellectual attack, and they probe more deeply into the nuances of the problem. Not only does it appear easier for Group A to develop a mode of attack but the group is capable of following up their hypotheses through a series of logical deductions. Group B responds directly and unpretentiously to the problem created by the unidentified object and relates it to their concrete and highly personal experiences. The level of abstraction among Group B students is not as high as among Group A students.

The similarities between the two groups are far more striking than the differences. Both groups exhibit a high level of interest in and great enthusiasm for this type of classroom experience. The high degree of motivation is demonstrated by (a) an increase in the number of students participating in classroom discussion, and a rise in the proportion of student versus teacher discourse,[9] (b) a sustained and relevant discussion over a period of three to five classroom sessions; (c) appeals to outside sources (e.g., other teachers, library reference materials, etc.); (d) informal discussion within the peer group outside of class. As we mentioned before, the groups proceeded through approximately the same cycle of operations; that is, object examination, problem identification, speculation, strategy formation, and so on. These operations, however, are not discrete and there is some overlap. It is also interesting to observe that there is a convergence of perceptions of the statue; that is, the fact that both groups tend to describe the object in similar terms implies a common organizing framework.

In these two episodes the teacher sought to establish an open climate of inquiry and capitalize on student potential for self-directed activity. It is apparent that he is more directive with students in Group

---

[9]One teacher reported that both the number of participants and the amount of participation nearly doubled during this kind of confrontation as compared with the traditional expository method of instruction.

B; in order to initiate and especially to sustain inquiry, he prods or "bugs" the students, gives hints or clues, asks for the reasons behind assertions, and heightens the suspense by denying them the missing parts to the enigma. In this particular case teacher involvement in the process of inquiry exceeded what it might otherwise have been since Group B was relatively inexperienced in giving full vent to their creative abilities. All other factors notwithstanding, it is conceivable that Group B would have needed much less teacher guidance if they had been exposed to previous classroom situations of a similar nature.

ARMS AND LEGS: A SCIENCE LESSON

Thirty-three urban sixth grade students of average ability were presented with a science lesson which focused upon the concept of adaptation. Each student was given a sheet illustrating a variety of human and animal limbs. These limbs were selected because each had special features unlike the others and each suggested an environment most suitable to its functions. For instance, the flipper suggested an aquatic setting, the ape's hand and foot an arborial environment, and the horse's hoof a grassland or open prairie type of place. The human hand and foot, by comparison, suggested a broad range of uses, wider and less specialized perhaps than any of the other creatures.

Students were seated in a semicircle around a demonstration table and asked to study each of the mammal limbs portrayed on their sheet. The teacher handled responses and questions in ways which encouraged student leaps of imagination and inference. The lesson illustrates how a teacher can exploit "ordinary" data to strongly encourage skills of hypothesizing and extrapolation.

TEACHER. What do you see on this sheet?
STUDENT. That one is hairy.
STUDENT. Is that a cat?
STUDENT. I didn't get a sheet!
STUDENT. Where is the cat?
STUDENT. I see arms and legs from different animals.
STUDENT. . . . and people, too!
TEACHER. Good, good!
STUDENT. I see a bear paw or maybe a dog's.
STUDENT. These are funny. Why no bodies?
TEACHER. I don't know. Why don't you make up what's missing!
STUDENT. These are limbs.
STUDENT. Yes, all ways of moving around on land, sea, air.
STUDENT. One of the feet is hairy—a gorilla?

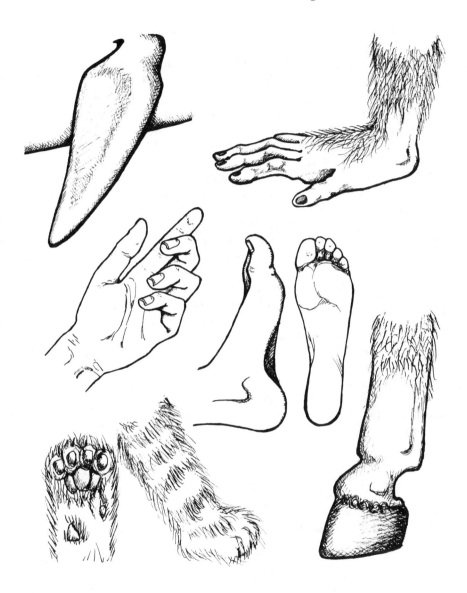

STUDENT. I see a seal flipper or maybe a whole fin.
STUDENT. I see a horse's hoof.
TEACHER. Are there any differences and similarities between the different arms and legs?
STUDENT. Sure there are.
STUDENT. There are many, many differences.
TEACHER. For instance?

STUDENT.   There are arms and legs, but none of them are for the same thing.

STUDENT.   But not everywhere. Those kinds of animals would live in open areas, like plains, where they could run away from the animals who hunt them.

TEACHER.   Are any of the hands or feet like each other?

STUDENT.   Yes, there is one that looks like a monkey's and one that looks like a human's. (*Points them out.*) They are a lot alike.

TEACHER.   That's good, but how?

STUDENT.   Both have hands with real fingers and a thumb. But people have feet that are flat on the bottom while the monkeys don't.

TEACHER.   Why do you think that might be?

STUDENT.   I think that the monkeys live in trees and their hands and feet are good for climbing. People could climb but wouldn't do as well as monkeys. Our feet are good for running.

TEACHER.   As good as the animal with hooves?

STUDENT.   No, but pretty good. I mean people who run the marathon can run miles and miles if they're in shape and most people are good walkers even if they can't run. I jog and it's easy.

STUDENT.   Yeah, I jog, too, and I can run pretty fast. I can almost catch my dog sometimes.

STUDENT.   The monkeys, though, couldn't run good at all. They'd be terrible out of a tree!

STUDENT.   Oh, I don't know, I'd like to live in a tree!

STUDENT.

(*Laughter*)

STUDENT.   We were monkeys once, but now we're better and smarter than they are!

STUDENT.   You are a monkey!

TEACHER.   Let's get back to the subject of feet and hands. Those were some excellent observations, but does everyone agree about the pictures shown? Why or why not?

STUDENT.   Yes, yes. I think that's what these pictures show. Each has a different use or purpose in nature. Each is built for a different purpose.

TEACHER.   But what about the human hand or foot. Is that as good as all the others? For swimming? For running? For climbing?

STUDENT.   My dog, for instance, has a paw that's good for running, but he can only pick things up with his mouth.

STUDENT.   Very few animals really can pick things up and handle them in a careful way.

STUDENT. You're right. Most use their mouths more like we use our hands.

STUDENT. I read in a book on early man that we probably evolved from apes, but changed to live on flat areas—plains. Walking upright helps in a flat area where there are few trees.

STUDENT. I read in *Guinness (Book of Records)* that people are excellent runners and can cover long distances even if they can't beat the fastest animals.

STUDENT. No, but our hands are better than those of almost any other animal.

TEACHER. Why?

STUDENT. Because we can use it to pick things up, make things, press things, hold, pinch, lift, use tools. . . .

STUDENT. Especially pinch. (*Reaches over to classmate.*)

TEACHER. Uh-uh!! Don't do it!

STUDENT. And we have a thumb!

STUDENT. What? What's the big deal with a thumb?

(*Laughter, kidding around, holding thumbs up.*)

STUDENT. Well, the thumb lets us hold things in a way we couldn't without it. I can't really explain it, but, for instance the monkey or ape in the picture couldn't really hold a pencil the way we can or use a screwdriver because he doesn't have a thumb.

TEACHER. That's a good point! Why don't all of us try picking things up or using a pencil or pen without our thumbs.

(*Laughter, monkey-like noises and grimaces.*)

TEACHER. Well, was it hard or easy? Hmmm?

STUDENT. Tough, you can't really control the pencil. You have to sort of grab it around with all your fingers and your writing is shaky.

TEACHER. Uh-huh!

STUDENT. Yes, and you can't aim too well if you want to throw something.

STUDENT. And you can't lift small or floppy things.

STUDENT. Yeah, I think . . . I think we should continue this experiment. I like it!

STUDENT. It's fun to pretend you're something else. I bet we couldn't swing in trees as well as monkeys, but I bet they couldn't use a knife or a saw or a drill too well!

STUDENT. What if we had hooves. I bet we'd never have evolved!

TEACHER. So what are your conclusions, if any, about hands and feet?

STUDENT. We can use our hands and feet for many purposes. Most animals can't do as much!

STUDENT. I think people can use their hands better than most animals and we can do a pretty good job of other things as well.

TEACHER. Great!

STUDENT. Our thumbs are like pincers. We can hold things from two directions. We can touch our other fingers with our thumbs, grab round things or straight or even square things.

TEACHER. For example?

STUDENT. We can run pretty well, though maybe not as well as a horse or antelope!

STUDENT. We can climb, too, but not like a monkey because we can only use our hands as they do but our feet are really best for walking.

STUDENT. People can swim, too. We learn how and some people are very good at it, even though whales, seals, and such do it better and can stay under water for long and are probably faster.

STUDENT. Oh, I get it, people can use their arms and legs for many purposes, while animals really can't. Each animal's arms or legs are suited for one activity like running, jumping, climbing, swimming but not for all. We can do a little of everything. Maybe that's why people can live in all kinds of places: hot, cold, wet, mountainous. . . .

STUDENT. Different types of hands and feet came about because each animal fitted into a different kind of place; some lived in water; some on land; others in the trees. Each developed to fit in nicely with their kind of place.

STUDENT. What do you think people would be like if we hadn't developed. . .

STUDENT. Evolved. . .

STUDENT. . . . Evolved hands with thumbs and flat feet with arches.

(Bell rings.)

STUDENT. We'd probably still be in the trees with—want a banana?

TEACHER. Why don't we continue this interesting discussion tomorrow. Where would we be without our type of limbs? Where will we be in the future? Where would you *want* to be?

We are offering the transcription of this lesson for several reasons: first, because it represents a teacher's effort to stimulate student thinking through a "discovery" mode of instruction; second, because it includes a gradation of questions and responses from relatively low to relatively high cognitive levels; and third, because it is based upon a use of curriculum that specifically fosters analytical thinking of a sort that we are advocating should be a daily feature of classrooms.

The picture used here was designed by the authors and drafted by Ms. J. Castiglione. It is constructed as a type of collage that stimulates divergent thinking about the concept of adaptive mechanisms in nature. Rather than offering a lecture on environment and adaptation, the content of the lesson immediately raises questions of comparison and contrast between different limbs and parts of mammalian bodies. Comparison, as discussed in other examples of inquiry and discovery, is a powerful device for sparking and sustaining discussions, particulary those in which several examples of a problem are being studied. Furthermore, we would argue that the picture is made far more interesting because it is incomplete and does not give every detail to the students. Showing the whole animal would reduce the focus of the lesson and perhaps provide more data than are necessary to provoke a discussion of adaptive mechanisms. Instead, just enough information is presented to evoke student questions, problems, and responses. Clues are carefully controlled to provoke responses, but not so much as to make the points involved immediately apparent, i.e., without the need for analyses and syntheses to take place in the students' minds. Hypothesizing, a key element in creative thinking, arises in our view out of problems that invite solution and not out of problems that are fully resolved or appear to be finished.

While the material for the lesson provides both evidence and motivation for starting discussion, the teacher demonstrates techniques of questioning and redirection which are particularly effective components in a) the process of sustaining ideas, b) guiding inquiry to successively more complex cognitive levels, and c) encouraging students to initiate their ideas about the data at hand. The teacher regularly rewarded responses, but more importantly, made use of and reflected students' responses without reprimands and corrections. Thus fostering and using students' ideas gives recognition and promotes production simultaneously. Using students' ideas also helps to create a classroom atmosphere in which "thinking out loud" is a legitimate and honored activity.

In addition, the teacher in this example moved the discussion forward by recycling the data through increasingly sophisticated questions that built up from an informational base through analysis to synthesis and judgment. In general, but not always, the teacher moved from lower to higher cognitive levels and back again. The students, interestingly, did not always reflect each level of questioning in their responses. In some instances, students gave information when reasoning was requested by the teacher, while other exchanges contained dramatic leaps from the data to relatively high-level inferences, e.g., toward the beginning of the lesson when a student drew an insight about the function of arms and legs from their appearance. When a question did not achieve a congruent answer or response, the teacher dropped back temporarily to a lower level and started forward again from a base or reasoning level that was easier for students to utilize.

Most significant, however, was the teacher's strategy of pressing for answers or questions that dealt with the more difficult problems in the lesson. This upward pressure acts as both a goal and motivation since students are strongly encouraged to use their own powers of analysis to solve problems, a situation that expands student's cognitive and creative skills and makes the classroom a fun place to be yet one that is intellectually demanding as well.

ANALYZING POPULATION DATA

Population data were used as a springboard for discovering in this case study. As before, the following outcomes are claimed as a result of emphasizing discovery in the classroom: (a) it increases the students' intellectual competence, (b) it motivates learning from within rather than from without, (c) it promotes the acquisition of modes of intellectual attack on learning how to learn, and (d) it enables the participants to retrieve related information with facility.[10]

The first hypothesis deals with student ability to develop and refine cognitive skills in selecting and applying information to the problem at hand. The second proposition states that when a person is involved in discovery his/her behavior is competence-oriented and self-rewarding; the desire to solve the problem becomes its own reward. The third hypothesis suggests that while knowledge of the formal aspects of inquiry is important, the individual needs to be involved directly in the processes and techniques of problem-solving. Direct participation in inquiry will lead to learning how to organize data and develop systematic strategies to attack a given problem. The last claim indicates that information used as the basis of inquiry is retained more completely by learners because they relate the information to the process itself. Thus content and process become inseparable components of the total learning process. In sum, self-initiated and self-sustained inquiry helps develop individual human capability to its fullest.

[10] Jerome S. Bruner, "The Act of Discovery," *Harvard Educational Review* 31:21–32, 1961.

To test the foregoing hypotheses, the investigators conducted a series of discovery episodes that were planned and executed in two Chicago public high schools over a period of approximately two years.[11] The particular study reported here took place in a United States history class composed of 30 juniors of slightly above average intellectual ability. The general approach of the course was directed toward the critical analysis of original sources and historically controversial material; the course followed broadly the sequence of events in American society. Intermingled with the formal-analytical aspects of instruction there were a few discovery sessions mostly of a documentary nature; that is, a document was presented, the origin, referent, and author of which were carefully deleted; the students were encouraged to find the missing details. The material serving as a springboard dealt with birth and death rates in four diffeent countries, covering a time span of approximately 70 years. The statistical information was given to the students in chart form as reproduced on pages 106 and 107.[12]

Except for the charts and the notes, no other clues, instructions, or guidelines were given to the students by the teacher. In a discovery situation the teacher's control of the teaching-learning situation is not of the traditional type; it is mostly nondirective. Any kind of structuring of the learning experience is in the selection and development of the initial curiosity-generating material and in the teacher's continuous encouragement of student self-directed activity. The teacher's main task is to facilitate the flow of discussion by recognizing students, rephrasing statements, redirecting questions, and rewarding imaginative thought.

The discussion that ensued from the confrontation with the statistical information was recorded and transcribed by four stenographers. Because of space limitations, only selected parts of the transcriptions are reproduced here.

First Day

(Teacher enters room and distributes two dittoed sheets to each student. Each sheet contains two graphs. Each graph represents the

---

[11] For a report of an earlier experience see Byron G. Massialas and Jack Zevin, "Teaching Social Studies through Discovery," *Social Education* 28:384–387, 400, November, 1964.

[12] The charts are drawn on the basis of data derived from Kingsley Davis, "Population," *Scientific American* 309:63–71, No. 3, September 1963; *Statesman's Year-Book*, London: Macmillan and Company, 1890, 1900, 1920, 1948; *U.N. Demographic Yearbook: Population*, New York: U.N. Publishing House, 1960; *The Statistical Yearbook of Egypt*, Cairo: Egyptian Ministry of Finance, Statistical Department, Government Press, 1882, 1897, 1907, 1919.

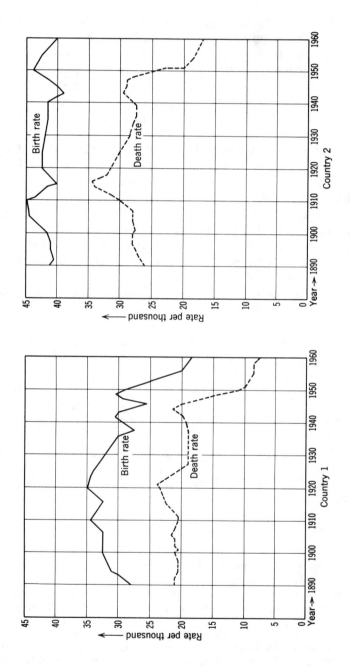

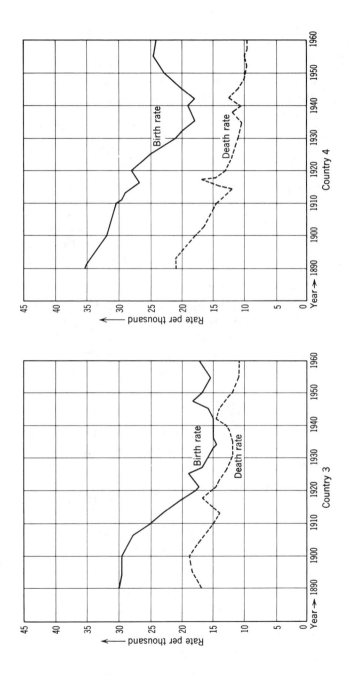

birth and death rate for a different country; however, the exact country represented is not shown.)

SEVERAL
STUDENTS. What are we going to do with this?
TEACHER. Read the information you have. Then decide what you want to do with it.

(A very long pause; approximately ten minutes. Students apparently studying the charts carefully.)

ROBERTA. Aren't these the birth and death rates for different countries?
TEACHER. Yes—they are given for the years 1890 until 1960.
ROBERTA. Well, the rates change a lot for the different countries.
GAIL. Not only that, but the rates are different for each country.
NANCY. Each of these countries must be very different because the rates show this.
TEACHER. Well, why not?
TED. Well, many of the countries seem to be affected by the wars. I mean about 1917 or 1943 there is usually a rise shown in the death rates and a lowering in the birth rates.
ALAN. I think country number two may be a bigger one than country number three because its birth and death rates are higher.
JAN. Can that be so?
TEACHER. Well, can it? Someone think about this! Any suggestions?
STEVE. I don't think that's right. We can't tell the size of the country or how many people are in it from these graphs.
MARIS. Why?
STEVE. Because these are graphs of rates or proportions. The graphs tell us how many people were born or died in proportion to the total number of people in that country. We can't tell what the total was though.
GAIL. That sounds right. At the side of each graph it tells the number of persons per thousand of the countries' population who were born or died.
DORIS. Each of the four countries might be small or large or medium sized. Is there any way of telling?

(pause of several minutes)

STEVE. I guess not. We can tell that the population is getting bigger or smaller by subtracting the death rate from the birth rate. The bigger the number we get the bigger the population is getting.

JAN.	That means that the bigger the gap between the two rates, the more people there are in that country.
TAMMY.	Well, what does that tell us about each country? What is each country?
JAN.	I don't know.
TED.	I still think that of all these countries were affected by the two great World Wars.
TAMMY.	But doesn't each of them seem to be affected in different ways, some more and some less?
TED.	Yes, no two of the countries are exactly the same although all of them do show rising death rates and lowering birth rates in and around the World War periods.
MARIS.	When were the World Wars?
BRUCE.	The First World War lasted from 1914 to 1918.
LEE.	Wait, that depends on the country. If I remember rightly, the United States wasn't really involved in World War I until about 1917.
BARBARA.	World War II lasted from about 1940 to 1945 also depending on the country.
NANCY.	Then, too, different countries wouldn't be affected as much as others by the wars. For instance, if a war were being fought within a country's territory, then the death rates would be much higher than it would be for a country that was fighting the war on someone else's land.
DONNA.	Well, how can we tell what each country is?
ROY.	Yes, we don't even know what kind of a country each one is.
KARYN.	This is too hard!
TAMMY.	We need help.
DORIS.	We only have birth and death rates to go by. We need some hints.
TEACHER.	Well, I don't think you're trying hard enough. Think it over tonight and we'll continue tomorrow.

As noted in the foregoing dialogue, the greater portion of the first day was spent in an effort to understand and interpret the graphs. The discussion that opened the discovery episode was an orientation into the problems presented by the given material. Since the class was not familiar with this type of information (graphs, etc.) some time was given simply to reading and correctly interpreting the statistical data. As the discussion evolved, the behavior of students became more and more purposeful and they began to set for themselves specific goals: for example, Tammy's demand to relate the data and the inferences drawn from them to the identification of the country in question.

Toward the end of the first day they were determined to figure out which countries are represented by the birth and death rates. Generalizations formulated by Ted and Nancy regarding the four countries (e.g., wars affect the death and birth rate of a nation) were only partially developed and explored. The first day ended with a feeling of unresolved difficulty and some frustration. The teacher obviously did not do anything to lessen apparent student anxiety.

Second Day

TEACHER. Well, any new suggestions today?

GAIL H. Maybe country number two is the United States because it has a high birth rate. I think a wealthy country would have a high birth rate.

BRUCE. But look at the death rate. Would an advanced country like the United States have such a high death rate? Compare the death rate for country number two with the other countries.

NANCY. Wouldn't a well-to-do country have a high birth rate, though?

JAN. That does seem right. I don't know.

ROBERTA. Poor people have a lot of children. I think right now the government is thinking of giving many poor people here birth-control advice.

GAIL. Maybe poor countries are the ones with high birth rates, not wealthy ones.

RUTH. Now we're contradicting ourselves. Is it rich ones or poor ones that have more kids?

(*pause*)

GAIL. Maybe both.

TEACHER. Why?

GAIL. I'm not sure why. When people are better off, they want to bring up more kids.

NANCY. But don't many parents have fewer kids so they can give them more things and a better education?

STEVE. Yes, I guess so. Then a rich country would have a lower birth rate than a poor one.

NANCY. But why would poor people want to bring so many kids in the world?

STEVE. I don't know, but I have a suggestion: countries that have been poor for a long time usually have high birth rates, as do groups of poor people in various countries.

LEE.   There's a word for it. Oh yes, people living on a *subsistence* level often have many children. They are always poor.

DORIS.   But we're still stuck with the contradiction and I'm not so sure which answer is right.

RUTH.   I think I know. We've been on the birth-rates too long; let's look at the death rates. A very poor country would have to have a high death rate and a wealthy country would have a much lower one.

TED.   Yes, especially the farther back we go. Richer countries would have more doctors and hospitals and services to save people so they would have to have low death rates no matter what their birth rates were like.

ROBERTA.   Then country number two could not be the United States at all. From what we have said, it must be the poorest of the four countries because it has the highest over-all birth rate and death rate.

NANCY.   If country number two is the poorest of them all, then that might explain why poor people have lots of children. Maybe they have more deaths, especially of babies, so they have more children to outrun the deaths.

DONNA.   That sounds like a good idea, but look, country number two's death rate has been dropping very fast since 1948, but its birth rate has dropped much more slowly. How can we explain that?

TAMMY.   Maybe more people are being saved in country number two. Maybe modern medicine has been introduced recently.

ROY.   Maybe they've built a lot of hospitals.

STEVE.   Maybe the country is getting wealthier so the birth rate is high and the death rate is getting lower.

BRUCE.   I don't know about that! I think country number two might be in bad shape. Remember we said the bigger the gap between the two rates, the faster the population is growing. There are more people surviving in country number two since about 1950 than at any other point on the graph. They would have to get a lot better off to keep all those new people fed and clothed and housed.

GAIL H.   It's got to be a poor or backward country because of its high death rate. That we know even if we can't decide about what the birth rates tell us.

MARIS.   All right, so we know it's a poor country and has been for a long time, but can we possibly decide exactly which country it is?

During the second day discussion is centered around the development of models representing a poor country and a wealthy country. The students draw from their own experiences and they go beyond the data given to them by making numerous logical inferences. They now suggest several factors that contribute to poverty or affluence of a nation, as related to birth and death rates. In trying to develop a reliable indicator, the students examined critically many contradictory statements or generalizations. For instance, although Gail H. suggested that a wealthy country would have a high birth rate, both Lee and Gail brought up a contradictory proposition, namely, that poor countries are the ones with high birth rates. It is apparent that the dilemma presented by these propositions involved more students in a discussion and eventually it caused the group to shift strategy. This shift was prompted by the realization that they had reached the limits of grounded conjecture and that they needed to have a more reliable index of national development. Hence, Ruth's proposal to emphasize death rates rather than birth rates is readily accepted by the other participants. The students constantly criticize or complement each other's hypotheses, and at times they appear to proceed in logical sequences or units. For example, Ruth's statement is given evidential and inferential support by Ted; Roberta offers a conclusion based on the preceding dialogue.

Throughout the deliberations the students give evidence of both creative and analytical forces at work. The creative elements are apparent when they attempt to make a leap into the world of hunch and conjecture; the analytical elements are evident when they engage in syllogistic reasoning, and in developing if-then generalizations supported by experiential and factual evidence. The students constantly seek to apply interpretive principles to the resolution of the puzzle. The generalizations drawn from the given data and from the verbal exchange operate as working hypotheses. Such hypotheses as "poor people have a lot of children," "the bigger the gap between the two rates [death and birth], the faster the population is growing," or "the poorer the country, the higher the death rate" serve to organize the material, to outline the strategy of attack, to separate the relevant from the irrelevant, and to indicate pertinent validating criteria.

Third Day

TEACHER. OK, let's get down to business. Come to order.

MARIS.   We know that country number two is a poor country.

TED.   And we can see that it was affected by both World Wars.

GAIL H.   Maybe it's India.

TEACHER. Why?

GAIL H.   Because I think India was in both wars[13] and is a poor country with a high birth and death rate. Furthermore, I believe India is being helped out now by other countries. Better medicines would account for the drop in the death rate after World War II.

NANCY.   But why couldn't it be China?

ROY.   Yes, China must be about the same.

STEVE.   But I don't think China was affected by World War I.

ALAN.   Well, I'm not so sure it's India. Whatever country it is, it wasn't affected by the Depression.

DONNA.   What depression?

ALAN.   The depression that took place in the 1930s. I'm pretty sure many, many countries around the world were affected by it.

ROBERTA.   But not country number two.

TED.   Country number two might be Russia. After the Revolution in 1917, Russia started its own new economic system and I don't think it would be touched by the Depression like the U.S.

GAIL.   But I don't think Russia was *that* poor, was it? Anyway, why would Russia show such a sharp decline in deaths since 1948?

NANCY.   And why would the Russians' high death rate last until 1948?

LEE.   Doesn't sound like it's Russia.

GAIL H.   I still think it's India.

STEVE.   Maybe it's Italy.

ALAN.   But wouldn't Italy be affected by the Depression?

ROBERTA.   Country number four must be a rather advanced country because it has a low death rate. It's down to about 10 per thousand in 1960.

STEVE.   For some reason it has a high birth rate compared to the others except that country number two is higher.

NANCY.   The birth rate seems to be dropping generally.

GAIL.   There is a very sharp drop from about 1930 until 1945.

GWEN.   The death rate is going down, too, except for humps at about 1915 or 1917 and 1938 or 1942.

TED.   Wait, wait, I know which country number four is! It must be the United States. The U.S. entered the First World War late and this graph shows a sharp rise in the death rate at

---

[13]While this conjecture is not quite borne out in the sense that India was not independent and did not participate directly, India did provide manpower to the British war effort, especially during World War II.

about 1917 or 1918 and a small drop in the birth rate at the same time. The birth rate keeps falling after 1930 to a low point that lasts until about 1944 or so. This would be caused by the Depression and World War II. People wouldn't have many kids during a bad time or during a war. Then the birth rate rises after the war. Say, we're part of those figures!

TAMMY.   Yes, we're all postwar babies!

The third day represents an intensified effort to name the countries that correspond to the statistical charts and their own interpretation of them. At this stage they take one country at a time and they examine it from many viewpoints, bringing in other relevant information. In the introductory phase of the third day the students appear to engage in a guessing game. India, China, Russia, and Italy are offered as possible choices without strong supporting evidence. However, as the focus of investigation shifts to another country, the discussion is less haphazard and moves toward a higher level of interpretation. This level of analysis is illustrated by Ted who tried to match the known or inferred characteristics of country number four (e.g., it was involved in the two world wars, it was affected by the Great Depression, and it had a high post-World War II birth rate) with a specific country, in this case the choice being the United States. The discussion of the third day perhaps suggests that while the method of discovery encourages the student to tolerate ambiguity and uncertainty, a point of high indeterminancy may be reached that causes a random response to release mounting tension. However, this indeterminancy usually leads to a shift of strategy or a quest to find new data.

Fourth Day[14]

TEACHER.   You haven't tried country number three yet. Since you're stuck on one, why not try three? Who would like to start?

BARBARA.   Country number three shows a steady drop in both birth and death rates over the long run with a big drop from about 1900 until 1915 or so. Maybe that's when the medical advance hit this country. Also, it seems that people started limiting their families. This country has a very low over-all birth rate compared to the other three countries.

[14]Because of space limitations we have not included much of the discussion of the fourth day. On this day there was a continuation of the same type of classroom discussion as on the third day. The focal point, however, has been directed toward countries one and three, following the same general pattern as on the preceding day; the change of country came about only after an impasse concerning country one had been reached.

NANCY.   It must be a fairly advanced, civilized country. I mean, well-off. People must have been having small families to better their financial position. Nothing especially bad seemed to have happened during 1900 to 1915 because the death rate is falling. People must just have had small families by choice.

ROBERTA.   All this comes down to this being a very advanced country even in 1900, providing all our reasoning is right.

TED.   Country number three was in both World Wars and was affected by the Depression because the birth rate reaches a low point in 1933.

JAN.   Country number three is rather different, though, because World War II hurt it more toward the beginning of the War than toward the end. Why could that be?

PAT.   Yes! The birth and death rates almost touch each other. That means that there was almost no population increase in 1941 or 1942.

NANCY.   The war must have hit them hard then.

DORIS.   Maybe they were invaded at the beginning of the War?

RUTH.   Then it could be one of many European countries.

TED.   Maybe it's Poland. That was invaded at the start of the War.

GAIL.   But it could also be Holland, Belgium, or Czechoslovakia, or maybe even France.

MARIS.   Or Russia—Russia was invaded.

JAN.   I think we can leave Russia out. Russia was not that advanced in 1900 and Russia was not affected much by the Depression. This country was. Then, too, the death rate drops after 1918 and this doesn't fit in with what someone said about a civil war in Russia after the Revolution.

MARIS.   OK, I give on Russia.

On the basis of previously developed hypotheses and inferences, a list of possible choices of countries is now emerging. The students delimit the range of choice, however, by introducing negative evidence. For instance, Russia is eliminated because the facts known about her do not harmonize with the theoretical formulation advanced by the students. More important, although the participants continually reconstruct their ideas, they always build on their cumulative experiences. Their exploratory behavior seems to be integrative; and it is self-sustaining so that students provide their own rewards. Actually, teacher-induced external rewards are practically nonexistent.

Fifth Day

GAIL.   I think we're in a bad spot again. These are very hard to understand.

TEACHER.   Before we go on, perhaps someone would like to summarize what has been accomplished.

DEBBIE.   Well, I think we're in a kind of a mess. We're fairly certain that countries with high birth and death rates for a long time are chronically poor countries. Countries with lower death rates are more advanced and are better served by medical services. So we know that country number two is a rather backward nation, while the other three are more or less advanced. Country number three would be the earliest advanced country, while country number one would be the one showing the most recent advances in medicine.

TED.   I think we've established that country number four is probaby the U.S. Then we thought that country number one is either Japan or Russia. Country number three is probably a European country like France or Holland.

DEBBIE.   Or England or Belgium.

MARIS.   Country number two is probably India or maybe China.

ROSLYN.   I found out that India had trouble after World War II. They had trouble with an independence movement and Pakistan separated from India. There were many people hurt or killed during that time. That might explain why the death rate stays high until 1948 in country number two.

BARBARA.   But I looked up China and there was a civil war there after World War II between the Nationalists and the Communists.

ROSLYN.   India seems a better choice because country number two was affected by World War I and I'm pretty sure that China wasn't.

BARBARA.   The book I looked up on China said they weren't part of it. You're right.

TED.   I think I have found one of these countries for sure. Country number four just has to be the U.S. No other country seems to fit the graph and furthermore I found out from a yearbook that the U.S. had a birth rate of 24 and a death rate of 9.5 in 1960. That fits in exactly.

LEE.   All right, that's one we have.

TAMMY.   Yes, what about the rest?

DONNA.   We seem to be stuck on one, two, and three.

PAT.   It's too hard. Give us a hint.

TEACHER.   I think you've done very well. You don't really need any hints.

NANCY.   Well, but we're stuck.

(The bell rings amid a great deal of screaming and yelling.)

The behavior on the fifth day is highly task-oriented. The conversation clearly demonstrates a high degree of motivation that was generated by this discovery episode. The fact that the students are most eager to pursue a line of inquiry begun five days ago even though the materials are relatively complex and, at times, frustrating suggests that this mode of classroom operation has its own self-sustaining goals. Also, there is a feeling among the participants to marshal some kind of documentary evidence to allow them to arrive at a conclusion, however tentative. This observation is indicated by a number of students (e.g., Roslyn, Barbara, and Ted) who have sought outside sources in their quest for a more definitive interpretation.

By the end of the fifth day the class in general felt that they had reached the limits of their exploration and psychological endurance. This feeling produced an intense situation where the class demanded to be supplied with either additional clues or specific information to solve the puzzle. The participants shared the belief that they had developed the most defensible hypotheses possible under the circumstances; to achieve a feeling of self-satisfaction or fulfillment, they demanded to know how close they were to the precise country involved.

It is possible that the high level of complexity of statistical data in the charts generated a feeling of inadequacy to deal effectively with the task. The apparent frustration and exasperation was carried into the sixth day when a few half-hearted attempts to explore further and to summarize the findings did not produce a complete feeling of achievement. The general sentiment of the class is expressed by Barbara who said, "I looked through lots of history books, but I couldn't come up with a good choice," by Gail who said, "Yes, we've been in suspense, oh, so long," and by Lee who concluded, "We refuse to go any further!" The discovery episode was terminated at the end of the sixth day when the teacher helped them to resolve their quandary.[15]

---

[15]The countries represented by the charts were Japan, Egypt, the United Kingdom, and the United States, respectively.

DISCUSSION

On the basis of our observation in this episode the four hypotheses suggested for investigation in the beginning have largely been confirmed. From the dialogues reproduced, it becomes increasingly evident that the intellectual potency of the members of the group is maximized. The students respond constructively to problematic situations by analyzing data, by recognizing existing gaps and missing information by developing strategies of attack, by formulating and testing hypotheses, and by drawing logical inferences and conclusions. As they proceed to investigate the problem they are constantly involved in the construction and refinement of a conceptual framework which guides their work, provides missing clues, separates relevant from irrelevant information, harmonizes contradictory data, and serves as a logical base of operations. Students operate as bona-fide explorers, capable of ordering their own learning and capable of producing new ideas.

Throughout the various phases of inquiry students build on their on-going activities without losing sight of the end-in-view. They capitalize on and draw from a variety of sources; for example, the given data, classroom discussion, personal observations and experiences, and primary and secondary material. Our research generally supports Bruner's proposition that when facts and details are placed in a structured pattern of thought they are retained longer and are easily retrieved. This case study suggests that even though the discovery episode may be extended through a week or more it develops a unit or a pattern which integrates all experiences in an organic and cumulative fashion.

The psychological climate prevailing in the classroom was characterized by ever-increasing degrees of interest in and motivation to resolve the indeterminacy. The observed behavior was goal-oriented and largely self-sustaining, on an individual and a reciprocating group relationship. The high level of student motivation to explore ideas may in part be explained by (a) the gamelike situation that is engendered by the discovery episode; (b) the adamant attitude taken by the teacher in refusing to give direct answers; (c) the understanding that the discovery process is a legitimate educational experience and it is not linked directly with either external rewards or punishments: and (d) the encouragement of the free flow and counter flow of ideas.

The concept of "right or wrong answer" is not relevant to the process of discovery; rather the idea of developing defensible and reasonable theoretical models and schemes of interpretation becomes the crucial element. Even factually and logically erroneous postulates are eventually rejected or corrected in the open forum of ideas. The point is that the task of verifying and accepting propositions rests with the students. In their desire to reach a reliable interpretation of the evidence they constantly check and carefully scrutinize all ideas, hypotheses, and information. They develop a spirit of educated doubt in that they refuse to reach definite conclusions without sufficient validation. This classroom climate induces the students to learn to live with uncertainty and leads them to investigate a wide range of alternatives to a problem.

In a situation such as this teachers do not exercise direct control over the flow of discussion but they perform more subtle and yet very important tasks. Their main contributions are in providing a nonthreatening environment which is conducive to receptive listening, and planning for and selecting the perplexing initiatory activity which may be given in the form of a document, a graph, an artifact, a piece of music, or a picture. Also, the teacher is on hand at all times to reinforce the perplexity and prod the students into defending or explaining their ideas. Teachers generally minimize their role of giving specific directions, but they may suggest new paths of inquiry when a stalemate is reached.

THE DISCOVERY OF GEOGRAPHIC PRINCIPLES

Geograpy is a rather complex subject that deals with the relationship between man and his environment. The environment could include such varied items as topography, fauna and flora, water supplies, climatic conditions, and even the political boundaries of human existence.

Ordinarily this subject is presented to the students as a mass of details and statistics—weather reports, average snowfalls, capitals of nations, location of cities, length of rivers, height of mountains, and so on. Explanations of the results of the interaction between man and his environment are generally *supplied* to the students after they have "mastered," usually by memory, the basic subject matter or data of geography. This method falls short of promoting student awareness of the process by which man reacts to his environment and to the principles with which to interpret goegraphic factors.

The purpose of this case study was to discover if students could grasp some of the basic problems involved in relating man to his environment, whatever that environment might be. The study was also designed to ascertain if students could understand these relationships by working in autonomous group units. Autonomous inquiry, in this case, may be understood to mean that after the presentation of the material to be studied and the problem to be solved the students receive no direct aid from the teacher.

A set of materials was constructed to give only a limited amount of geographic information, namely, (a) topography, (b) rainfall, (c) vegetation, and (d) temperature ranges. Since the students were asked to relate man (as they were left free to define him) to this specific set of geographic conditions, no information whatsoever was offered about the human population of the region in question. Thus, to solve the problems that were given them, the students would necessarily have to develop abstract generalizations of principles that would help to explain how man in general would go about adapting to a set of general environmental conditions. To reinforce the abstract qualities of the prepared materials, no specific names were given to any area or point on the maps that constituted the raw data.

On the other hand, the materials were constructed and selected in such a manner that students would be faced with a set of real environmental factors which other men have actually had to deal with in order to survive. The situation confronting the students thus necessitated the solution of abstract geographic problems, yet, at the same time engaged them in discovering the actual environmental difficulties faced by the people of a real country. Two different lines of inquiry were being pursued simultaneously without the students being directly aware of it. This had the advantage of encouraging the student groups to give free rein to their imaginations and creativity in the solution of a general rather than a specific problem. A second advantage of the twofold nature of the problem would be that the information supplied by the teacher and the conclusions developed by the students could be discussed and studied later in both their abstract and concrete aspects.

The maps that the students produced were later compared in class with the actual geography and history of the Soviet Union; that is, additional maps were handed out to the students for purposes of comparison with the maps they had produced. Discussions took place in which the students tested out their ideas against what has happened in the U.S.S.R., and the validity of various geographic principles were tested against the real situation. All of these discussions culminated in a general discussion about the relationship between the people of Russia and their environment.

The various groups worked together for four to six class periods to complete the reports, and several of the group leaders reworked the reports at home. For the most part the groups stayed together to work on their problems, which were often different from the tasks given their neighbors. However, a great deal of fraternization and discussion occurred between members of the various groups, although not all of it could have been connected with the problem at hand.

Each participant received an identical set of prepared materials consisting of five maps showing, respectively, the topography, vegetation zones, average summer rainfall, and July and January isothermal lines of temperature of a country called "X." These five maps appearing on pages 122–126 constituted the basic information availale to all students concerning the unknown country.

Country "X" is, in reality, a distorted upside-down reproduction of the Soviet Union with generalized and slightly altered versions of its geographic and climatic conditions. No other information, either general or concrete, was presented to the two social studies classes involved in this study.

All of the students involved in this project were enrolled in contemporary history, a high school course generally offered to seniors. This course offers a wide range of topics from Russia and Communism to urbanism, race relations, and civics; much of the selection is left to the discretion of the teacher. Two entire classes and part of a third (described below) participated in this experiment. Each class was divided arbitrarily according to row into five committees of five or six pupils. To these ten groups was added an eleventh composed of seven students from a third class who volunteered to solve a problem utilizing the maps. With very few exceptions, the students were seniors ranging in intelligence from average to very bright. The average IQ of each group was approximately 120, with the exception of the volunteer group in which the average was approximately 100.

After the groups were organized they were allowed to spend one class period studying the five maps that described country "X"'s environment. At the next class meeting the students were presented with general directions and specific problems—a different problem for each group in the class—which were constructed to force the student investigators to come to grips with both the specific assignment confronting them and a more general problem involving the relationship between human societies and the geographic region influencing their existence.

Geography Problems for Country "X"

1. If people living at the point marked "X" on the map began to migrate *or* expand, where would they go and what direction might they take? (see map on page 127.)

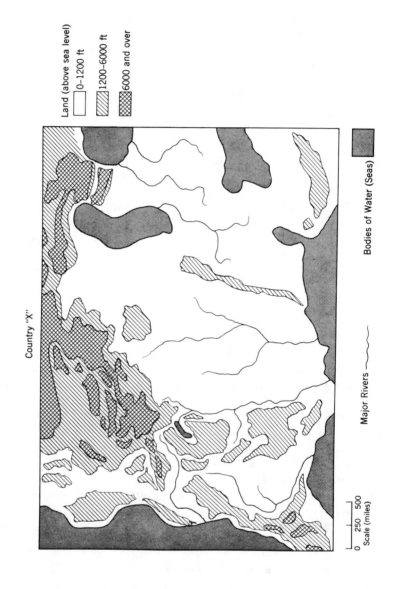

Country "X"

Land (above sea level)

☐ 0-1200 ft

▨ 1200-6000 ft

▩ 6000 and over

Major Rivers ⌇

▨ Bodies of Water (Seas)

0 250 500
Scale (miles)

122

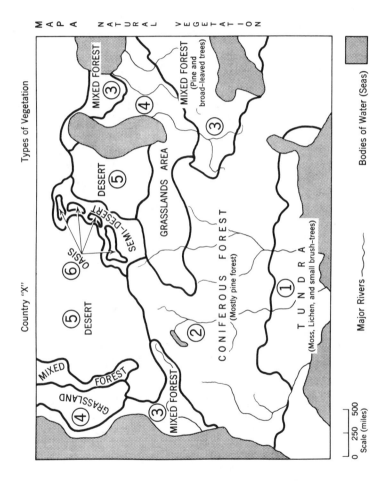

MAP A — NATURAL VEGETATION

Country "X"

Types of Vegetation

MIXED FOREST ③

④

MIXED FOREST
(Pine and
broad-leaved trees)

③

DESERT ⑤

GRASSLANDS AREA

SEMI-DESERT

OASIS ⑥

DESERT ⑤

MIXED
FOREST

GRASSLAND

④

MIXED FOREST ③

②

CONIFEROUS FOREST
(Mostly pine forest)

T U N D R A
(Moss, Lichen, and small brush-trees)

①

0   250   500
Scale (miles)

Major Rivers ——

Bodies of Water (Seas)

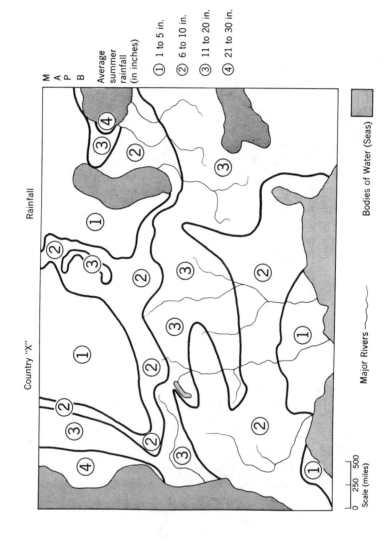

Country "X"   Rainfall

M
A
P
B

Average
summer
rainfall
(in inches)

① 1 to 5 in.

② 6 to 10 in.

③ 11 to 20 in.

④ 21 to 30 in.

Bodies of Water (Seas)

Major Rivers

0 250 500
Scale (miles)

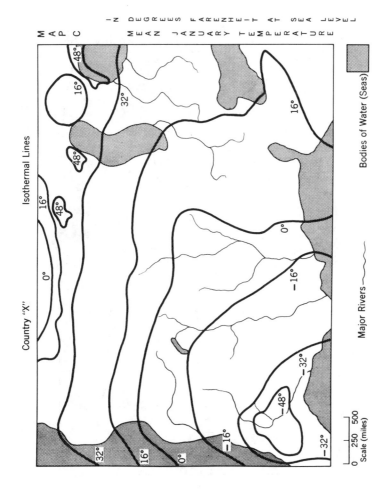

Country "X"   Isothermal Lines

MAP C

MEAN JANUARY TEMPERATURE AT SEA LEVEL
IN DEGREES FAHRENHEIT

Bodies of Water (Seas)

Major Rivers ————

0   250   500
Scale (miles)

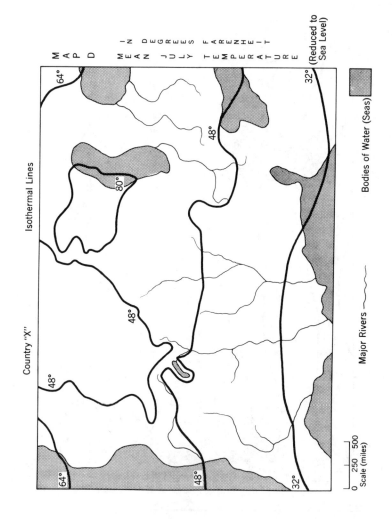

Country "X"

Isothermal Lines

MAP D

MEAN JULY TEMPERATURE IN DEGREES FAHRENHEIT
(Reduced to Sea Level)

64°

48°

80°

48°

48°

48°

64°

48°

32°

48°

32°

Major Rivers ——

Bodies of Water (Seas)

0   250   500
Scale (miles)

2. If people at the point marked "X" on the map began to move *or* expand, where would they probably go and what direction might they take? (See map on page 128.)

3. What would be the distribution of population in country "X"; that is, where would many people live, few, and so on?

4. Where would large cities develop in country "X"?

5. How would you judge country "X"'s economic potential; that is, what areas might be best for development, which worst, and so on?

General Directions. You have each been given a map of a country "X" on which to illustrate your solution to the problem presented to you. Draw your map carefully. After you have decided on a map, draw up a report explaining the reasons for your particular solution to the problem given to your group. Use as evidence the five maps of country "X" now in your possession.

Each group was requested (a) to decide on a solution to their specific problem, (b) to illustrate it geographically on a topography map of country "X," and (c) to write a report explaining and defending the map they had produced and to justify their solution. Although no time

Country "X"

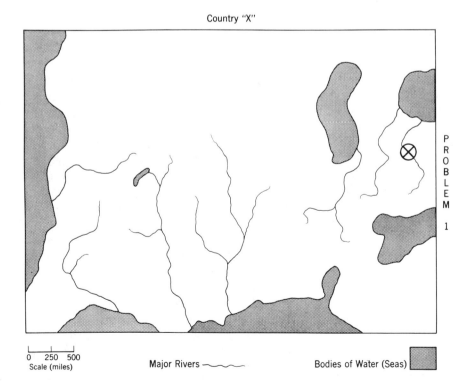

0   250   500
Scale (miles)   Major Rivers ～～～   Bodies of Water (Seas)

Country "X"

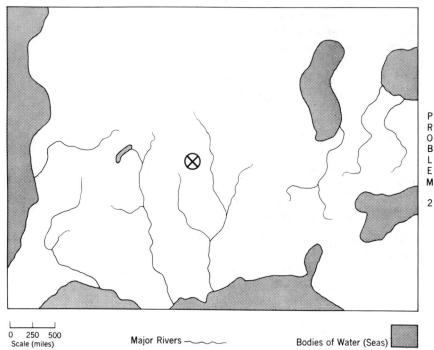

P
R
O
B
L
E
M

2

```
L__L__J
0   250  500
Scale (miles)        Major Rivers ‾‾‾‾‾‾       Bodies of Water (Seas) ▓▓▓
```

limit was specified for the solution of the problem, each group took approximately three class periods to complete both the maps and the written reports. Of these, seven maps with accompanying reports are reproduced on the following pages. The first five maps-with-reports (numbered one through five) are the total product of the five committees comprising one entire contemporary history class (See pages 128–138.) The work of this class was chosen to give the reader an understanding of the entire range of creative production possible in a single class of about thirty students dealing with a set of geographic problems. The last two assignments reproduced (numbers six and seven on pages 139–144) were chosen to demonstrate characteristic variations between the products and conclusions of the different class committees working on the same problem and using identical information.

First Group: Population Expansion *(Map on page 129)*

BASIC ASSUMPTION.   Although able to make small adjustments in environment, these people will try to expand and move into an area as similar to their own present situation as possible.

SECONDARY
ASSUMPTIONS.

We believe that these people have evolved a way of life suited to their present environment. We postulate that this has taken a long period of time in which they have become specially adapted to a particular kind of habitat.

PRESENT SITUATION.

1. There is a river supplying them with fresh water.
2. They are living in the forest, but near the grasslands.
3. Rainfall is moderate: 10 to 15 in. summer average.
4. Temperatures moderate: January average is 24 degrees and July average is 64°F.

We may thus predict that they will move into a forested, well-watered region with a generally moderate climate. Perhaps they depend on lumber for their way of life. They may also be engaged in small farming and the hunting of forest animals for fur clothing. They are probably not too advanced industrially. Perhaps they are avoiding

Country "X"

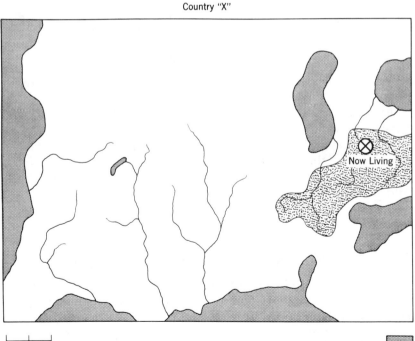

POPULATION EXPANSION

0 250 500		
Scale (miles)	Major Rivers ⌇	Bodies of Water (Seas)

Country "X"

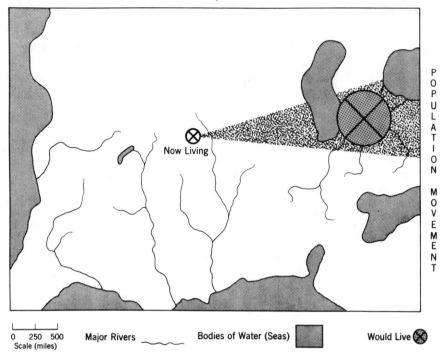

| 0   250   500 | Major Rivers ‾‾‾‾ | Bodies of Water (Seas) ▮ | Would Live ⊗ |
| Scale (miles) | | | |

the grasslands because they are not specialized farmers or there is danger there.

Conclusion. These people will most likely take the path of least resistance and most similarity to what they already are adapted for. Therefore, they will move into adjoining forest regions, mostly to the south along the three great rivers there until the climate becomes too cold. Perhaps they need the rivers for their logging enterprises and would not go very far from them in any event.

The area they will most likely live in after their expansion is indicated by 🮕 on the map of country "X."

Second Group: Population Movement (Map on page 130)

1. Migration would be almost due east. The people are now living at the edge of the grasslands; therefore they are engaged in farming or raising animals (sheep, cattle) or both. We believe that if they did move, if they were following this way of life, they would choose an area similar to their own in every respect possible.

2. Migration would not be south. Conditions are not satisfactory. The area to the south is either forest or tundra, the temperatures are too cold for either farming or cattle raising, and the annual rainfall is quite low. This area would probably be a lumber district.

3. Migration would not be north. Conditions are unfavorable here because they would either run into a very mountainous region or a large desert. In either case there would be too little water and not enough grazing land for the people living at "X" to survive as they are used to surviving.

4. Migration would not be west. Migration to the west, even though there are some grasslands located in the northwest, would not be likely because it would mean that these people would have to cross both a mountainous region or a heavily forested region to get there. Furthermore, there is little possibility that they could settle along the way if they wanted to keep their old way of life: farming and/or herding.

5. Migration would be east. Migration would follow the grasslands area stretching from the center of the country to the northeast. These people would be near water for their crops and animals, and the grasslands would provide suitable farming and grazing conditions wherever they would go in this area  . They would most likely settle in the area marked with a large "X." We believe this because this area is located near abundant water resources for crops or cattle, there is good rainfall, the temperatures are not too extreme, and this would be the largest and best grasslands section.

6. *Conclusion.* Migration would therefore have to be almost completely due *east*, around or across the long sea, because of the logical deductions stated above.

Third Group: Population Distribution (Map on page 132)

We believe that the statements below are true if one's opinion is based on the following knowledge: climate, rainfall, altitude, water locations, and over-all topography of the country named "X."

1. The highest population would be found in the northeast around the shores of the large round sea, of which part is shown on the map. This area has a fairly warm climate, good rainfall, and is fed by two rivers. This area would be good for fishing, boating, and shipping of goods out of the country as well as into the interior. There would probably be many ports in this area, especially at the outlet of the two rivers. Furthermore, the area is a low plain which would provide good farmland as well as level land on which to build port cities. Also, high

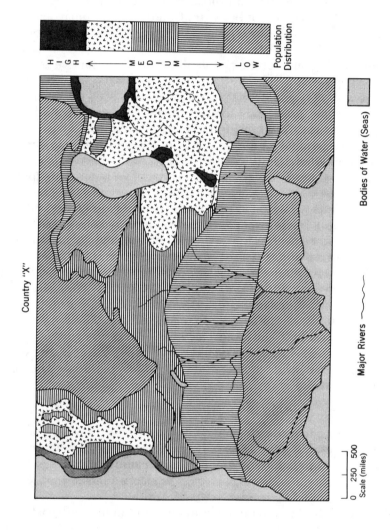

Country "X"

Population
Distribution

H-I-G-H ← M-E-D-I-U-M → L-O-W

Major Rivers ——   Bodies of Water (Seas)

0 250 500
Scale (miles)

population areas would be found at two other points in the northeast: one at the point where a large river runs into the long sea that is completely inside this country, and the second area would be at the fork (with two branches) of the river that runs into the long sea. The densely populated area on the long sea would also be a port area and have pretty much the same advantages as the region surrounding the other northeastern sea. We believe that the densely populated area at the place where the river branches into two other rivers would be a kind of convenient central location for the whole country—a kind of trading post. Probably a big city would grow up in this place because all the things produced in the northern region could be shipped inland from here in two different directions, while all the things produced in the southern region could be shipped to all the people living around the long lake. The climate and the topography would not be as good at the place where the river branches into two as it is around the two seas, but we think it would be a convenient central location nevertheless.

Finally, the last highly populated region would be along the northwestern sea coast because it is fairly warm and would make a good trading and port area. It is also near grasslands which would be good farmland and near forests which would provide building materials, fuel (?), and the basis for many other products. The coastal area could, therefore, draw from, and do business with, the surrounding farm and forest regions.

2. The next areas we would consider to be fairly well populated, but not densely populated. These areas would have about the best climate and rainfall when compared to the rest of the country. One well-populated area would cover most of the northeast, extending west into the grasslands until the weather becomes too cold. The other well-populated region would be in the northwestern grasslands region. The grasslands regions of this country seem most protected from the elements. The northeastern region is further aided by very good water supplies from three rivers. Finally, the grasslands are lowlands which would be easiest to farm or build on.

3. A moderate amount of people would live in areas bordering those with heavy population. These areas would be somewhat colder average temperatures than the better areas or they would be found in low mountain regions in or near the better areas. The climate in these areas might be fair, but the land would be forested or mountainous,

making living conditions less suitable than in the lowlands. As the temperatures get colder and the terrain higher, the lower the density of people living there.

4. The next area of lower population would be between the grasslands and the tundra. We feel that this land, being forested and having a cold climate, would not be high in population due to the fact that transportation would be very difficult because of the bad weather and because the river system would be frozen most of the year. Furthermore, cold earth would not be so good for farming, especially if you always had to cut down trees and tear out stumps to create a farm. Another area of lower population would be found in the low mountains bordering the desert region in the North; that might be slightly more livable than the desert since there would most likely be streams running down the mountain from the melting snows higher up.

5. The most sparsely populated region is the lowest section of the country: the tundra. This area would be unsuitable for living for all but a very few people. It is very cold and the water that would fall as rain would turn to snow. The many river systems would be frozen all or most of the year. No farms could be set up in the area. The whole lower section of the country would be in the same geographical condition, and it would be very low in population. The most northerly areas would also be very low in population because of the high mountains and desert regions, low rainfall, and lack of lakes or rivers for water or transportation.

Note. The lower mountain regions might be almost livable if they are not located in a very cold climate, if they have some streams or water supplies, or are not too far from grasslands regions which could supply them with food. It would also be easy to transport things over grasslands but not in high mountains, or over frozen tundra.

Fourth Group: Location of Cities: 1 (Map on page 135)

We, the people of this problem, feel that the large cities would be at the following locations for the following reasons:

1. The rivers provide a means for procuring food and lumber.
2. The cities are centralized so they may trade with large surrounding areas by land or water transportation.
3. The cities are located in region with decent climates, not too hot and not too cold. None are too far South.

Country "X"

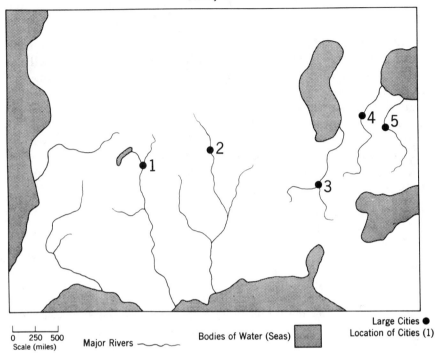

		Large Cities ●
0 250 500	Bodies of Water (Seas)	Location of Cities (1)
Scale (miles) Major Rivers ‿‿‿		

4. The cities are in the more productive region, either grasslands or forests, or, if possible, near both.

We have chosen the specific locations for five cities for the following reasons:

1. Cities 1 and 2 were chosen because they can take advantage of the huge forest near them, and become great lumber-processing centers. Furthermore, they are far enough up on the river to make use of it. We don't think that the river will be frozen more than part of the time at these locations.

2. City 3 is central to the whole livable area of the country and might be the biggest city. You could ship things to and from this city for long distances by water since it is on a forked river that flows into a sea. It is also in a forest area and near grasslands; therefore, it could be a market center for all these products and goods.

3. Cities 4 and 5 were chosen because they will have very good climates, both with respect to temperatures and rainfall. They are also located to take advantage of both farm and forest regions, as well as

river and sea trade. We believe that these will be popular cities to live in. They will be industrial centers and trade centers.

None of the cities will be in the open grasslands because we think this would leave them unprotected from the elements. They will all be located on the edge of the forest right near the grasslands. This way they will not use up valuable farmland but will be supplied by the neighboring farms. None of the cities will be in the mountains because they are too cold and too high. None of the cities will be too far south because this area is too frozen. Finally, none of the cities will be way over on the West coast because that is too far away from the rest of the population and would necessitate crossing several mountain ranges.

Fifth Group: Economic Development of Country "X": 1 (Map on page 137)

We have discovered an unexplored country which we shall temporarily call country "X." Our country's wealthy businessmen have hired us to explore this new area and determine if it is suited for farming or industry or both. We have worked out a map of the potentially useful areas for farms or industry. This report will help you understand the map and also sum up country "X's" economic potential.

Key. Potential farm areas ▱▱▱ are subdivided into six lettered areas.

Potential industrial ▨▨ areas subdivided into five numbered areas.

Farming.

AREA A. Farming should be quite good the year round; we find fertile soil, good, average temperatures (i.e., not too high or low), and an adequate to heavy annual rainfall.

AREA B. Farming should be as good as area A during the warmer part of the year but the winter is quite cold; rainfall not so good as in area A but rivers provide plentiful water supply.

AREA C. Should be the *best* farming area because it has the best water supplies; the highest mean annual temperature except for the desert; the most fertile soil because most types of natural growing plants and trees are found there.

AREA D. Could be a good farming area except the soil really must be well cared for since little plant life was found growing and mean temperatures are lower than one likes for farming.

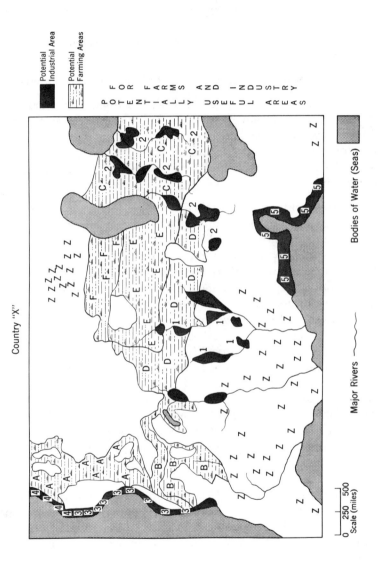

Country "X"

Potential
Industrial Area

Potential
Farming Areas

POTENTIAL FOR FARMS AND FUTURE INDUSTRY

Major Rivers ⌒

Bodies of Water (Seas)

0 250 500
Scale (miles)

AREA E. This is a very fertile area but annual rainfall is low; good mean temperature; flat level grassland would indicate this might best be a grazing land for livestock; good for grain crops.

AREA F. This area has unfertile soil but the highest yearly temperatures; could be irrigated with some effort; too hot to live there comfortably.

Industry. Industrial potential was judged on the following bases:

1. Nearness to large bodies of water for import-export trade.

2. Nearness to streams for electric power and intracountry transportation of raw materials and by-products.

3. Nearness to natural resources.

4. Type of living conditions for workers and the possibility of high population.

AREA 1. Good industrial area except for low winter temperature; it is near the D farming area but has three large river tributaries; major problem would be the support of working populations because living conditions are far from good.

AREA 2. The *best* area for industry because it will be the most highly populated; best living condition in entire country found here; surrounded by natural resources; adequate water for transportation and drinking; this should be the center of all country "X"'s activities.

AREA 3. This could be a good industrial area but temperatures are colder than one would like for normal living.

AREA 4. Meets all the requirements for a good industrial area; warmer than Area 3, except it is small and isolated.

AREA 5. This would be a good industrial area except for two reasons—lack of natural resources and cold mean annual temperature; living condition poor, "nice place to visit but I wouldn't want to stay."

The areas represented by black Z's are completely unacceptable for farming or industry. The small area above the F farming region is much too hot and dry. The large Z areas in the lower left of the map are unbelievably cold with a mean temperature of −48°F. in the winter—much too cold to live.

For the size of country "X" we find extremely few good possibilities for farming (except area C) and few for industry (except for area 2). Thus we conclude that country "X," on the whole, would not fare too well economically.

Sixth Group: Location of Cities: 2 (Map on page 139)

This is a very cold country and due to this we have located most of the larger cities in places where they are protected from extreme temperatures. A large city should also be located near a fresh water supply and a supply of water power. Rainfall is not too much of a problem unless it is too low as it is in desert areas. Most of the large cities will be located in moderate temperature areas for more comfortable living. Cities are more likely to grow up in grasslands regions due to the ease with which the land may be cleared. Cities are also likely to grow up near large bodies of water (seas, lakes, or oceans) because these may serve as trade routes. Large cities usually serve as some sort of trade and transportation hub. Finally, because of transportation problems and temperature inclemencies, large cities are unlikely to "sprout" in mountainous territories.

1. City No. 1 is located in the most moderate climate zone, and would probably be the largest, or one of the largest cities in the country. This city has a fresh water supply, a water power supply, is located

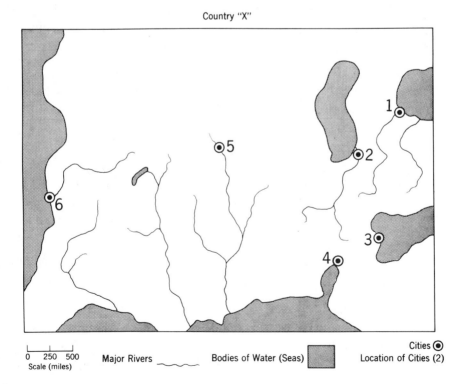

Country "X"

0 250 500 Scale (miles)	Major Rivers ⌢ Bodies of Water (Seas) ▨ Cities ◉ Location of Cities (2)

at the mouth of a 1200-mile river, and is on the coast of a sea flowing into adjacent territory. This city thus offers (a) good climate, (b) transportation inland by riverboats, (c) international trade possibilities, and (d) power for industry. This city could be an industrial, mercantile, and financial center.

2. City No. 2 is also located in the grassland area, thus allowing easy building construction. It has advantages similar to City No. 1 because it is at the mouth of a long river with two branches that flows into a large sea. This city also has a supply of fresh water, water power, and it is a possible transportation and seaport center. City No. 2 could draw upon both the farm products of the grasslands and the wood products of the forest area for its manufacturing base.

City No. 3 is located on an inlet to the sea which affords it some protection from the climate. It is in a cool region, but is located on a sea flowing into adjacent countries, thus making it useful for trade. Since it is in the forest area, it might be a lumber export center, but would probably be considerably smaller than the other large cities. It might also have a fresh water problem since it is not on a river.

4. City No. 4 is important as a port. Although the natural conditions are not good, they are the best of any along this southern coast, being somewhat protected from the weather by being on a large bay. There could be a fresh water problem unless there are small lakes in the area. It is located on the border between the tundra and the pine forests, thus lessening clearing problems, yet providing some relief and needed wood products not found in the tundra. This port would probably not be too large, but at least it would be open most of the year.

5. City No. 5 is located in the central grasslands region for strategic reasons. It might serve as the connecting link between the two settled and most heavily populated areas of this country. It would be a stopping place and trading center between the long West coast region and the area between the three Northeastern seas. The climate is fairly good there, and it does have fresh water supply and is located in the grasslands, thus providing the city with farm products and level land.

6. City No. 6 is located on the western coast of the country. It is also on a large river which gives it a fresh water supply, power for manufacturing, and access to the central portion of the country. It is in the moderate rainfall area and has "comparatively" warm summers and cold winters. The river would freeze in the winter but would remain open much of the year. Its coastal position would give it immediate access to the resources of the western region and to the more northern portions of the coast which are quite comfortable, as far as the climate

is concerned. Produce could be shipped up and back on the river and out to sea, thus making this city a port and trading town.

There might be other cities chosen but these appear to be the most likely to be of large size. Another city might have been built at the mouth of the most northeasterly river, but City No. 1 would probably give it too much competition. All the large cities woud be engaged in the following activities: shipping, transportation, commerce, and manufacturing. Except for No. 5, the large cities would be seaports engaged in export-import trade. Probably sizes would be as follows beginning with the largest and running to the smallest: 1, 2, 3, 6, 5, and 4.

Seventh Group: Economic Development of Country "X": 2 (Map on page 142)

We have hereby appointed ourselves the economic planning committee for our country. We shall try to develop our country using all of the most modern equiment and techniques. We pledge ourselves to develop our country, called "X" by its inhabitants, to its maximum potential—to make it rich and prosperous.

We shall now point out what we intend to do with our country, and why we think our plans are the best possible solutions. To facilitate matters, we have carefully studied our country and have decided to divide it into different zones, each of which is to be developed differently. The zones are as follows:

1. Seaport areas
2. Agricultural areas
3. Oases (warm climate) agriculture
4. Irrigated regions
5. Industrial region
6. Railroads
7. Lumber industry
8. Mining industry
9. Useless areas (white)

1. We are placing our main seaport area on our West coast because of the extremely long coastline and because of the relatively mild climate. The other long coastline is in the South, but that would be frozen almost all year round, making it useless.

2. We are going to spend a great deal of effort to develop our two best agricultural regions: one in the Northwest grasslands, and the second in the northeastern and central grasslands. Grasslands would be like the United States' great plains, containing rich soil and good

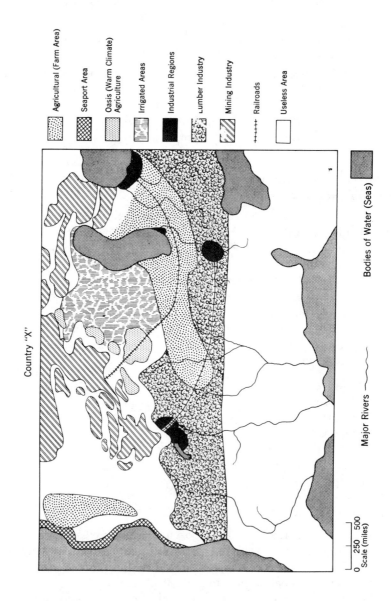

Country "X"

Legend:

- Agricultural (Farm Area)
- Seaport Area
- Oasis (Warm Climate) Agriculture
- Irrigated Areas
- Industrial Regions
- Lumber Industry
- Mining Industry
- Railroads
- Useless Area

Bodies of Water (Seas)

Major Rivers

0   250   500
Scale (miles)

farmland—none better in our country. They are also luckily in moderate climate zones escaping the extreme cold of the south.

3. The oases would be located just off the desert region which we intend to irrigate. These would not be too large but could provide us with some delicacies; for instance, fruits and vegetables that need a very warm climate. We would also have a rail line running to the oases to supply this food to the mining, farming, and industrial workers.

4. We intend to irrigate the desert because it is near a large body of water and not too far from some large rivers and it does have a nice warm climate which should not be wasted in this cold country. We will plant oasis crops throughout the whole desert when the irrigation system is finished.

5. We intend to develop four major industrial regions in our country. They will be located on rivers or ports and will be connected by railroads to food- and mineral-producing regions. They will also be transportation centers to other parts of the country. The one to the West will be conveniently located near the main mineral-producing region, the industrial port on the peanut-shaped sea will be conveniently located in the farming region, and the one at the branching of the river running into the peanut-shaped sea will be the center for the lumber industry. The last one, in the far Northeast, will be the main export-import region connecting most of the other regions by railroad. We plan to have all the main industrial areas in fairly central locations and moderate climates, and near rivers or bodies of water.

6. The railroads will connect the main industrial centers with their sources of supply and with each other. We did not feel that it was worth it to build a railroad to the seacoast region because we can ship industrial products to them by river and then over the sea. The seacoast area will export farm products. What else can it do?

7. The lumber industry will be located in the heavy forest region and should be very successful since we have such a huge forest. There will be lumber mills all across this area, but we will not build anywhere it it too cold to work.

8. The mining industry will be found scattered throughout our many mountain ranges, especially in the big mountain range to our North. We believe that all the different minerals we will need for our industries will be found here, although the mining might be difficult in places because of the height.

9. Finally, a big chunk of our country is not much good for anything. This we have left blank. However, we put great trust in our workers and scientists to come up with something in the future that may allow us to develop this region. We are not giving up completely; we are working on it.

Conclusion. Most of Country "X"'s economic development will be located across its middle portion in a wide band of industry and agriculture. We feel that our country's main problems are its size and the cold weather. Because of its size we have developed the long railroads to connect our different resources.

Suspicion. We have thought about what country this might really be. We now think that it is Russia. We turned the map upside down and it bears a resemblance to Russia, but we weren't certain. Are we right? Please tell us.

Although it should be kept in mind that the students responsible for producing the preceding maps and reports were seniors in high school with at least two years of social studies experience, it also ought to be pointed out that none of them had had any formal instruction in geography because it has not been offered as part of their school's curriculum. Considering this, the results of the groups' inquiries are strikingly perceptive and well-reasoned. The group interaction and cooperation that went into the creation of these maps and reports must be called successful solutions to the problems posed. There were, of course, no "right" or "wrong" answers relevant to this project. The approximation of the various maps to reality was not the main thrust of this experiment, although many of the maps produced do correspond very closely to the actual arrangement of life in the Soviet Union. Rather, the methodological criterion for success was the level of defense achieved in support of cartographic decisions. In other words, a perceptive and an intelligently drawn map would be one in which every decision was based on logical assumptions and environmental evidence. In addition to demonstrating logical operations in defense of geographic interpretations, the reports contain many highly imaginative and creative passages in which students have apparently given free play to their inventive powers. Since the human factor was totally absent from all information about country "X" until the introduction of the problems, each group had to rely on its own resources to create, develop, or assume the particular type of society that might exist in the geographic region being studied. In each case of the reports, whereas the geographic regulants of human behavior are analyzed and interpreted, the human behavior itself is open to supposition and invention, keeping imagination within the bounds of that which is possible.

The urge to defend their interpretations by logic can be seen in every report. Some of the reports even contain defenses of basic assumptions and principles, thus demonstrating a working knowledge and deep understanding of the problems encountered when dealing with a rather new and ambiguous geographical topic. There appears to be a constant effort in all the reports to develop valid geographic ideas that would serve as predictive and interpretative devices for whatever problem might arise within the realm of geography.

ANALYSIS

Each of the reports contains several items that should be taken into account to understand fully the processes by which the student groups arranged and solved, however tentatively, the problems posed to them. A brief analysis of each report follows.

Group One

The first and second reports represent solutions to what is basically the same question: how a population would move about from a given point within a specific region. Two different starting points were designated by an "X" on the maps given to several different groups.

The report of group one immediately opens with a set of postulates or basic assumptions. The group apparently believed that it was logical to assume that human societies became "adapted" or "acclimated" to a particular environment. Group one decided that the people living at point "X" would be engaged in such work as lumbering, farming, or hunting. Implicit in this is an image of a rather technologically backward group of people inhabiting the forest region. Group one predicts that the people of place "X" will expand farther into the zone of forests because they have developed occupational categories especially suited to a forest area. Thus the first group's report includes a wide range of generalizations, most of them concerned with human behavior. They have invented a particular society, the members of which are engaged in occupations suited to their environment and who will most likely move into areas similar to the ancestral forest lands to which they have grown accustomed.

The students logically and explicitly state the assumptions or principles that serve as their conceptual tools of analysis. The group has decided that a population adapts to its particular environment, whatever that environment may be. They follow this through with a corollary, to wit: when expanding, a population chooses an environment as similar to its own as possible since its members are already adapted to it. The student committee then studied the area in which the population originally resided, established the type of habitat to which the people had grown accustomed, and on these bases predicted the region most suitable for expansion. Thus the first group had developed the logical pattern of deduction they used to solve the immediate problem facing them.

Group Two

Problem two resembles the first, but the original location of the population of country "X" was placed in a different region and vegetation zone. Thus somewhat different conditions were created than were present in the problem encountered by the first group of students.

It is interesting to note that group two interpreted their problem differently than group one. Whereas the first group had speculated about the *expansion* or *spread* of their original population over wider territory, the second group apparently interpreted their problem as one of *movement* or *migration*. Group two, proceeding from an explicit assumption that migration was taking place, investigated all the possible areas into which the people of place "X" could move. First the students studied the kind of area inhabited, then the surrounding regions, and finally they selected, by eliminating unsuitable possibilities, the best territory for settlement. Thus the second student committee adopted a method of elimination to reach their conclusion. However, group two made some implicit assumptions in their report before solving their problem. They appear to have assumed that the population of point "X" had developed a way of life particularly well-suited to the grasslands region. A set of occupations and cultural conditions was supplied to the population of the country. On the basis of the character provided for this population and the surrounding topography, climate, and vegetation, the students decided that the most likely solution to their problem was the migration of the people of point "X" to the most attractive grasslands region in all of country "X."

Group Three

The third student group tended to emphasize climatic and topographical factaors in all their decisions concerning the population distribution of country "X." Although the first two groups spent considerable time creating specific characteristics for the people residing in the country, the third group made no explicit reference to any supposed way of life. They seemed to assume that geographic condition would so strongly influence the general distribution of population that the technological level of the inhabitants—whether high or low—would not produce that much of a difference. This student committee reasoned that higher population densities would be formed in regions with good water supplies, moderate climate, plentiful food, abundant building materials, and useful trade and transportation routes. Sparse populations would be found in mountain, desert, and tundra regions. Priorities were set up for areas that would be best, in-between, and/or worst for settlement as far as geographic conditions are concerned. If anything, this group of students indirectly assumed the population to be sedentary rather than nomadic, but they refrained from giving any further details.

Group three, having given great importance to the geographic factors regulating human settlement, apparently studied the few pieces of data given them very intensely. Climatic and topographical data were used to support almost every inference made by this group. It should be noted that at one point at least group three produced a generalization to explain the relationship between the density of human settlement and varying geographic conditions; that is, section three of their report contains the rule that, "As the temperatures get colder and the terrain higher, the lower the density of people living there." This group, therefore, has discovered the idea that population gradually diminishes over vast areas as climatic conditions worsen. This demonstrates a rather high level of understanding and conceptualization.

Group Four

Group four, given the task of locating the great cities of country "X," began to solve their problem by immediately establishing a four-point criterion for locations most conducive to the formation of metropolitan areas. Cities were thus to be placed at strategic locations designed to take advantage of the commercial, agricultural, and industrial possibilities of vast surrounding regions. Five locations were chosen. However, it may be observed that group four appears to have selected city sites with a view to the internal development of country "X" rather than for external or international trading activities. All five of the cities are located at points bordering on both forest and grasslands regions. In other words, they have been located to take advantage of the products of the lumber industry and the produce of the likeliest and richest agricultural areas. Each city also is located on a river for ease of communication, both upstream and downstream.

To round off their report, group four, having stated the likeliest location for big cities in country "X," pointed out the areas eliminated from consideration. Reasons were given for each of the regions eliminated as unsuitable for the growth of large cities. This student group has shown, in a reasonable way, *where cities are most likely to rise and where they are not*—thus having explicitly solved their problem.

Group Five

The fifth group produced a highly imaginative report in which they pretended that they were exploring and evaluating country "X" for their own country's wealthy businessmen. They then divided the country into three types of area: (a) farming ▰▰▰ ; (b) industrial ▰▰▰ ; and (c) almost worthless (in black "Z"'s). Each of these areas was then subdivided, and each subdivision evaluated, by taking into account all geographic factors. Although an explicit criterion was set up for industrial areas, none was stated for agricultural regions. Group five apparently assumed grasslands regions would make the best farmland and that areas bordering on the grasslands in which weather was colder or drier would make poor but usable agricultural lands. Section D of their report represents a misreading of their information, for they state that "little plant life was found growing" in an area partly forested. The evaluation of industrial areas is much more carefully done (perhaps this is the group's real interest); for example, a criterion for the most suitable industrial location is developed and then applied to five different regions; each region is then evaluated individually and judged for the amount of potential in relation to the criterion already established. Finally, the group rejects certain regions of country "X" as not worthy of development at all.

At the end of the report is found an over-all judgment of country "X" by the investigators, after what they believed to be a careful inquiry into the territory's economic potential. In connection with this judgment it should be noted that the students took a rather generalized view of the development of country "X," for they chose to seek out areas in the country suitable for industry and agriculture in general. Nothing specific was created by the group to give country "X" any particular industries or unusual agricultural produce. The group's purpose apparently was not so much to create specific industries or to choose distinctive crops for the "unknown" or "unexplored" territory as it was to identify those locations best suited to the development of a general type of activity, either industrial or agricultural or both. The students thus completed their own investigations with a general appraisal of country "X"; that is, the country might be difficult to develop as a whole and it would offer few really good economic possibilities.

Group Six

This group of students was attempting to solve the same problem as the fourth group, yet arrived at a very different set of conclusions. They agreed with the fourth group on only one choice for the location of a major city. All other choices were disparate ones. This group went into much greater detail concerning their reasons for the location of particular cities. Their choices for the location of large cities reflect the theory that cities in general are centers of trade and transportation. The cities on map six have an external orientation; that is, they are located to serve as export-import centers particularly useful for international or overseas trade; five of the six cities are located on seas, four of the six on rivers, and three are located in delta regions in which the rivers run into the sea. Thus all of the cities are designated as commercial centers located, if possible, for easy access from the interior of the country and from distant foreign nations. It is implied in the report that each of the cities will provide a link with the others and that each will be a manufacturing and processing center for the raw materials and crops produced in the interior of the country. The trade location, however, is so important that it dictates the location of a city even though (a) an adequate water power supply is not available, or (b) the climatic conditions are becoming rather cold. The students demonstrate that they fully recognize the extreme cold of most of country "X" and hope to locate the cities in "comfortable" regions, but apparently trade comes first.

Indirectly, the people of country "X" are being given a specific character: they are portrayed as quite advanced with respect to industrial technology and business acumen. The only items that the students have not explained in detail are the specific crops or manufactured goods that might be sold through the ports of this country. Otherwise a detailed account is given of both the advantages and the disadvantages of each city's location. Thus the students have developed an over-all theory to explain the *likeliest* areas for the growth of large cities. They then applied this theory to country "X," taking into account its special climatic and topographical conditions and produced a map based on a set of logical assumptions and criteria and on available cartographic evidence.

Group Seven

The final map and related report in this series was completed in response to the same problem of economic development presented to the fifth group for solution. The fifth group, however, did not delve so deeply or so creatively into the problem as the students of the seventh group.

The student committee responsible for the seventh map and report completed their project with a great deal of imagination and care. It should be noted that this was the group selected from an average class, yet it produced the most imaginative and comprehensive report.

They invested themselves with the role of "economic planning committee" for country "X," which they termed "our country." This demonstrates their identification with the country and its problems and may account in part for the understanding evident in many of the extremely creative and perceptive decisions concerning the development of "their country."

In addition to investing themselves with a personal role, the students also decided on the purpose of their endeavors: to make their country "rich and prosperous." To realize this goal "all of the most modern equipment and techniques" would be utilized. Thus the group had a personal stake in the problem, a purpose, and a method to achieve their end.

Subsequently, a list of nine undertakings was drawn up, including one project to identify those zones or areas of country "X" that would be of little or no value to develop. The undertakings listed ranged from the development of industrial regions to the building of railroads. In contrast to the solution of group five, these students identified very specific projects to be developed in certain selected areas of the country; for example, agricultural oases that might produce fruits and vegetables for the whole country. The planning committee apparently had a very concrete plan concerning what the country needed and what might be accomplished in the way of developing it to fulfill those needs. The student committee demonstrated a constant awareness of the relationship between the needs of mankind and the potentialities of a given economic region. Oftentimes the group decided to develop a given region even though natural conditions made it difficult to do so; consider their decision to irrigate the desert region to produce more warm-weather crops. Implicit in this kind of development is the idea that man is in a struggle with nature and may conquer it through his advancing technology. This indirectly bestows an aggressive industrial culture on the people of country "X." They, and the planning committee, are interested in developing the country to its maximum potential by utilizing the most advanced and powerful technology at their disposal.

The development of each area in the country is described, explained, and defended in great detail. Furthermore, all of the developments are linked with one another until a unified, integrated economy is developed in which each different region supplies its particular type of product to all of the other areas needing it. Thus the planning committee has created an interlocking and interdependent economic system of great complexity. Though reasons are given for each particular development in the country, the over-all goal is never lost sight of, and articulation between different regions and sectors of the economy is usually provided for by the planning committee; for example, railroads are strategically located to facilitate the movement of ore and minerals from mines to industrial areas.

The students also demonstrated a rather perceptive understanding of the major problems facing country "X" as a whole; namely, its size and the cold-weather characteristics of vast stretches of its territory. Furthermore, they concluded that the development of country "X" would take place primarily across its middle portion, for this wide band of terrain provided the best environment in which man could live and work. Thus the group's conclusion brings them back to an understanding of the relationship between man, as they have conceived of him, and man's environment, as provided for by the geographic information at their command.

Finally, this particular group was the only one to attempt to discover if country "X" did, in fact, represent a real nation. On the basis of their conclusions concerning the problems and prospects of country "X," the committee suspected that the Soviet Union was the country most like the unknown region "X." They ended their speculation with a plea for teacher verification of their theory.

In contrast to the other six reports this last one may be taken to represent a high point in both understanding and creativity. This group subjected the information at their disposal to extremely intensive scrutiny and thus achieved greater awareness of the magnitude of the task confronting them. To solve the problem of developing an entire country—a very large and cold one at that—a great deal of imagination was called for. Yet however imaginative and speculative the solution might have been, the students took natural conditions into account and offered a reason for almost everything they had done. This tendency countered or modified any far-fetched ideas that any individual member might have submitted. The seventh report and map were therefore the products of a series of logical inferences, suppositions, and deductions.

CONCLUSION

Although each report and map show many differences in emphasis, methods, and conclusions, an equal number of tendencies in common are discernible among the seven solutions:

1. The students displayed a great deal of creativity in interpreting the materials and solving their committee's particular problem. The variations in creativity ranged from the development of logical concepts to serve as over-all interpretative tools to the invention of a specific group role to be assumed in the solution of the problem.

2. Every group evolved a concrete idea of what the people of country "X" might be doing for a living. In a sense each student group invested the people of the unknown land with some type of technology and described them as engaged in a variety of occupations. Thus the students supplied the human beings living in country "X" with a society engaged in making some sort of use of their environment.

3. Each student group had carefully studied and analyzed the materials available to them; that is, the five descriptive maps. All of the maps created displayed a close correlation to the information about the climate and vegetation zones of the different regions of country "X." Apparently, each student committee had thoroughly analyzed, interpreted, and fused their basic materials into one integrated body of data.

4. Each report demonstrates the explicit or implicit tendency to develop a theoretical construct concerning man and his relationship to the environment. Each construct or generalization is then utilized as a tool or guide for the solution of the geographical problem being discussed by the students.

5. All groups concerned attacked their problems in the abstract, concentrating upon human and climatic problems rather than placing emphasis upon discovering if country "X" was actually a present-day nation. Only one group became aware of the reality of the country portrayed cartographically as "X."

6. One of the strongest emphases is on the use of logic or reasons to back up nearly all of the assertions and hypotheses found in the reports. All of the student groups appear to place great stress on the *defense* of their interpretations. They attempt to defend almost everything—from their generalizations and tools of analysis to their conclusions and general solutions of the problems. Very few clearly erroneous or illogical interpretations of the evidence are presented by the various committees in their reports. The groups tested almost all of their statements by logic and supported their conclusions with evidence.

7. The students appear to have reached conclusions that bear strong resemblances and, in some cases, are nearly identical to each other. Furthermore, all of the groups demonstrate an awareness of the way in which geography "controls" or "channels" human settlement and development, and they also appear to be aware of the ways in which mankind may take advantage of whatever is offered by its environment, or perhaps even control natural conditions.

Perhaps the convergence of conclusions is in part the result of group interaction in which a give-and-take occurs between its members which necessitates providing reasons for each suggestion. It should be remembered that the situation in which the reports and maps were devised was structured only through the materials that had been distributed by the instructor, and by the background experiences brought to light by student group interaction. Thus the students, working from a set of given materials, solved a set of different problems, by their own efforts, without any interference or direct aid from the teacher.

Whenever faced with difficulties, various individuals and groups would approach the teacher for more information, clearer explanations, and increased direction. Questions such as "What should we do?", "What does this mean?", "Is this right?", and "How should we draw the map?" all received the same type of reply; this might be "What do you think ought to be done?", "Do *you* think it's right?", or "This is your problem now. Why don't you try it yourselves?" The teacher appeared to cause students some anguish and apprehension, but he consistently followed the policy of answering a question with another question. The students were thus forced to act on their own and to make their decisions based solely on their background experience and the evidence in their possession. To understand the extent to which students are capable of (a) ordering their own behavior and (b) autonomously reaching their own conclusions, the teacher must consistently perform a nondirective role. If nothing else, the results of the geography experiment demonstrate that high school students, if encouraged to think on their own, are very capable of constructing logical and imaginative solutions to their classroom problems.

THE POET'S MEANING: EXPLORING
IDEAS IN AN ENGLISH CLASS

Many of the previous discovery episodes in this chapter reflect a social studies orientation, particularly toward the special problems and methods of analysis in history and the social sciences. The classes that we experimented with were often classes that tended to demonstrate a concern for concepts, problems, and goals characteristic of the social sciences.

The question, therefore, arises concerning the goals, problems, and concepts peculiar to different disciplines. Each field of inquiry, in a sense, creates its own special classroom milieu including language, domain, analytic methods, and special aims. In the case that follows, the group selected was an English class primarily engaged in the study of literature rather than grammar. The goal of the experiment was to ascertain the ideas and approaches characteristic of a literature class. In other words, the study addressed itself to the question: what might be the pattern of inquiry in a group concerned not with history, but with literary art.

The class selected was composed of high school seniors of average intelligence who were enrolled in a special program of integrated coursework. This class was following a program in which the English and social studies courses had been combined and were being jointly taught by a team composed of one history and one English teacher. It should be noted that although the investigator and the history teacher were present at the class session (a double period of eighty minutes) the English instructor presided over a large part of the discussion. The history teacher intervened only at strategic points to ask questions. Thus the English instructor performed the major teaching role.

The students in question were unfamiliar with the discovery method of teaching. The discussion was an isolated case in the interpretation of poetry. The class had been studying poetry before this session was held but had not been introduced either to Chinese poetry or to inductive teaching. The English teacher was asked to assume more of the leadership role in this discussion to compensate for the change in classroom method. The episode was followed up by giving the students the missing information about the poem. A short discusion took place in which the students reviewed their previous reactions to the poem in the light of the new information.

The material investigated by the class consisted of a single short poem of Chinese origin. This poem was selected because of its remoteness from the students' usual literary contacts. This particular poem (reproduced below) was also chosen because it lacked any specific identifying features that might immediately give away its cultural origin. Finally, this poem, which was written in the year 1927 by a young Chinese revolutionary named Wen I-to, was offered to the literature class because its dramatic qualities hopefully would raise student interest.

QUIET NIGHT[16]

This light, and the light-bleached four walls,
The kind table and chair, intimate as friends,
The scent of old books, reaching me in whiffs,
My favorite teacup as serene as a meditating nun,
The baby sucking contentedly at his mother's breast,
A snore reporting the healthy slumber of my big son . . .

[16]*Twentieth Century Chinese Poetry: An Anthology*, Translated and Edited by Kau-Yu Hsu. New York: Doubleday and Company, A Doubleday Anchor Book, © 1963, p. 62. Reprinted by permission.

This mysterious quiet night, this calm peace.
In my throat quiver songs of gratitude,
But the songs soon become ugly curses.
Quiet night, I cannot accept your bribe.
Who treasures this walled-in square foot of peace?
My world has a much wider horizon.
As the four walls cannot silence the clamors of war,
How can you stop the violent beat of my heart?

Better that my mouth be filled with mud and sand,
Than to sing the joy or sorrow of one man alone;
Better that moles dig holes in this head of mine,
And vermin feed on my flesh and blood,
Than to live only for a cup of wine and a book of verse,
Or for an evening of serenity brought by the ticking clock,
Hearing not the groans and sighs from all my neighbors,
Seeing not the shivering shadows of the widows and orphans,
And the convulsion in battle trenches, mad men biting their sickbeds,
And all the tragedies ground out under the millstone of life.

Happiness, I cannot accept your bribe now.
My world is not within this walled-in square foot.

Listen, here goes another cannon-report, another roar of Death.
Quiet night, how can you stop the violent beat of my heart?

Dittoed copies of this poem were presented to every member of the literature class. To enhance and heighten the students' interest in the meaning and background of this work of art the poem was rendered more ambiguous and unfamiliar yet by omitting the time and place of its creation, and the name of the author. The teacher was requested to adopt a nondirective approach throughout the entire class session. Complying with this request, the teacher refused to supply her class with any specific information about the poem, its author, or its historical setting. Furthermore, she refrained from explaining or clarifying any major points in the content of the poem. The meaning of any word, phrase, or sentence in the poem was left entirely up to the members of the class.

The factors mentioned in the preceding paragraph combined to create an ambiguous, somewhat confusing, yet unconstrained classroom atmosphere in which a fluid conversational state was created to allow maximum student participation in the interpretation of the poem. Because no standard for a right or wrong answer was imposed on the group, the students were encouraged to pursue any line of investigation that they believed to be interesting and productive. Each member of the class could interpret the poem as he desired, except that he might be called on to defend his particular point of view in a rational way.

The four excerpts that follow are the results of interaction of a group of English students, a problematic poem, and a seemingly uncooperative, nondirective instructor. Each of the excerpts was chosen to illustrate a different phase of the discussion, which ranged from analysis and interpretation to discovery and examination of values. The segments of conversation are presented in chronological order, the first example being drawn from the opening phase of the complete discussion.

Excerpt 1

LENNY.   He (the poet) is telling of the wars between other people and of the wars within himself. These things are not common with everyone. I don't think he is talking about a real war. Perhaps they are wars within the soul.

TEACHER.   Does anyone agree with this? Disagree? Do you think this is a real war or a symbolic one?

MAXINE.   I think you can take it both ways. It is quite confusing.

SUE.   I think it is a symbolic war. Life is a war, and death is his quiet boring life, but he still prefers life to death in this poem.

ROBERT.   You can take a poem and have it mean almost anything if you go too deeply into it. I think this poem is simply about the horrors of war and man's inhumanity to man.

HALEY.   Well, but perhaps it is about real life and a real war. The poet says that he would like to live quiet and peacefully, but can't. Does that mean he likes death, or that he is just moved by the problems of his fellow man? I think the latter is true of the peom.

TEACHER.   Does this poem recall anything to you from other literary works?

HAL.   I think it is a social protest poem like *September 1, 1939*.

MAXINE.   That's if it is about a real war.

HALEY.   It could be compared to *Cry, The Beloved Country*. When the hero of that book died he could not bear to hear the cry of his people. This book and the poem are both about the problems of mankind suffering from the oppression of other masters.

LENNY.   I think it could contrast with *Hedda Gabler*. She would have done the opposite of the poet and ignored the sufferings of the outside world.

SUE.   I think this poet is really trying to face the truth about his world: that it really isn't very pleasant after all. It is ugly and war-torn. In this sense the poet might be compared to Oedipus who wanted to know the truth, although it would kill him in the end.

JANICE.   The more I think about it, the more I agree that it reminds me of the hero of *Cry, the Beloved Country.* He was trying not to see the agony of his people at first, trying not to be part of them, but it didn't work and he couldn't escape helping them.

DON.   Yes, this is by some man who is deciding whether or not to give up his life to help the people who are suffering. He even decides to give up his security and material comforts to do this.

HALEY.   Whether the war is a real one or not, there are always terrible things going on in the world, and the poet is reacting to these events in a very special way. He is telling us to face them and do something about it.

SUE.   It works out so well as a symbolic poem of life and death and man's inhumanity to man because it really doesn't mention specific places or dates or events. It's general.

ROBERT.   Maybe it still means both real and symbolic wars. Can you really tell for certain which it is? I don't think so.

LENNY.   Well, our comparisons with other literature shows that the poet is definitely interested in what is going on around man. He is not keeping himself locked up in an ivory tower.

Having scrutinized the poem, Lenny poses a problem to his classmates and is promptly reinforced by the teacher who indirectly clarifies the difficulty; that is, is the poet describing a real or a symbolic war? Other students then attempt to solve the problem by a more intensive analysis of the poem as a whole. Before the students have resolved the aforementioned problem, the teacher raises a new problem, yet indirectly suggests a new method of approach to both the new and the old questions. The new method, literary comparison, is immediately grasped by several of the students and tried out. This method, however, leads to an incipient argument between different members of the class because each has developed a different theory concerning the problem of symbol versus reality. Don and Janice take the poet's concern with his fellow men at face value and assume that he intends to help them in their struggle to survive; Haley rejects the problem, stating that it does not matter whether a real or symbolic war is being described, since it is the poet's meaning or message that is of the greatest importance; Sue accepts the poem as symbolic because of its lack of specific identifying characteristics (e.g., time, place, and culture); Robert develops his own eclectic point of view that combines both the symbolic and realistic interpretation of the poem; and, finally, Lenny, the first one to suggest the problem, comes full circle around and points out that *Because* of the literary comparisons made by the other students this poem should be classed with those pieces of literature that are concerned with the actual and immediate problems of man's existence. It might be said that the last student to speak in this excerpt has rejected theorizing in favor of evidence based on literary comparison. It appears that the first phase of the discovery process in this class is devoted to the identification and clarification of problems inherent in the new literary work being studied by both teacher and pupils.

During this opening phase of investigation, the class also appeared to develop its own concepts with which to analyze the poem more carefully later on. Three main ideas dominate the remainder of the conversation: reality, symbol, and meaning or message. Applying their newly developed concepts, the class, with some guidance from the teacher, proceeded to interpret the poem line by line and word by word. The following is a representative passage from the second phase in which the poem is methodically analyzed:

Excerpt 2

TEACHER.   What does "light" mean in this poem?

LENNY.   Light is only on the inside of the poet's world. The outside is all darkness and horror. He is safe and comfortable on the inside.

HALEY.   Maybe light is also insecurity. If it gets stronger, it might extend into the night and show the truth to him. It might show him what is going on.

SUE.   Light might mean beauty and serenity and home.

MAXINE.   Light is all on the inside here because the poet is only seeing what is on the inside of his four walls—his little world.

JANICE.   Light is identified symbolically with the four walls to create an image of security and aloofness from the dark world outside.

ROBERT.   There is a constant comparison set up between the nice things lit up on the inside of his four walls and the miserable things out in the night.

TEACHER.   What might "dark" mean?

SUE.   Lightness is reality and darkness is escape.

MAXINE.   No, it is the reverse.

HALEY.	I'm not sure I understand. Light is on the inside, but dark is on the outside. However, the dark seems to hold all the terrors and the realities.
TEACHER.	Look again at the poem. Look more closely.
BOB.	The night is quiet, not terrible.
LENNY.	But the night also contains cannon-reports and the clamors of war.
SUE.	The night is also called mysterious by the poet.
TEACHER.	Why do you think that is so?

(*pause*)

MIKE.	The dark is the unknown and holds all those things of which we are afraid.
HALEY.	The night must be mysterious because it is really used in two different ways and has two different meanings. It contains the unknown horrors of war and suffering, but it *seems* quiet to the poet on the inside of his four walls.
LENNY.	The dark and the night are mysterious because they make you feel surprised and fearful of danger. Darkness and calm can make you feel very uneasy.
MAXINE.	The night is mysterious because it is dark out and very calm, and then there are hints of something terrible out there, like someone creeping up behind you. That is very unnerving.
JOHN.	I think we are getting confused because the poem changes its message. At the beginning it is all nice and lovely, but it changes later to something gory and horrible.
TEACHER.	Would you show us how you found this out?
JOHN.	The first stanza is all charming and peaceful. All the images are pleasant; meditating nun, snoring son, the smell of old books, and so on. This is all illuminated by the light. Then in the second stanza we get into "ugly curses" and the "clamors of war." Finally, in the third stanza, the whole tone of the poem changes to horror. Almost everyting in the third stanza brings out the change in the poet's outlook. He is now looking at all the terrible things going on in the world and has almost completely forgotten the nice things.
LENNY.	The poem changes from positive to negative feelings.
SUE.	The first stanza makes you want to doze, while the third stanza frightens you.
HALEY.	Toward the middle of the poem, all of the horrors crash in upon the poet through the darkness he has been trying to block out with his four walls and his light.

MIKE.   I think the poet is trying to point out that the calm night is really an illusion. How can it be anything else if it contains all those horrors like the "shivering shadows of widows and orphans" or "convulsions in battle trenches."

ROBERT.   The dark night really contains all the tragedies of life that the poet at first blocks out but later decides to face up to.

The second phase of the discovery episode is dominated by discussion about words—both their symbolic and their concrete meanings. However, this is only the surface appearance of the conversation which masks what the students are really concerned with. While it may be easily noticed that the members of the English class are debating word meanings (e.g., Sue, Maxine, and Haley arguing over Sue's statement that, "Lightness is reality and darkness is escape"), the students are also attempting to understand the way in which words function in the poem to create feelings and images (e.g., Janice's statement that, "Light is identified symbolically with the four walls to create an image of security and aloofness from the dark world outside").

The students move from the analysis of words and concepts to entire lines, and, finally, to whole stanzas. This is clearly demonstrated by John, who, toward the close of this excerpt, presents a long explanation of the radical change in mood and imagery from the first to the third stanza of the poem. Thus, as the discussion proceeds, the focal point of the investigation shifts from the identification of problems to the very careful analysis of the meaning and function of the various terms in the poem. The teacher constantly prods the students to explain their answers as well as to study the poem in ever greater depth. The search for meaning and the interpretation of words as image-creators continues throughout the session. However, toward the close of the inquiry, while debating the meaning of certain portions of the poem, the students shifted their ground dramatically to a discussion in which personal beliefs played an extremely important role. The following excerpt includes the debate over student values:

Excerpt 3

TEACHER. What does the poet mean by a bribe? What is the bribe for?

JACK.   A bribe is a payment made by one party to another to do something or to forget to do something.

SUE.   The poet is bribing himself, actually. At least, he was bribing himself at first, but later rejects the bribe offered him. He says the quiet night is the bribe.

TEACHER. Can anyone explain what that might mean?

HALEY.   The quiet night is offering a bribe of peace and quiet providing you stay inside your four walls with only light inside and darkness outside.

MAXINE.   Yes, that way you forget everyone's problems.

JOHN.   You remain in your own little world if you take the bribe.

ROBERT.   You don't help a soul. You don't even look at anyone in trouble.

HAL.   Maybe the poet is making fun of all those people who lie to themselves and withdraw into their own little private worlds not caring for anyone but themselves.

LENNY.   The poet's feelings, I think, are quite human, and highly probable under his circumstances. He doesn't want to face the terrible truth around him, but he also realizes that he cannot live for himself alone.

HALEY.   I think that, even though we should think of others, we also have our own security to think of. Of course, we are not usually doing as much to serve our fellowmen as we could.

SUE.   I think that the poet is coming out very strongly for helping others. He says, "My world is not within this walled-in square foot" and, "Quiet night, how can you stop the violent beat of my heart?" I take this to mean that he can no longer stand the cries of pain of his people, but must take immediate action.

JACK.   Oh! I don't know about that. Most people think only of themselves.

BOB.   I agree you think of yourself before you think of anyone else.

JANICE.   People do usually worry about themselves.

MIKE.   He is not being realistic. How many people would think of others before thinking of themselves? You can't do that.

LENNY.   There seems to be a lot of disagreement here. I'm not sure what to think now.

STUART.   I agree with Jack. It's unnatural for a person to think of others—strangers, before his own family.

TEACHER.   Now wait a minute! How do you explain the third stanza of the poem if you think that people only care about themselves or their families. For instance, look at the lines, "Better that moles dig holes in this head of mine, and vermin feed on my flesh and blood, than to live only for a cup of wine and a book of verse, . . . hearing not the groans and sighs from all my neighbors. . . ."

JACK.   Well, I am going to say something that you might not like. Can I go ahead and say it?

TEACHER. Why not?

JACK. I think the poet is an out-and-out hypocrite. I think this because he is advocating all those fine things for others to do. That is very easy to do, but what about what he will do for the others. All he does is write fine verses and keep out of the real trouble.

MAXINE. Well, I don't know if he is going off to war, but I think he is still writing powerful poetry designed to make us want to go out and go to war or help our fellowmen in some way since there is a war on.

STUART. So he wrote the poem. What does that prove? It shows he has fine ideas, but it doesn't show that the poet himself is doing anything to help others.

LENNY. Is there anything in this poem that would make you believe that this man would not do anything about what he thinks?

MAXINE. I think this man is a real thinker, otherwise why would he picture himself the way he does? He is actually cursing himself if he does not personally do anything. He says, "Better that moles dig holes in this head of mine." What do you think that is? Do you still think he is being hypocritical?

JACK. It is beautiful and everything but it just stands as it is. He is really trying to get others to help out. Is he really trying to do anything himself except spread fancy thoughts for others to follow?

SUE. Well, don't you know anyone who doesn't do as Jack and Janice and Bob say?

ROBERT. Maybe Martin Luther King or President Johnson.

JACK. President Johnson is a politician. He helps people to get votes.

TEACHER. Does Jack speak for the whole class? Is everyone that cynical?

HALEY. No! The poet is trying to make us think—not of ourselves, but of others.

SUE. He is not trying to make the problem sound beautiful, but brutally realistic, to make us want to go out and *do* something about it. The poet is saying that if we cannot realize that the problems of others are our problems, too, then we might as well be dead.

At the beginning of the third phase of the inquiry, the students appear to be primarily interested in deciding on the meaning of the word "bribe" and the way this concept functions in the poem. Haley points out, "The quiet night is offering a bribe of peace . . . providing you stay inside your four walls. . . . This analysis is based wholly on the grouping of words within the poem itself. However, a short time later the same student is engaged in making a personal value judgment, though this judgment is, of course, closely related to an issue raised by the poet; that is, Haley's statement, ". . . even though we should think of others, we also have our own security to think of." As the discussion progresses, the interpretation of the poem slips into the background, and the controversy raised by the poet within himself becomes the object of classroom debate. The issue, as the group defines it, appears to be twofold: (a) selfishness versus selflessness, or should you primarily help yourself or others? and (b) action versus words, or will the poet (and, implicitly, other persons) act upon what he is suggesting others should do? The controversy causes many of the members of the class to state their personal ethical codes with respect to this issue. Statements like Jack's, "I think the poet is an out-and-out hypocrite" become characteristic of the kind of value judgments made by the students concerning the poet's philosophy.

Both favorable and unfavorable comments are made either supporting or refuting the poet's point of view, and the argument expands into broad disagreement about human nature and the relationship between words and deeds. A rather large number of students participate in this phase of the discussion and spend most of their time arguing about the various positions that have been developed by several members of the group. A lively dialogue between the students themselves arises out of the controversy. The teacher, while retaining the role of guide and interrogator, approaches the position of a participant in the inquiry.

It is extremely interesting to observe that the class used nearly the entire period (a) to investigate the symbolic and the real meaning of the poem; (b) to analyze the poet's language; and (c) to discuss the poet's general philosophy concerning his own and other persons' behavior. Very little attention was paid to placing the poem in time and space. The latter phase of the general inquiry did not occur until the very end of the discussion. A portion of the last phase follows:

Excerpt 4

LENNY.   It's not completely a dog-eat-dog world. The poet says we should think of our fellowmen and come to their aid. I think he would too.

HAL.   I know a woman who helps mentally retarded children without pay on her own free time. Many people do similar things.

MAXINE. The whole world isn't selfish. Can't you believe that people do come to the aid of each other in many cases of need.

JACK. But you still can't prove it.

STUART. The poet's just handing out a line.

HALEY. The poet is trying to change people's behavior by changing their minds. This shows his mind is changed also; therefore, he would aid others. If he didn't sincerely believe it, why would he write such a poem stating it the way he does.

MIKE. Yes, you're calling the poet a liar He's one of the best liars I ever read. I couldn't write something so convincing if I didn't believe it.

JOHN. Everyone must do their part in the world if it is to be a better place to live. That's the poet's message.

MAXINE. We usually think the best thing in the world is whatever is for ourselves, but the poet makes us think otherwise. Why do we think that people who are thinkers do not act? You cannot say he does not sound like he believes in what he says and you cannot say that he did *not* act on it. Even if he didn't, think of all the people he moved to action on behalf of others. Even if the poet didn't do anything else, he has caused a great deal of good.

SUE. Many times we help others without thought of material reward because we feel it right to do so or because we are all part of the same society and would like kindnesses done to us in return some day. Helping someone across the street or aiding someone who has too many packages to carry would fall into the category I'm talking about.

JACK. I don't know. When you need a helping hand, people usually try to avoid you or else they block you out altogether.

LENNY. But that's exactly the poet's point. We shouldn't do that. We *should* notice each other's problems.

TEACHER. Where do you think the author of this poem comes from?

SUE. I think that the poet is English because it sounds like it was written during World War II.

MIKE. It was written in 1943 in England.

MAXINE. I think it is from the World War I period because it mentions trenches at the end of third stanza.

BOB. Then the poet might be French or German because nearly all the trenches were in France and manned by Frenchmen or Germans.

LENNY. I do not think it would be from Germany because it sounds like the poet's country is the one being attacked. Germany was the attacker until the end of the war. Also, this poem

	does seem to have been written at the beginning of the war since the poet is trying to block out the first signs of battle.
DIANE.	Perhaps it is from some period in Russian history, maybe the First or Second World Wars.
JOHN.	I don't think it would be Russia because the poet speaks of 'meditating nuns.'
HALEY.	There might be nuns in Russia. A lot of people over there still belong to the Orthodox Church.
MAXINE.	I do not think it really matters what country the poem is from. It is a poem telling us to help our fellowman when he is in trouble. It also shows us the horrors of war in all countries, so it doesn't really matter where it is from.
HAL.	It is a poem that expressed a universal problem.
STUART.	That makes it very hard to place in a particular time or country.
LENNY.	The poet is someone who believes in the same things that we believe in.
JACK.	We believe in those things as ideals. I'm not so sure that we practice what we preach.
HALEY.	If it is translated from a foreign language, that would make it twice as hard to place since many of the words we are basing our ideas upon might be changed from their exact meaning when turned into English words.
MIKE.	I have thought it over, and I think that the author might be a Russian because the poem sounds like propaganda. It is very forceful and is designed to arouse people to action during a terrible war.
SUE.	It might even be from Viet Nam.
JACK.	It sounds like a poem that might be written by Stephen Crane.
STUART.	It is definitely an action poem. Maybe it is a modern anti-war poem. I'm still not absolutely certain it is about a real war.
ROBERT.	It is pretty realistic, though. I think the poet is referring to a pretty big war: an attack on this country. He says *all* his neighbors are affected by the war.
DIANE.	It has to be from a war-torn land. The author sounds like he might even be a leader against the enemy—if he lives up to his views.
LENNY.	I don't know. I think I agree with Maxine. The author is generalizing from the war he knows to produce a picture of universal human misery. That's why it is so hard to tell where this is from.

BOB.

All we can say is that it is from a modern or fairly modern time and from a country under attack during a big war. That takes in a lot of ground.

TEACHER.   How do you know this is a recent poem?

BOB.

The poet mentions clocks, battle trenches, and cannons. The rest of the things he mentions could be from any time, but these make me believe the poem is fairly recent.

DIANE.

I still say it is from one of the countries attacked during World War I. The things Bob mentioned make me certain of this.

MAXINE.   But does it matter?

DIANE.

I suppose not, but it would be interesting to know. I'm all curious to know now.

MAXINE.

Whenever and wherever it is from, it is still a beautiful piece of poetry. I think we've gotten its message.

HALEY.

It is written by someone who sounds almost like a revolutionary propagandizing his people to defeat the enemy. Maybe it is Russian. Or French.

SUE.

The author is getting his people to fight their oppressors, whoever they may be.

JANICE.

He might just be saying these things to make them sound noble.

SUE.   Well, even so, that's better than not doing anything at all.

MIKE.

I think we'd have to look through many, many history books before we locate the right place. Even then I'm not sure we could find the origin of the poem.

TEACHER.   Why not?

MIKE.   Not enough to go on.

The main line of inquiry in the last phase of the discussion was to discover the cultural origin of the poem by carefully gleaning and testing various phrases and words as clues to historical context. The words of the poem constitute the evidence used to support student assertions concerning the poet's probable membership in a particular society. Outside evidence, such as a historical event, is brought to bear on the material in the poem in an attempt to gain a more precise idea of the poem's actual setting in time and space.

Wherever the social and cultural identification of written material might serve as the focal point of investigation of a social studies class, the English class, apparently, focuses on the meaning and imagery found in written works. Even though this particular English class was accustomed to studying literature from historical perspective, they still approached this poem primarly as a literary work of art, and as a part of their own personal experience. The latter two tendencies may be observed in student remarks even when they are supposedly engaged primarily in cultural identification (for example, Stuart's remark, "It is definitely an action poem"; Robert's statement, "It is pretty realistic . . ."; and Lenny's comment, "The poet is someone who believes in the same things that we believe in"). Mike's comment, "I have thought it over, and I think that the author might be a Russian because the poem sounds like propaganda. It is very forceful and is designed to arouse people to action during a terrible war," is characteristic of the union of historical and literary analysis. The first part of his statement relates cues in the poem to a specific social setting, while the second sentence proceeds to analyze the poem's purpose as a work of literature. The student gives good reasons, usually of an analytical or interpretive nature, to support both of his sentences. It may be observed, however, that the general method of defending answers adopted by students is to resort to the analysis of word functions and the study of the images and meanings these bring forth. Outside evidence is seldom used, except for comparisons with other literary works, and an occasional reference to a historical event such as the first or second world war. The study of language and meaning is the dominant preoccupation of the class.

Thus, this discovery episode passes through four noticeably different phases, though none of these is mutually exclusive. It would be more correct to call this episode cumulative in nature since the conversations represented by each of the different excerpts build on the previous ones. The concepts and conclusions developed at the beginning of the experience recur again and again, though often in different form, throughout each phase of the discussion. Keeping this in mind, the conversation may be said to have moved through four stages, each with its own special emphasis.

PHASE 1. Exploring the new material and identifying the problems connected with it.

PHASE 2. Analyzing and interpreting the language of the material.

PHASE 3. Searching for meaning and examining values related to, or arising from, the literary work.

PHASE 4. Discovering the social and cultural origin of the work of art.

On the whole, this sequence of events compares closely with what happens in a social studies discovery episode, but there appears to be far more concern with meaning and symbol in the English class which is quite unusual for a history group. Not until the symbolic, linguistic, and stylistic factors have been carefully weighed, and the poet's purpose debated, does the English class inquire into the age and locale of the literary production. The powrful desire to discover the social and cultural setting of evidence that becomes one of the major motivating forces for a history class plays only a minor role in the English group's investigation of a poem completely new to them. A gamelike situation does result from inquiry into this poem, but it is directed toward discovery of meaning and purpose, not time and place. The emphasis on meaning in an English class operating in an open-ended atmosphere for discussion goes so far as to take the author's or poet's message to heart, and the poet's message in turn becomes the subject of debate in immediate and personal terms as well as on a symbolic and literary level.

CLASSROOM EXPERIMENTS IN RADIATION BIOLOGY

There were eight groups composed of three or four students, each from a physics class that was given five weeks of radiation biology in a pilot program of the Board of Education. They were almost all sophomores of *high quality* (honors class in physics).

The first six experiments referred to were designed to give a working knowledge of the technique of radiation detection and some of the physical limitations to be taken into account when attempting to determine the rate and strength of radiation of particular radioactive sources.

In the following experiment each group was assigned a single source whose identity was not known to them. There were two pairs each of four different sources, some liquid, some solid, and some powdered. They were coded 1A, 1B, 2A, 2B, 3, 4, 5, 6. The teacher alone knew the identity of each source. In addition each group was provided with a chart of the half-life of some 50–60 radioisotopes and the characteristic type of radiation emitted by each. The members of each group received, as a class, a short lecture on the technique of determining the half-life of an unknown substance. From that point on they proceeded to determine the half-life.

In the suggested curriculum for this experimental program in Chicago only two possible sources were suggested for this experiment. Here the teacher went further, using four and keeping the identity of the sources unknown to the experimenters, a procedure followed by some, *but not all*, of the other teachers involved in the program.

The level of interest in the identification of the sources was very high and sustained and it was, from the teacher's point of view, emotionally rewarding. The shifts from independence to dependence by

the students during the experiment came out clearly in the dia-
logaues.

KATHI. We've got an awfully weird source. A couple of days ago it
was 600 and now it's over 700. The machine is driving us
crazy.

TEACHER. I wonder why that's happening.

RICHARD.
(*another*
group). Which one on this list would it be? This seems to have a
half-life of six days: 144 hours and 20 minutes. We got the
same count twice.

BRIAN. Here are yesterday's counts and here are today's counts.
Today's are higher. How can this be?

TEACHER. What might be going wrong to produce those results?

BRIAN. I don't know. We'll run it again.

(*The above dialogue was voiced similarly with a member of another*
group.)

KATHI. Why do our counts go from 600 to 300 in the space of a few
minutes?

TEACHER. I don't know. What do you think might be happening?

KATHI. I like when teachers don't tell me the answers, but every
once in a while you could say something. We might be here
for a thousand years.

TEACHER. Well, grandma, your grandchildren can finish up for you.

TEACHER. (*going over to another group in the lab*) How are things
going here?

WILLIAM. All right, we started at 164 two days ago and now the count
is down to 118. (*This source is uranium with a half-life far*
longer than our life span.)

TEACHER. Which one do you think it might be?

RICHARD. I don't know. There are so many.

TEACHER. Well, maybe you can narrow it down by applying what you
learned from your previous experiments.

RICHARD. Oh, if it's an alpha, beta, or gamma source?

TEACHER. That's one possibility.

RICHARD,
ROBERT,
and ED. It must be a beta-gamma source because the amount of
radiation coming through is cut down enough to fit neither
one separately. And this means that it must be either cal-
cium or silver. Is it?

TEACHER.	Are you sure it is beta-gamma radiation?
EDWARD.	But silver isn't a liquid at room temperature. And neither is calcium.
RICHARD.	Is it Iodine 131? It's the only other half-life close to our six days. It's 8.03 days.
TEACHER.	Eight days seems pretty far from six days, doesn't it?
RICHARD.	What's bismuth?
TEACHER.	I don't know.
EDWARD.	May I go to the chem lab to find out?
TEACHER.	Go ahead, take my pass.

EDWARD.	We found out. It might be silver nitrate, or calcium, or bismuth, since they can all be put into liquid form at room temperature. So what is it?
TEACHER.	Back in the hole again.
EDWARD *and* RICHARD.	Yeah!
TEACHER.	Well, how can the previous experiments help you?
GROUP.	Which ones?
TEACHER.	One through six.
GROUP.	But that's all of them.
GROUP CONVER- SATION.	It couldn't be the first three, so it must be four or five since six is absorption and that tells us only that we have a beta-gamma source. But four and five are the same. They aren't. One is the range and the other is the inverse square law. No, they're the same because if they were different we couldn't use the gamma data in four for number five. But they are different. I can't explain it but I know it. Mr. H., tell them they're different.
TEACHER.	Are they?
GROUP.	Ohhh!

[*Teacher's note: At the end of the period the group wanted to stay to "pick my brain" but I sent them on to their next classes, for they had already stayed on past the end of the period so often that I did not want the other teachers "on my neck" for missed work in their classes.*]

RICHARD,
ROBERT,
and
EDWARD.   Well, it must be silver, we've decided. Because the half-life was in between seven days and eight days and the only other possibility is Iodine 131. Which is it? We're going to choose silver, because it's too much to go through to try to tell the difference.

TEACHER.   If you think that you have the answer, OK.

WILLIAM.   *(from another group referred to above)* Look, Mr. H., yesterday we were getting readings of 55 to 60, and today it's 130–140. I can't understand it.

BRIAN.   Did you get the right source?

TEACHER.   Well, what might be the trouble?

BRIAN.   We don't know. Let's take some more counts.

RICHARD.   *(referring to another groups efforts) They're* getting iodine. Their results are more exact than ours. They're getting a more steady drop.

TEACHER.   How come you're here?

RICHARD.   I'm helping them with my vast experience.

I've noticed that the sources are numbered 1B, 1A. Now silver is Ag and I is iodine. Is that your system?

TEACHER.   Why would I use such a simple code?

RICHARD.   Tell us. We're sure it's silver, but tell us.

TEACHER.   Next week.

EDWARD.   Can you imagine Strauss not sleeping all week wondering if it *is* silver?

TEACHER.   How about you? Is it silver?

EDWARD.   Sure it's silver.

TEACHER.   OK.

After encountering frustrations the various groups fell to calculating the intention of the teacher rather than to attacking the problem again. When no solution was forthcoming from the teacher, back they went to the problem.

Each student group tried, with the equipment available, to find its "unknown" by the trial-and-error method. It should be noted that the participants often sought direction and additional information from their instructor in their attempt to arrive at a satisfactory conclusion to their task. However, they were always encouraged to seek their own conclusions while checking over their work until it seemed to explain the data collected about the various unknowns. All groups involved took several days to do this. At the end of the period of experimentation the different groups had either worked out an accurate conclusion or one approximating the identity of the unknown element. At this point the students' results were compared with those of the instructor. After the comparison the discussion centered around the nature and process of scientific investigation, concepts of science, and the general problems met by scientists. The question was raised about the problems the class would have to face if they were investigating a real unknown. After this discussion the class turned to new work in the area of biophysics.

Searching for the answer to an unsolved question creates a gamelike atmosphere in the classroom and has a highly motivating effect on the students. In this class little or no encouragement was needed to keep them working at their task, no matter how puzzling or difficult it became. The more data the students collected, the more it seemed they wanted to formulate a conclusive theory that would explain the entire problem. The instructor's unwillingness to give specific information or direction to the participants further complicated their difficulties but prompted them to work more and more on their own and to rely on their own knowledge and techniques of investigation. Each member of the group contributed considerably to the total outcome to the experiment. Also, the students learned the value of teamwork and pooled their talents and labor.

In a sense, searching for an unknown is similar to many scientific investigations and closely parallels the actual activities of scientists. Although the students presumably were learning how to use scientific apparatus to acquire knowledge of the elements, they were also learning to form more important ideas. They were being put in the position of having to think systematically and logically as well as critically about their data. The exercise served as an introduction to the process of scientific reasoning, although it was certainly not on the level of an advanced practicing biologist or physicist. Thus, this one classroom activity led the students to a knowledge of content, process, and technique, simultaneously.

STUDYING SOCIETY THROUGH MUSIC

Twelve musical selections were played for a group of thirty-two above-average high school seniors enrolled in a contemporary history course. The class was engaged in studying a very elaborate unit about Communism and Russia. The folk music was used as an introduction to the diversity of a people living in the territory now controlled by the U.S.S.R. The music was also used to demonstrate the size and complexity of the area taken over by the Russian government. Each of the musical pieces was a folk song or folk dance representative of a specific culture and region in the Soviet Union. Each piece of music derived from a somewhat different cultural tradition. The twelve selections formed a kaleidoscope of subcultures residing within the Soviet Union.

The music was chosen because of its dramatic, and possibly shocking, quality. It was anticipated that the folk songs and dances would awaken student interest and provide evidence for conjecture and interpretation. Since the context of inquiry was the history class mentioned above, the relationship between society and music would be the main line of investigation rather than the study of music itself. The cultural origin of each piece of music was as follows:

1. Armenian	2. Turkmenian
3. Uzbek	4. Tartar
5. Kazak	6. Great Russian
7. Byelorussian	8. Moldavian
9. Ukrainian	10. Georgian
11. Azerbaijanian	12. Baskkir[17]

Thus, the folk music taped for the history class was the product of traditions very divergent from our own popular musical heritage. On the first day of this episode, the instructor aroused the students' curiosity by playing the tape recording in class and by providing suggestions for further inquiry into the nature and origin of the folk music. Not until the second day, however, did the class have time to explore the relationship between the sounds they had heard and the cultures responsible for their production. A transcribed record of the events of both days follows.

First Day

TEACHER. I am going to play a tape of twelve musical selections. See if you can decide what type of music you are hearing. Also, take a guess at the place of origin of each musical selection.

EUGENE. Are they all from the same place?

MIKE. What do you mean by "type of music?"

TEACHER. Listen to the tape and decide for yourselves.

MIKE. I still don't understand what is meant by type of music. Does that mean something like classical, folk, popular, religious, jazz, or country and western?

[17]Music drawn from *Folk Music of the U.S.S.R.*, compiled and with notes by Henry Cowell, Ethnic Folkways Library, Folkways Records FE4535, 1957, New York, New York.

TEACHER.   I suppose so. Now listen to the tape.

(*The tape takes about 35 to 40 minutes to play.*)

Second Day

TEACHER.   Does anyone have anything to say?

MIKE.   Those were weird.

GAIL.   I think the first one was oriental.

TEACHER.   That covers a lot of ground.

GAIL.   Well then, Middle Eastern oriental, not Chinese oriental.

DEBBIE.   Number eight sounded Greek.

DENNIS.   One of them, number seven, I believe, seemed Slavic, Russian, or Polish.

NAOMI.   Some of them seemed Far Eastern in origin, maybe number five or number ten.

ROSLYN.   Number one was definitely from some Middle Eastern country, Arabia, for instance.

BRUCE.   Number eleven might have been a prayer, perhaps a Moslem prayer.

JANET.   I think most of them were folk songs because of their nice quick beat and because of the few instruments involved in each selection.

MIKE.   Some of those sounded like something I never heard before.

ETTA.   Much of the singing in those selections was quite rough, and that's why I think it was folk singing.

MARC.   Several of the catchy selections might have been popular. Some of the players are obviously very good at manipulating their instruments. The twanging selection, number four, seemed almost like a hillbilly piece.

LARRY.   Really, this is very aggravating. We're getting nowhere fast. Those songs could have come from anywhere. How should we know their place of origin?

GAIL.   Well, you can tell that they are probably not from the United States or from Western Europe. I didn't hear anything that sounded Spanish, or German, or English.

ROSLYN.   There wasn't anything that sounded African, was there?

LARRY.   All right, granted we can rule out some large areas, but how can we possibly pinpoint their exact places of origin?

DENNIS.   Larry does have a point there. We really don't know what we are doing.

EUGENE.   It's not quite that bad. I think I noticed that there are at least three or four different musical traditions represented among those twelve selections. Numbers one, three, and eleven seemed to be similar. Six and seven also seemed similar in many respects. They are oriental more than anything else.

KAREN. This still does not get us very far along. . . .

DON. Where did you get these recordings?

TEACHER. Where do you think?

DON. Oh, come on! How am I supposed to know?

STEVE. Are these recorded? I never heard anything like them before.

DON. That's not impossible.

TEACHER. There are even recordings of Australian aboriginal music.

STEVE. See, they were recordings!

ROSLYN. I think most of them are from the Middle East, or maybe India.

KAREN. We really need a hint.

CLASS. Give us a hint! . . . hint! . . . hint!

TEACHER. All right, just one hint. What would you say if I told you that all of these selections were recorded in the same country?

MARC. That would have to be a very large country . . .

PATRICIA. For a country to produce such a great variety of music, it would have to contain many different peoples.

EUGENE. There couldn't be too many countries like that.

GAIL. No, only the United States, China . . . India . . .

BRUCE. Russia.

ETTA. But which one is it? Could it be the United States?

LARRY. No. Where would all that Eastern music come from? We don't listen to music like that either as folk music or as popular music.

ROSLYN. I don't think it would be China because that country doesn't really contain that many kinds of people. Furthermore, I don't think we heard any Chinese music on that tape.

EUGENE. I agree. I've heard some Chinese music and it doesn't sound like anything we heard, although I'm not sure what we heard. Chinese music is more nasal and percussive. The music we heard relied on stringed instruments a lot.

TAMMY. Maybe India? But wouldn't that be completely oriental-sounding type music? I think some of the pieces we heard were European or Slavic.

LARRY. Then that leaves only the Soviet Union.

TEACHER. Then what would be the moral of this lesson?

LARRY. That the Soviet Union contains many different peoples in its total population, and that they probably come from at least several different language and musical traditions, but they are all part of the same country.

GAIL.   Yes, I see the point clearly. All Russians are obviously not Russians, or I mean Slavic Russians. There are many other, rather strange and different, people living in the Soviet Union with the Russians. The Russians possibly conquered them at some time in the past.

KAREN.   Now will you tell us the origin of each of the musical selections?

TEACHER.   Should I?

(*A resounding "Yes" rings out from the class.*)

The students' curiosity was aroused in anticipation for the tape, and they immediately attempted to elicit additional information from their instructor. Further aid and direction, however, was denied the class until the day after the whole tape had been played. Members of the class began their discussion of the twelve selections either by guessing at their probable cultural origin or by commenting on their exotic and foreign qualities. They began their discussion by giving expression to their intuitive ideas and feelings about the sounds they had experienced.

Soon after the guessing phase of the inquiry many students began analyzing the twelve selections in an effort to define the type or category of music represented; that is, were the selections popular, folk, or classical pieces or a combination of each type? While this issue was being debated, other students shifted the strategy of inquiry to that of elimination and began ruling out those cultures that could *not* be responsible for the music being investigated. They narrowed the field of possibilities by rejecting those that were not supported by any available evidence. For supporting data the students drew on their analysis of the music and on their own musical experiences. The students contrasted their experience and musical knowledge with the new sounds they had encountered.

After dimissing several cultures as poor choices, the students again called on the teacher to provide additional information that would lead directly to the discovery of the origin of the music. They apparently believed that not enough evidence was available to solve the problem, and complete the puzzle. A momentary impasse developed when two students questioned the instructor about the recordings in the hope of obtaining new clues or "tricking" the teacher into giving away the missing information. At this point the instructor intervened to offer a hint that simplified the task considerably, though it did not constitute a direct answer. The hint immediately rekindled the process of inquiry, leading the students to develop hypotheses that ultimately resulted in the discovery of several social implications of the different musical selections. Three of the most important hypotheses used by the discussants as analytical tools may be condensed from the conversation into these statements:

1. Each culture produces its own unique musical sounds which may serve as an identifying feature of that particular group of people.

2. Widely divergent musical sounds are indicative of a variety of cultures.

3. If very different folk songs and dances may be heard in a single country, that country must contain many different peoples with distinct musical and cultural traditions.

Thus, even though many students felt unsure of themselves and complained about the complexities of the task and their lack of musical knowledge, they were still able to develop several insights into the relationship between culture and music, society and musical expression. Inability to find a direct and specific solution to the problem led the students to adopt a method by which they narrowed down the field of choice until their goal was reached. Furthermore, motivation was high throughout the discussion because of the novel and striking nature of the evidence, and because of the students' desire to discover the unknown.[18] The students evinced a desire for closure and for a solution to the problem. Thus, rather than simply being told about the vastness of the Soviet Union and the diversity of its peoples, this group of students was encouraged to arrive at an understanding of the variety of Soviet cultures by studying a set of their divergent musical products.

CONCLUSION

From our limited, but varied, sample of classrooms, we would suggest that a process of structured inquiry or discovery can successfully be developed by teachers in many subject areas and at different age and ability levels. The classroom transcriptions we have used as illustrations show that students with limited experience in an inquiry framework can be easily motivated to analyze unfamiliar materials— whether musical performances, scientific data, statistics, or historical

[18]Several students later requested permission to record the music for their own collections.

documents. These examples show that teachers who wish to stimulate creativity and encourage insightful leaps of thought may accomplish this by following a few crucial rules in planning and carrying out their lessons.

First and foremost among these rules for teaching creatively is that imagination and insight are best achieved in an atmosphere of freedom, i.e., a classroom in which it is both legitimate and desirable to "think out loud" and to make mistakes jumping to conclusions. An inquiry process requires that its participants freely speak their minds without fear of punishment. Of course, decorum must be observed so feelings are not hurt but it should be noted that argument is a consequence of free expresson although this in no way implies either lack of a discipline or disorganized discussion. The discovery episodes presented in this chapter include numerous intuitive "guesses" and flashes of understanding, but nearly always follow a pattern of development that includes analyses and recapitulates the evidence under discussion. In no instance did students or their teachers exhibit a pattern of tangential reasoning or go off in seven directions at once. Intuitive suggestions were almost always followed by testing and ideas were defended by logic and supported with evidence.

A second rule in teaching creatively has to do with the way in which subject matter is presented. Beginning a lesson with new and puzzling evidence creates a situation in which interest will be awakened and run high *throughout* the lesson. A gamelike atmosphere develops when there are gaps or "unknowns" in knowledge because students are often driven to find or fill in the missing information. The missing information is avidly sought by students since it alone will provide a solution or conclusion to a problem. The need for closure creates a powerful intrinsic motivation to work with the material provided, however puzzling it may seem at first glance. Puzzlement usually gives way to fascination with a problem. The resulting search for the unknown and the indeterminate is the heart of the discovery process.

A third key to creative teaching and the flash of discovery involves the teacher's behavior pattern in the classroom. Since the goal of discovery involves searching for the missing pieces of a puzzle, it is vital that the teacher supports the inquiry process through a) reflection of students' ideas, i.e., paraphrase, redirection, and elaboration, b) praise and reward for the production of ideas, c) asking probing questions of increasing difficulty, and d) allowing for "wait-time," i.e., silent periods, between questions and responses. The teacher should offer as little direct aid in the way of answers and directions as possible during a lesson, instead relying on the more indirect behaviors described above. Self-direction is inversely proportional to the extent of teacher direction in a classroom. The more work completed by the instructor, the less reasoning needs to be done by the students. Help from the teacher ought to be extended only when a point of impasse or a high level of frustration has been reached when insight is blocked. At the point of blockage, a redirected question, a point of clarification, or the presentation of supplementary data or resources is appropriate and useful. Once the peak of frustration is passed, students can continue on the path of inquiry under their own power.

As in almost every learning process, atmosphere, teacher, and materials impact significantly upon the learner. We have demonstrated that insight and high-level inference can be dramatically increased by emphasizing the following: indirect teaching behaviors; thought-provoking materials that engage student interest by incorporating unknown and open-ended questions in daily problems; and an atmosphere conducive to the free expression of ideas and insights, even if questionable or unusual. Inquiry and discovery, contrary to much popular lore, are not undisciplined processes nor the property of unique individuals. Rather, creativity can be fostered and shaped by teachers willing to plan for it. Creative questions or answers develop out of hard work and close analysis of information. Only with practice can conclusions or hypotheses be honed against new data or alternative theories.

In each discovery episode discussed in this chapter, specific conclusions were reached using music, poetry, artifacts, statistics, or historical documents. More importantly perhaps, learners were enabled to go beyond the data given to identify relationships between evidence and theory, process and product, that could serve as generators of further inquiry. In the various lessons, students investigated relationships and connections between music and culture, history and literature, geography and human settlement, biology and social attitudes. Disciplinary lines were crossed in the pursuit of knowledge, although the structure and focus of each lesson remained well-defined. We would argue, along with Dewey, Bruner, and others that the identification of relationships leads to insight into the working of humankind and its world, and that these insights or hypotheses form the driving force toward further inquiry. In effect, students in each episode have learned something about *how to use, interpret, and apply evidence*—whether drawn from the arts, philosopy, science, or social science—in short, to solve problems. In some instances, students created their own questions and problems to solve. Therefore, we conclude that the discovery process is very much a part of teaching creatively and that students of varying ability and level can, under encouraging circumstances, identify problems, give meaningful interpretations, develop procedures, draw valid hypotheses, and test these against new information and conjectures. Process-oriented teaching, as illustrated by both analytical and discovery teaching episodes, is far from being haphazard and unpredictable. Problem-solving methods, whether dealt with rigorously and analytically or creatively, follow a pattern and impose a structure of their own, yielding deeper meaning and clearer insight for most students as a result.

CHAPTER FOUR

Examining Values

While values and beliefs are omnipresent in human existence, the examples of classroom interaction offered in the previous chapters dealt principally with problems of a cognitive nature. Analytical episodes stress reasoning and attention to particular bits and pieces of information which we are trying to understand. Assumptions are identified, meanings clarified, and interpretations developed. Discovery lessons emphasized the techniques and types of materials that most strongly contribute toward the formation of hypotheses, generalizations, and insights: the synthesis level as defined in Bloom's first, or cognitive, *Taxonomy of Educational Objectives*. Because primarily cognitive skills were employed in both analytical and discovery classroom sessions, the examples that follow illustrate the ways in which teachers and students deal with issues and controversies rooted in philosophical or value differences, an area we have not discussed in detail and one seldom seen consciously developed in classrooms.

Two points of clarification are in order with regard to values. First, all expressions of opinion or taste are by no means identical with high-level judgments, rationales, or evaluations. Value judgments of great power are the products of extensive knowledge and considerable thinking, representing cumulative development including awareness, response, valuing, organization of values into a framework, and finally a full-blown expression of philosophic outlook. This process must begin with the verbalization of views and feelings. These feelings are not to be denigrated or dismissed, but neither should low-level opinions be seen as achieving the goals implied in thorough examination of value preferences. Thus, we may encourage students to express their views on issues ranging from food through poverty to nuclear energy, using these beliefs as the starting points for developing positions which explain and defend an outlook on a whole class of problems or on life itself. For instance,"I like ketchup" can be the beginning of an examination of tastes and preferenes dealing with health, nutrition, and culinary philosophy. "I hate the poor" could serve as the springboard for discussion of the reasons behind dislike (or sympathy) for those who are needy, and lead into a study of the causes and consequences of support or denial. The slogan "No Nukes, no nuclear power or weapons ever!," might presage an extensive study of the data for or against nuclear energy and lay the groundwork for an intensive debate concerning ethical implications for society if development occurs or is stalled.

The second point of clarification concerns the essential unity and interrelatedness of cognitive and affective processes. Neither is ever wholly omitted from a conversation in which the other dominates. Cognitive-oriented lessons, stressing mainly analysis or discovery, are usually driven by a need for fulfillment that is largely psychological and emotional in origin, a need to obtain satisfying answers. Conversely, classroom teaching in which affective goals dominate also include a great deal of comprehension, analysis, and synthesis. The peak of affective inquiry, or value examination, is the formulation of a defensible viewpoint, but much of the discussion leading up to and interwoven in the leap to judgment is cognitive. The close connection between creative insight and surprise, curiosity, and emotion is supported in the work of scholars from science, philosophy, and education.[1]

Given these connections between cognition and affect, values and knowledge, the classroom examples in this chapter share a common goal of stimulating discussion about beliefs and belief systems. Although cognitive skills (to use Bloom's distinction between the domains for analytical purposes) are very much in evidence, each discussion moves from a set of facts or an account toward the expression and defense of opninions and views about a variety of subjects including politics, economics, philosophy, science, and racial attitudes. The teachers in charge of the different lessons have boldly stepped into the realm of philosophical inquiry in which values, beliefs, and ideals are treated as topics open to examination and study. Questions call for students to freely express attitudes and prejudices, in an atmosphere where self-study and cross-examination by others is encouraged, yet

---

[1]John Dewey. *Human Nature and Conduct.* New York: Henry Holt, 1922, 1930. Michael Polanyi. *Personal Knowledge.* New York: Harper & Row, 1962. Israel Scheffler."In Praise of Cognitive Emotions" in *THINKING: The Journal of Philosophy for Children,* Vol. 3, Number 2, pp. 16–23.

carried out in a reasonable and disciplined manner. In short, the teachers opt in the long run, for "light" over "heat" by challenging students to identify, analyze, and evaluate their own values and the values of their society.

A CASE ON CITY BOSSISM

This class of juniors was engaged in the study of United States history. They were quite used to the discovery method, having been exposed to it for a period of six months. Throughout this time the group had been leaning toward the introduction of more and more comments on values and attitudes in the daily discussions. The ability of the group ranged from average to slightly above average, no one having less than 100 IQ nor more than 125.

At this particular time the students were studying the growth of big cities in late nineteenth-century America. One of their sources was a paperbound book entitled, *Plunkitt of Tammany Hall: A Series of Very Plain Talks about Very Practical Politics*, edited by William L. Riordon, E. P. Dutton & Co., New York, 1957. Because the book was moderately priced, a quantity was ordered and sold to the students at the school bookstore. The class began by reading and analyzing various statements in the book. The period of analysis was followed by attempts to generalize about the nature of politics in a large American city. The major goal of the group in examining the material was to understand the machinery of the political system in the urban community. During the evolution of the discussion there were several occasions during which the students expressed approval or disapproval of certain practices brought to light by the material. When the students expressed their own feelings, and views about something in the book, they were actually involved in the act of making value judgments. Here we have selected a few relevant episodes which demonstrate a change in the flow of response from the cognitive domain to the affective or the valuative.

As we mentioned before, the discussion is based on a book containing a series of impromptu interviews regarding the rules of the political game as seen by Plunkitt. Plunkitt was a leading machine politician and ward boss in New York city and a state senator at the close of the century. In essence the book incorporates a set of principles of political life; for instance, one should always keep in mind the difference between honest and dishonest graft (preferably engaging in the former), and that careful adherence to this conduct will result in success. We are including a few representative passages from Plunkitt's "talks" in order to give the reader something of the flavor of his thought.

"Everybody is talkin' these days about Tammany men growin' rich on graft, but nobody thinks of drawin' the distinction between honest graft and dishonest graft. There's all the difference in the world between the two. Yes, many of our men have grown rich in politics. I have myself. I've made a big fortune out of the game, and I'm gettin' richer every day, but I've not gone in for dishonest graft—blackmailin' gamblers, saloonkeepers, disorderly people, etc.—and neither has any of the men who have made big fortunes in politics.

"There's an honest graft, and I'm an example of how it works. I might sum up the whole thing by sayin': 'I seen my opportunities and I took 'em.'[2]

"Say, the people's voice is smothered by the cursed civil service law; it is the root of all evil in our government. You hear of this thing or that thing goin' wrong in the nation, the state or the city. Look down beneath the surface and you can trace everything wrong to civil service. I have studied the subject and I know. The civil service humbug is underminin' our institutions and if a halt ain't called soon this great republic will tumble down like a Park Avenue house when they were buildin' the subway, and on its ruins will rise another Russian government."[3]

In the selected exchanges that follow we can detect the range of feeling toward Plunkitt in particular and bossism in general as well as the logical and affective operations the students perform in presenting a grounded point of view.

TEACHER.   Now that you have read what Plunkitt has to say, how does he keep in power and what do you think about it.?

STEVE.   I think he keeps up his power by doing political favors for people, especially his own voters . . . those in his district.

TED.   He also belongs to an organization which helps him and all of the political bosses do a lot of favors for their constituents.

WENDY.   He helps people by giving them what they need, for instance, rent money, a place to stay if they get evicted or burned out of their homes by a fire, a job, food. . . .

MITCHELL.   He also does things that people like. He goes to weddings, funerals, bar mitzvahs, confirmations, and he also gives gifts. People like this and vote for him.

ROBERTA.   He also helps get people's kids out of jail.

---

[2]William L. Riordon, *Plunkitt of Tammany Hall*, New York: Dutton, 1957, p. 3. Reprinted with permission.
[3]*Ibid.*, p. 13.

JAN. He actually helps people. He depends on poor people for his votes. His district seems to be occupied mostly by poorer people who are also immigrants. He's got a kind of Robin-Hood complex: Plunkitt takes from wealthy New York City and gives to his poor district. . . .

BRUCE. He's also crooked and takes for himself. He may help, but he also cheats and takes for himself in an underhanded way.

JAN. That not so. He says plain out that he takes for himself and even tells us exactly how he got rich.

TED. But he still certainly isn't honest.

GAIL K. You are all missing the point. Plunkitt is really helping people and as he says he really gets things done. These immigrants in his district have all kinds of the worst problems and need help, and he gives it to them.

TED. In return for their votes. . . .

GAIL K. Maybe so, but doesn't he still do good for them at the same time? Isn't that what's important: clothes, food, housing?

BRUCE. I think you are excusing him. He himself even says that "I seen my opportunities, and I took 'em." That sounds like honesty?

ROSLYN. But Plunkitt also points out that he never got caught because he never did anything illegal. Maybe he took for himself, but he never took illegally.

STEVE. But he did pull some awfully good stunts, like buying land for a park before anyone else knew that a park was going to be built there. He, of course, had a tip from his organization. Is that fair?

GAIL K. Didn't he deserve a reward for his good deeds? Well, he took his own rewards.

BRUCE. Couldn't he be honest, and do good for people, too?

GAIL. If he did everything legally and honestly, maybe it would have taken too long to pass in time to help the people of his district. He would probably get bogged down with paperwork and red tape. Or, maybe he wouldn't even be given the money he needed.

JAN. What he does is sneaky, but it works.

STEVE. Remember that according to his book, the other party controlled the State Legislature of New York and they didn't like the City of New York and taxed it and mistreated it to benefit their own people, the "hayseeds."

ROY. The whole system sounds bad. It shouldn't have been that way.

ROBERTA But it was. So what could he do about it?

ROSLYN.   If everyone had been willing to treat their fellowman and the poor better, New York wouldn't have needed a "Boss."

MIKE.   To help the poor would have called for government interference like President Johnson's anti-poverty program is doing now.

ROY.   They probably didn't want to shell out to help the poor or the immigrants because they were down and out and foreigners. A lot of people are prejudiced against foreigners.

BRUCE.   Plunkitt still acted immorally!!

ROSLYN.   Listen! That's still not the point. Human needs were taken care of by the Boss—any way he could—and in return, because of gratitude, votes were cast his way.

LEE.   That sounds fair. Give and take. I can see why the immigrants voted the way they did—they knew which side their bread was buttered on.

BRUCE.   That's just my point. Plunkitt was taking from people, paying off others, giving favors, getting votes, keeping money for himself, getting his pals jobs through politics—not because they deserved it, but because they could get votes for him.

JAN.   But he still got immigrants jobs. Those people couldn't read or write sometime—or even speak English. He helped them adjust.

TED.   You make Plunkitt, the politician, sound like Robin Hood.

JAN.   Well, I don't think he was so bad. He never hurt anyone if we can believe his own story.

BRUCE.   I understand that these people had problems, but Plunkitt solved them in an unethical, dishonest, and dirty way. He wanted votes for his help

MIKE.   He certainly wasn't noble about it—or very worried about ideas.

GAIL K.   I still say so who cared? The immigrants needed help desperately and he gave it. They took it, remembered it, and repaid it. Is that wrong? Should they care where it came from if it was put to good use?

WENDY.   It's good to do things right always, but I don't think he could under the circumstances of 1890 or so.

JAN.   If society was so moral minded, why didn't it do something to put bosses like Plunkitt out of business?

MIKE.   I don't know.

BRUCE.   I would have tried to find a more honest way of helping.

GAIL K.   What if you couldn't?

BRUCE.   I'd try.

GAIL.   I guess no one tried hard enough in those days to help the
            poor groups, considering how well Plunkitt did.
TEACHER.   Is that your final analysis of this problem?
BRUCE.   Sounds like it to me. I've had enough.
PATRICIA.   Let's go on to something else. We'll probably never get any
            agreement on this one.

Classroom discussion of this particular phase of the book is prompted by the teacher's opening question. The question seems to elicit
two categories of response, the first analytical-explanatory and the
second affective-normative. The analytical type of response is ex-
emplified by those remarks which (a) describe the functions performed by a city boss as in Wendy's or Mitchell's statements, "He
goes to weddings, funerals, bar mitzvahs, confirmations, and he also
gives gifts," (b) explain the behavior of the political boss in terms of
political necessities or altruistic motives, for example, Jan's suggestion, "He depends on poor people for his votes," and "He's got a kind
of Robin Hood complex," or (c) integrate different bits of evidence
regarding Plunkitt's operations into a broader problem of society having both cognitive and affective implications, such as Gail K.'s idea,
"Plunkitt is really helping people. . . . These immigrants in his district
have all kinds of the worst problems and need help, and he gives it to
them." The affective or normative category of response is demonstrated by those statements which (a) indicate awareness of a sensitivity to a social problem or issue; for example, can the political action
of a city boss be justified, which Bruce implies in a form of a question,
"Couldn't he be honest, and do good for people, too?" (b) express a
value judgment about the entire social system of that period, as in
Roy's remark, "The whole system sounds bad," or express a judgment
about the inherent morality of an act, such as Bruce's comment,
"Plunkitt still acted immorally!" and (c) contain emotionally charged
terminology and display a strong personal feeling; for example,
Bruce's reference to Plunkitt's approach as "unethical," "dishonest,"
and "dirty" or Jan's rejoinder, "If society was so moral minded, why
didn't it do something to put bosses like Plunkitt out of business?
    The foregoing illustration represents a typical case of classroom
discussion which began as an analytical exercise but gradually
evolved into a combination of analytical and affective discourse. Because by its very nature social studies is conducive to controversy,
there are frequent instances in which materials and classroom discussion evoke a wide range of response, including statements of opinion,
emotion, and criticism as well as of a descriptive or explanatory nature. It is quite common to have both components, the affective and

the analytical, integrated into the same statement. Although it is important to be conscious of the fusion of empirical and value statements at this general plane and to try to separate the two, it is equally important to link value judgments to observable reality in order to validate and support personal viewpoints. Obviously, reference to empirical data helps at various points of the judgmental process but does not, in and of itself, enable one to make the final personal choice.

GOOD AND BAD SAMARITANISM

The issue discussed here calls for a more direct and personal response than the issue of city bossism. Although the preceding case is a combination of analytical and judgmental processes, this case focuses more on the personal attitudes and values of the participants. An incident of bad Samaritanism is within the range of everyday experience, whereas machine politics is a fairly remote experience for the average person. However, a certain amount of description and analysis of the event, as reported in the newspaper, is interwoven in the discussion.

The conversation reported here is the product of a group of very bright high school juniors enrolled in a United States history course. No one in the group had an IQ of less than 120. These students were very well acquainted with the inductive method, for the discussion took place toward the end of a whole year of United States history which had been taught by the inquiry approach. The students were among the most academically and socially active of all their classmates.

As we see from the recorded dialogue, the discussion was initiated by the teacher, who asked his class to read a newspaper report of a case of robbery in which the bystanders did not involve themselves at all. This kind of incident is getting more coverage in the daily papers and national magazines. It appears that wider publicity given to helping others under threat has increased public awareness and caused considerable public concern. Since the late 1960s and early 1970s, many states and communities have passed "Good Samaritan" laws that offer rewards and financial help to crime victims and those who go to their aid.

TWO ROBBED IN OLD TOWN AS PEOPLE WATCH[4]

"There must have been a dozen people sitting on the porch across the street who saw us get robbed. Then when we started to walk over to ask if we could use their phone to call the police, they all got up and went inside and slammed the door."

Robert J. Spinney, 33, a production engineer, told of the incident Sunday in relating how he and his 67-year-old mother were attacked and robbed after a stroll through Old Town.

[4]Chicago *Sun-Times*, Monday, May 24, 1965, p. 24. Reprinted with permission.

The outing was planned as a birthday celebration for Mrs. Spinney, a widow, of Buffalo, who was visiting her son and his family at 28 Tuttle, Clarendon Hills. Since her birthday was Friday, Spinney took his mother to dinner Saturday evening at the Stock Yard Inn. Then he drove to Old Town and parked in front of 226 W. Goethe so they could see the sights.

"There were so many people around that I didn't think there possibly could be any danger," said Spinney, who works for the Continental Can Company. When they returned to their car shortly after 10 p.m., however, three youths accosted them.

"I was bending over putting the key in the door lock when one of them grabbed me around the neck," said Spinney. "He spun me around and a second one held a knife against my stomach." Meanwhile, the third youth attempted to wrest Mrs. Spinney's purse from her. When she resisted, he hit her across the mouth and flung her to the ground.

They took $21 from Spinney plus Mrs. Spinney's purse containing $36 and a valued rosary and a St. Jude medal.

"I know all the people across the street saw what happened,"said Spinney, "because we were right under a street light. I guess it's understandable they didn't come to help us, but at least you would have thought they'd let us use their phone. I suppose they didn't want to get involved."

Spinney drove to Wells St. where he saw a foot patrolman. The policeman directed him to the East Chicago Ave. Station. Mrs. Spinney was taken by police to Henrotin Hospital, where she was found to be suffering from bruises and a pulled back muscle. Spinney, who was unhurt, toured the area in a patrol car with a policeman in an unsuccessful effort to spot the robbers.

"I just didn't think I'd ever be involved in anything like this," he said. "You hear about these things happening, but you always think they happen to someone else."

Spinney said he was not bitter about the failure of the people on the porch to help but merely mystified by their lack of concern.

The foregoing article was dittoed and distributed to the class. The discussion that ensued is illustrative of the ways in which young people adjudicate value conflicts.

First Day

TEACHER.   Well, what do you think about this article?

MIKE.   I would have called the police. This is only if I didn't have to give my name.

TEACHER.   Why not give your name?

MIKE.   So I wouldn't have to get involved. Once you get involved with the police, there are messy consequences: trials, investigations, expenses, too.

MARC.   The police often get whoever helps into trouble. I know of a few cases, personally. The law doesn't seem to be on the side of the person who helps other people out. The others aren't even grateful, sometimes.

JOHN.   Even so, is that really the issue raised by the article—our inconveniences, or the trouble caused by involvement with the police?

TEACHER.   What are the issues?

JOHN.   The issue, I believe, has to do with moral duty, but it also has to do very much with the situation confronting the person watching a robbery or an attack.

RONNA.   It seems to be a very difficult problem with all kinds of psychological problems and consequences.

DAN.   Yes, for instance, someone's interference might cause the robbers to get more excited, and perhaps, many people would get hurt.

MARC.   The people watching the robbery might have been afraid and no one wants to stick their necks out and get hurt. Maybe the people watching have families to care for and worry about.

DAVE.   No one says those people have to intervene. They just, at least, should have called the police. They didn't even let the people in trouble use their telephone to call the police themselves.

PAM.   They probaby didn't want to get involved with the police.

DAVE.   Why couldn't they have called anonymously?

ILYSE.   Would the police have come on an anonymous tip?

DAVE.   I'm sure they would, especially if it sounded urgent enough.

LOIS.   Maybe they didn't have time to think.

LARRY.   They thought long enough to close their doors when they saw the robbed couple approach their houses. They knew they were purposely not getting involved.

TEACHER.   What do you think about "not getting involved?" Do you approve of the bystanders' action?

CLASS.   No!

TEACHER.   But you seem to be justifing their actions.

MIKE.   Well, I can understand their problem and thoughts in seeing this.

PAM.   They didn't want to take the risk in helping out.

DAVE.   Yes, any risk at all. There were at least twelve people watching this robbery. If even a few of them had walked over, or yelled, the robbers might have been frightened away.

JOHN.   Or they might have shot somebody.

RONNA.   But isn't there a moral obligation to do something—anything—however slight—to help your fellowman in trouble?

EUGENE.   These people wouldn't help to even the slightest degree.

LARRY.   Many people say that in the same situation, no one would help them, so why should they help these people.

DAVE.   That's just great! It doesn't say much for our society or our safety. What can you count on? Certainly not other people if they believe such a philosophy.

RONNA.   Something should definitely be done about this. We all do live together in a society, and if it would always work like this, wouldn't it be a horrible place in which to live?

MARC.   Perhaps the people watching were some kind of ghouls. Maybe they enjoyed seeing people suffer.

JOHN.   There are plenty more of such cases. I could bring a few clippings in to show you.

RONNA.   Maybe there are too many of such cases. I would guess that such instances are quite frequent.

LOIS.   Can't something be done about this? This is a pretty frightening discussion!

RONNA.   In some countries, if you don't come to the aid of someone in trouble, the law can make you an accomplice to the crime.

JOHN.   These countries, like Germany and France, don't have any less of a moral problem than ours. However, due to these laws protecting and favoring good Samaritans, people feel safer helping others. According to a poll written up in *Time* magazine, a much larger percertage of persons in countries with these good Samaritan laws now favor such laws, while people in the United States, which does not have any laws of this kind, tend to be much less in favor of such laws. I think this demonstrates that the law can encourage people to act in different ways. Furthermore, such laws do protect those people who do aid their fellows.

JIM.   Would such laws really bring about a change within people?

ILYSE.   At least the law would protect those who have or would aid others.

LOIS.   But the people over there care enough to have those laws.

They must have been interested in encouraging good Samaritanism and punishing bad Samaritanism or the failure to do one's duty.

TEACHER.   Do you mean that we, in this country, do not care about morals or helping one another?

LOIS.   I'm not sure of it.

EILEEN.   People don't care enough about it because it doesn't concern them. If people don't care, these laws will not be passed or, if passed, will not be enforced.

MIKE.   I don't think the government is concerned. If they were, the police would be more helpful toward the good Samaritans.

ILYSE.   Wouldn't such laws be good, though? They might not affet us very much, but they would have a great effect upon future generations.

MARC.   It would take a long time to change men's minds and hearts. Even then, I'm not sure it would work.

ILYSE.   But, at least it would be a good head start. Don't we have to start somewhere or do you agree with the action of those twelve people described in the newspaper article?

MARC.   I certainly don't agree with their total neglect of their moral obligations, but I wouldn't want to say how far they should have gone.

LARRY.   The majority of people can't be very excited about this problem or we would already have such laws on the books.

RONNA.   Maybe so, but the fact that we are discussing this now shows that we do care and that this is a current topic of discussion. There were just some conferences on this entire problem at the University of Chicago. The conference lasted several days and the people participating in it all recommended immediate legislation to protect the good Samaritans and to encourage all people to help their fellowman and not be afraid of the legal consequences.

JOHN.   There has also been a great increase in the number of magazine and newspaper articles on this topic. I have seen many myself.

MIKE.   Come to think of it, I have been noticing more about this lately. Maybe we will have a law pretty soon, but I'm not so certain of its good effects. Most people might still be afraid of risking their lives in such situations.

DAVE.   What about just making a phone call?

MIKE.   Well, I didn't disagree about that!

DAVE.   I'm dissatisfied with this discussion. There is something missing from it.

TEACHER.	What do you think is missing?
DAVE.	Our own commitments.

Second Day

DAVE.	I think all of you are moral weaklings. You have avoided discussing your own actions. I think you are all chicken.
MIKE.	Well, what would you have done?
DAVE.	I would help. I would try to do the most I possibly could, even more than just call the police or let some one use my phone. That isn't much at all. That isn't really help.
JOHN.	But aren't you overlooking the complexities of the situation?
DAVE.	What about doing what is right? You are all too worried. Would all of you help? What would you do?
MARC.	It's hard to say. It depends on so many things. I don't know what I'd do.
LARRY.	It's still awfully risky. What about the guy who did help out some girls being attacked here on the South Side. He was cut up and wound up with big hospital bills and loss of income. He was a cab-driver I think and had a family, too.
ILYSE.	Yes, but I read that someone recently paid all his hospital bills by anonymous donation.
LOIS.	See, we have at least two good Samaritans, three including Dave.

(*some laughter*)

LARRY.	Dave, would you even go so far as to run into a situation that was really dangerous to help out? One where you might even get hurt or knifed?
DAVE.	I think I would.
MARC.	But how can you be so certain? I sure wouldn't know what to do.
JIM.	Often, even if you do want to do good, it doesn't work out. There are cases where people take advantage of other persons' good natures and pretend to be hurt or in trouble, and then rob those that come to their aid.
DAVE.	Something like that almost happened to me once. We were being signaled to stop our car by what looked like some kids who had been in an accident. As we slowed up, a bunch of kids came from behind their car and began yelling, approaching our car, so we sped up again and got out of there. I guess they wanted to swipe our car or just make trouble, or do something to us. You have to be careful.

PAM.   Yes, you have to look out for yourself, too.

BERNIE.   Other people may get you into big trouble, while you wish to help them. I agree that the whole situation is very complicated.

RONNA.   We all can't be as sure as you are Dave. I would like to be, but I just honestly can't.

JOHN.   I have a clipping I can show you of a case of good Samaritanism repaid with criminal behavior on the part of those receiving the help they didn't deserve but were counting on getting.

TEACHER.   All well and good, but what would all of you do in such a situation as that described in the article handed out the other day? You are not really answering Dave's question.

JIM.   What if the incident Dan has described involved a real accident?

MARC.   I would have helped. But that's not really a good example. It doesn't involve much danger. It's the dangerous situations that call for a difficult decision. I don't know whether I would intervene actively. I would call for the police.

RONNA.   I think we all would want to help, but can't be sure of what we would actually do since we are discussing a hypothetical situation. All kinds of factors have to be weighed before we take action.

DAVE.   Isn't that declining to do much of anything? Don't all the doubts show your fear and the probability of inaction?

JOHN.   I don't think so. We are just being honest and realistic. Everyone can't be a hero.

LOIS.   Everyone would, or should, at least do something to help, however little that help is.

TEACHER.   How many of you would do something?

(*All raise their hands. Much private discussion is going on.*)

TEACHER.   How many have doubts as to what they would do in an actual situation?

(*Almost all raise their hands again.*)

TEACHER.   How many consider themselves to be of sound morals and would *want* to help in such a situation?

(*All again raise their hands, amidst much mumbling and an exchange of personal comments.*)

DAVE.   I would have helped.

MIKE.   Even if it meant getting hurt, or possibly getting hurt?

DAVE. I think so.

JOHN. You don't just rush in to aid someone until you have at least sized up the situation.

JIM. Some might. And have.

(tremendous outburst of small-group discussions and heated comments)

ILYSE. This is a really tough problem. How can we solve it if the authorities and professors and clergy can't?

RONNA. The conferences at the University of Chicago on this topic took days and days. How can we be so certain of our own actions having never been faced with such a difficult decision?

TEACHER. But might you not become faced with such a situation in the future?

DAN. It's still hard to decide.

PAM. Maybe it's emotional. Some people are just built to act bravely, and others not.

JOHN. But don't you think that good laws would encourage citizens to help each other when in danger, at least to the extent of calling the police?

EUGENE. We certainly can't uphold the actions of the Old Towners. I wouldn't want to be the one in that kind of a spot.

DAVE. Exactly.

LARRY. Right now, you still have to buck all kinds of difficulties to help someone. Most of the weight of the law, society, personality, physical and financial consequences are against your intervention into such a dangerous situation. You only seem to be backed up by morality.

ILYSE. Isn't that important?

LARRY. That seems to be the problem. How important?

MIKE. Important enough to get us all pretty excited and steamed up.

JOHN. It's still an extremely complex problem. I think we all believe that we should help each other when needed, and that what those people in Old Town did was wrong, but then you are faced with the real situation and it seems different. There are so many forces at play upon you that influence your decision at that precise moment, that it's hard to say what most people would do. I'm not sure what I would do. It is a very, very deep problem. Many want to help, but can't. I don't think a majority of people are really indifferent or callous, just frightened of their own lives and the consequences of interfering. After all, it is dangerous to do so, and as of now, the law isn't especially helpful to the good Samaritan.

DAVE.   But could you live with yourself after completely giving up your responsibility?

ILYSE.   Don't give it up completely. Do what you think is right, but do what you also think won't cause you actual harm. Do what you can handle in a given situation.

MIKE.   I think we all want to do what is right, don't we?

(*Most heads nod agreement.*)

JOHN.   But it does seem that the reality of such a situation causes great indecision and anxiety and people wind up doing nothing at all.

For the most part the first day is spent discussing the issue as a group and contributing their thoughts to the clarification of the problem. They spend some time in putting together bits of information and trying to get a general idea of what is involved in a problem situation such as this. While some students take individual positions (e.g., Mike), the majority of them focus on the behavior of the bystanders, attempting to explain why they showed no concern whatsoever for those being victimized. In this connection a whole range of possible reasons is examined; for example, they did not want to get involved with the police, interference might cause many people to get hurt, they did not have time to think, they enjoyed seeing people suffer (they were mean), or they were simply afraid.

Actually, the broader social issue is identified by John who suggests that the problem stems from the conflict between the "moral duty" of citizens to help people in distress and the individual's desire for survival. Ronna adds to this by pointing out the magnitude and complexity of the problem. The complexity of the problem is further shown by the inherent difficulty in producing a concrete solution to the problem.

It is during the second day that several students take a more direct position on the matter and express more sharply their personal feelings. But even during the first day there are some who take a stance rather openly. The positions on the issue seem to range from complete noninvolvement to total cooperation in behalf of harassed or endangered persons. On a continuum, the positions may be shown by direct student comment. Dave, on several occasons, indicates his willingness to help without qualifications. Larry stands perhaps on the other extreme by implying that each individual should look out for himself and by saying "no one would help them, so why should they help those people." In between the foregoing polar position there are such statements as, "Everyone would, or should, at least do something to help . . ." (Lois), "I would have called the police . . . if I didn't have to give my name" (Mike), "I don't know whether I would intervene actively" (Marc), ". . . can't be sure of what we would actually do . . ." (Ronna), ". . . Do what you also think won't cause you actual harm" (Ilyse). It is obvious that the majority of the students do not want to commit themselves beyond "Surely we will help but the extent of our help will depend on the circumstances." Constantly they weigh the consequences of their involvement; they feel, generally, that the anticipated personal consequences tend not to warrant involvement. On the other hand, there is a vocal minority who appeal to "moral duty" (John), "moral obligation" (Ronna), "doing what is right" (Dave), "failure to do one's duty" (Lois) in order to justify intervention of some sort. This group seems to imply that there is a universal morality or ethical norm which is above the individual and which impels members of a society to reciprocate with each other for the common good. It seems that the projected behavior of the students is based on two sets of criteria—the reluctant or uncertain group tends to apply personal criteria, the more action-oriented group applies ethical and social criteria and is concerned with what is right. However, toward the end of the second day the discussion indicates that both groups see each other's position and underlying rationale; for example, John's remark, "We are just being honest and realistic," followed by a show of hands indicating both willingness to help and an expression of doubt as to what they would do in an actual situation.

It is worth noting that the group as a whole has a good grasp of the problem, and it makes a genuine effort to introduce new elements that would resolve the conflict. For example, the problem is seen from a legal perspective; that is, the extent to which law may promote good Samaritanism. It is asserted by John that people in countries in which such laws have been enacted "feel safer helping others." This claim brings up the whole question of the effectiveness of law and the extent to which an unpopular law may be enforced (what is commonly known as "sumptuary legislation"). In effect, the discussion of the place of law is presented when the class is exploring alternative courses of action and it is by no means complete. Their appeal to legal protection is also part of their search for a standard of behavior which they can use as the basis for their own decisions. The pluralistic nature of our society is to a degree reflected in student response; that is, the range of opinion as well as their difficulty in finding a commonly accepted norm indicate the complex milieu of our society.

The discussion is at times haphazard as far as following up a logical sequence of ideas is concerned and it appears to be based on an expression of feeling rather than on a thorough factual investigation of the topic. Nevertheless, the discussion as a whole moves toward a greater classification of the problem and increased agreement with respect to the ethical standard of behavior of the participants.

As shown by the recorded dialogue, all students were highly motivated to participate in the discussion of the issue. While their enthusiasm with the topic in question was about the same as that of a discovery episode, student motivation is sustained without any decrease in momentum. After the first contact with the material, interest reaches a very high level. This is further demonstrated by their search in the library and elsewhere to produce more information or material that would support certain viewpoints. An example of this is a clipping from a newspaper describing the case of a good Samaritan whose good intentions were taken advantage of. Here is the article as delivered to the teacher by a student:

BANDITS TRAP, ROB SAMARITAN

A Hammond steelworker leaving town on a vacation stopped early Monday to help two women apparently stranded by car trouble on the Eisenhower Expressway.

But as he stopped his car on the shoulder, two men jumped from the women's car and robbed him at gunpoint of $350 in cash, all his vacation money.

James Prather, 28, of 4747 Baltimore, Hammond, told police that he was on his way to LaGrange to pick up his wife when the women flagged him down.

When we compare this discussion with a discovery episode, we see an emotionally charged atmosphere in both cases. However, emotional involvement is of a different order in a social issue such as this, for it bears directly on the daily life of the discussants and it calls for the development of a value judgment that reflects one's personality and expected behavior. The fact that the topic is controversial, lacking clarity and consensus, creates a psychological climate which stimulates students to participate as well as encourages them to bring their values to a conscious level and examine them critically. Students in this case come close to "knowing themselves" in the Aristotelian sense. Hopefully, sensitivity and commitment to the issue and its rational examination will transfer into actual behavior in life.

Generally, the role of the teacher in dealing with values is similar to the role performed in connection with discovery episodes. The teacher presents the basic material or springboard, moderates discussion, prods students, asks for the defensibility and explanation of positions, legitimizes the free expression of ideas, and generally refrains from taking a stand, at least in the beginning. In addition to these common tasks, the teacher puts greater emphasis on (a) the student becoming aware of social values, (b) his ability to explain fully his own ethical stand on the matter, and (c) his ability to tolerate other positions and negotiate them openly.

Because of the limitations of this study, the authors cannot make any claims regarding social or psychological factors that influence students to respond and react to moral issues in the way they do. Such a study would entail a thorough research into the ethnic, socioeconomic, religious, geographic, and individual personality components of each student—something well beyond the purpose of this series of studies.

A DEBATE ON PUBLIC POLICY

The class debating public policy was composed of high school seniors, ranging in ability from average to somewhat above average. These students were enrolled in a course called contemporary American history, which is generally devoted to the study of present-day social problems, controversial issues, and international affairs. The course usually lasts an entire year, although some students take it as an elective for only one semester. In this class the vast majority were enrolled for a year and their discussion was held after seven months of the academic program had been completed. The students therefore were accustomed to the free and open discussion of ordinary materials as well as of controversial issues involving personal beliefs and values.

The students were encouraged to determine, by a poll, those current issues they would most like to discuss. The most popular choice reflected a concern for United States involvement in the Viet Nam war and for the demonstrations that have accompanied the growth of this serious problem. Several days after the poll had been taken the instructor decided to rekindle class interest in this subject by providing each student with a copy of a recent article describing the deliberate destruction of a draft card by a young protestant. This particular *Time* article (shown below) was selected because it was both topical and laden with value judgments.

AN INVESTIGATION INTO THE PROS AND CONS
OF NUCLEAR ENERGY

The lesson that follows concerns the pros and cons of nuclear energy. This complex problem has increasingly occupied public attention in the United States and throughout much of the world. Demonstrations have been held in many areas to protest the development of power plants, to express displeasure with the storing of nuclear wastes, or to deflect the placement of nuclear weapons. Yet these outcries have often been met with counterpressures from other sources who want to see nuclear power become a major source of energy. When voters in several states have been asked to place a moratorium on development, they have indicated disapproval; in other words many are unwilling to support a law forbidding all future building of reactors as energy producers. The controversy over nuclear power is clearly an issue with two major sides to it, each containing many points of view and shades of opinion on subissues. Adversarial problems such as the nuclear one offer strong potential for discussion since the questions are open, the policies debatable, and the data amenable to criticism and cross-checking.

For these reasons, the question of nuclear power was selected for study and debate. The students investigating the nuclear problem were enrolled in an eleventh grade American history course in a New York suburban high school. The classroom group was average to slightly above average in reading level and the school's population was racially and ethnically heterogenous, but tended to be largely middle-class in terms of socioeconomic status.

To spark discussion, the teacher selected a passage from *The Nuclear Question* by Ann E. Weiss.[5] This book, written for young adults, is an attempt to present a relatively unbiased and objective account of the development of nuclear theory and the argument for and against this energy source as a practical power supply. Several passages were used to focus and structure subsequent discussions. One of these is reproduced below to give the flavor and style of the author's presentation.

Should the United States push on with nuclear power? Or should we declare a moratorium and slow down the growth of the industry? Should we search for alternate energy sources so we can afford to give up commercial nuclear power altogether? These are questions all of us will be helping to answer in the months and years ahead.

[5] *The Nuclear Question.* New York: Harcourt, Brace, Jonanovich, 1981. pp. 134–135, pp. 141–144, pp. 150–152.

Many people believe that nuclear power is so unpredictable and so hazardous that the only safe course is to shut down all the nation's nuclear plants immediately. Dr. Helen Caldicott shares this feeling. Others take a less extreme position, calling for an end to new plant construction and for a gradual phase-out of existing plants. The nation's growing antinuclear movement includes men and women with both points of view.

Since the accident at Three Mile Island, over three-hundred organizations have joined forces to work for the eventual end to the use of nuclear energy for both civilian and military purposes. Operating as the Coalition for a Non-Nuclear World, organization members are finding ways to make their views felt at the voting booth and in the halls of Congress, in state and local government, and throughout the news media.

A Nuclear World?

Another argument that nuclear proponents use to try to convince Americans that they ought to go ahead with nuclear development is that other countries are doing it. West Germany has ten nuclear plants, Sweden has six, and Canada, eight. Japan is reprocessing some of the spent fuel rods from its twenty nuclear power plants. Brazil, Argentina, and Mexico are in the process of constructing nuclear power reactors. England has found places to temporarily store wastes from its thirty-three plants. France, with fifteen plants already on line, is building more. Currently, the French are assembling the world's first commercial breeder. Built with the cooperation of West Germany, Italy, and England, the French breeder should be generating electricity sometime during the 1980s. By the year 2050, one American nuclear advocate says, three fourths of the world's energy will come from breeders. Worldwide, there will be five thousand reactors, producing nine times the total energy we generate today.

More convincing—at least at first—is the American nuclear industry's argument that we must continue with nuclear power in order to meet the nation's future energy needs.

That our demand for energy will rise in the next decades is accepted as fact by those who urge nuclear development. They point out that the country's population is increasing. More and more people are going to need more and more jobs, food, clothing, homes, recreation equipment, and so on. It's going to take a growing economy to supply those needs. A growing economy, nuclear supporters say, cannot exist without ever increasing amounts of energy to fuel it. Oil is costing more and getting scarcer; coal threatens the environment. That leaves nuclear energy as the best, in fact, the only possible answer to our future energy needs.

Nuclear opponents do not accept this argument, either. They believe that we have many other potential energy resources, enough to fill all our demands without resorting to either coal or foreign oil.

So, should the United States continue to increase its use of nuclear energy? Congress, Presidents, and the nuclear establishment urge us in that direction. Our needs demand it, they say, and the technology is there. But other forces push us the other way.

Americans have reduced their demand for oil and electricity. Many are now aware of the dangers of nuclear power. They have learned to look at nuclear advertising and P.R. with a more critical eye. They are asking their Congressmen and women to reconsider their past support of unlimited nuclear research and development.

Some business people, bankers, and utility owners are also beginning to think twice about nuclear power. Plant construction is getting more and more expensive, and it commonly costs 100 percent more to build a plant than was originally estimated. One plant now under construction on Long Island is expected to cost $2.2 billion before it is finished—eight times the figure quoted in 1969, when the plant was proposed. This makes investors wary of putting more money into nuclear power. Owners of plants under construction are having trouble coming up with the cash to finish the facilities and get them on line. New-plant orders are slowing down. A sort of moratorium is in effect despite the reluctance of Congress to call for one officially.

What about the future? Will we go on with nuclear power and find it means a world set free? Or will a nuclear world prove to be a world headed for grief?

The debate continues, and the decision—nuclear or not—is up to us. We must endeavor to decide wisely, to choose the best way for a world like our world, in a time like our time.

The discussion as a whole covered nearly a week in scope and was organized in a variety of ways, including periods devoted to research, student discussion, and small group analysis of additional data. Each activity was designed to create a balance between discussion of values and the collection of relevant data. Both "heat" and "light" were expected and encouraged by the teacher, but in an overall atmosphere of respect for well-grounded argument.

First Day

The first day set the tone for the debate that was to follow. Students read excerpts from *The Nuclear Question* and were asked to react to the ideas and problems raised by the author of the book.

TEACHER.   What are some of the questions brought up in our reading?

TOM.   Safety, really safety is the thing she is worried about.

SUSAN.   I think it was need. Do we really need nuclear power?

BOB.   Pollution is the main idea. Will nuclear power pollute us out of existence?

TEACHER.   Were any of the problems most important or were they all about equal? How do you see it?

SUSAN.   I still think the basic issue is need. Nuclear energy can be expensive to develop and we already have other sources to choose from.

JOHN.   Yes, but, I think the nitty-gritty problem is safety. What people are really worried about is their health. Nuclear power is scary because of the radioactivity. Don't you think that's really it, Sue?

SUE.   I'll have to think about that. Maybe you're right but it seems more complicated than that.

RICHARD.   Yeah, it seems *very* complicated. The real problem is who's telling the truth and who is lying about the dangers of nuclear power.

PAT.   From what we've read so far, you can't tell anything except the questions. I don't even like to talk about it because it's so scary.

SARAH.   The more worried you are, the better it is to talk about it, I think! I never even thought about nuclear anything until I saw the movie *The China* something with Jane Fonda.

TEACHER.   What was that movie . . . I think the title was *The China Syndrome* . . . about?

SARAH.   It was really good! Frightening! The story was mainly about a nuclear energy plant where everything went wrong. People caused the problems and the machinery failed, too!

JEFF.   I read about a real case "Three Mile Island," where the reactor burned out or something, but it didn't blow up. Cost a hell of a lot of money, though. I guess things like that started people worrying, even though most people I know aren't *very* concerned—yet!

TEACHER.   Why do you think the whole problem has been noticed lately? Do you think it's really worth discussing?

JEFF.   Well, it's worth talking about because they're building more and more power stations, but I don't see people really steamed up over the whole bit.

FLORA.   Well, maybe they should be! I mean radiation doesn't just go away. If you soak it in you will really suffer or your children will suffer. That's what the people are really worried over—the future.

MIKE.   Yeah, but a lot of know-how went into these projects. We must need the power or the government and industry wouldn't put up all that money to build these. Think of the oil storage. We need our own power so we don't have to depend on oil so much. Our scientists will watch over the nuclear plants and see to it that there is the least possible damage or harm to people.

FRED.   It sounds to me like you're for the whole thing! I don't know whether to be for or against. What we read didn't help me. It only confused me. After hearing all of you talk, I only see more problems, but no answers.

SUE.   I think Fred's got a point. We really don't know much of anything. I mean, what is the big deal? Maybe it's not really worth worrying about and the people who are against it are just terribly scared.

MARGE.   I agree too. We are worried, but not sure of what to worry about most!

TEACHER.   Maybe what we need is more information. Let me hand out a bibliography for you to use. Most of these books are in our library. Please share them and feel free to bring in anything else you have come across. Let's get to some reading right now. Then I want to hear your own opinions tomorrow, OK?

The first day's discussion, as you may have observed, was exploratory in nature. Students summarized their reading, brought in experiences of their own from films and news stories, and generally attempted to sort out the problem. Passionate argument was not in evidence, nor was there much expression of independent judgments concerning nuclear power. The students did not put forth their own views, tending rather to speak of the viewpoints of others or of developments "out there." It is also interesting to note that several participants exhibited feelings of confusion in the face of a complex social and ethical issue. Reasons for confusion stressed lack of knowledge to make a decision, complexity of the problem, and a surprisingly early awareness of the controversial many-sided nature of the questions posed in the article on nuclear energy. A few students were already searching for biases in what they had read, heard, or seen about nuclear issues—a search that will not go unrewarded in subsequent portions of this examination into values.

Second Day

After reading from the books and magazine set aside for them in the school library, the students returned to their classroom. As soon as they entered, the teacher asked them to look at an exchange of views on nuclear power in a local newspaper, comparing these with their own research. Reproduced below is the nuclear energy article from the newspaper and the answering letters which appeared in subsequent issues. Each author expresses quite a different view of the issues and projects very dissimilar feelings about nuclear development.

WHAT OPPONENTS OF NUCLEAR ENERGY FORGET

By Bertram Wolfe

Except for the creation of mankind, it is hard to identify a technical subject that has received more public attention and debate than energy. Indeed, arguments about energy, and nuclear energy in particular, rival in intensity those about creation. Yet I am not convinced that these public arguments illuminate the central issues.

The difficulty with much of the energy debate is that it focuses on technical issues, such as radiation effects or radioactive waste disposal. The central underlying philosophical questions are obscured.

When considered in isolation, as is frequently the case, people's concerns about offshore oil leaks, the hazards of liquefied natural gas, the dangers of natural-gas pipelines, western coal mining, nuclear waste disposal, environmental effects of shale oil, high-voltage transmission-line effects and the role of solar power—all these lead nowhere. The risks associated with each of these activities can be viewed with fear, but they can be meaningfully discussed only when they are balanced against risks from alternative energy sources or from lack of energy.

One who believes that the future welfare of society is dependent on new domestic energy supplies will see large advantages to the development of nuclear power, offshore oil resources and western coal, even at some risk and inconvenience. Those who believe that society suffers because it already uses too much energy will not accept even minimal risk or inconvenience in order to supply more energy.

Many of the major "no-nukes" organizations, for example, also oppose coal development, shale-oil development, LNG facilities, additional hydroelectric facilities and offshore oil development. In the past, they opposed exploitation of the present Alaskan oil fields; today they oppose exploration for new Alaskan oil.

There is no argument about the desirability of developing solar resources. Almost everyone, including myself and my company, General Electric, advocates solar development. But, as anyone can verify by getting an estimate from a local solar contractor, even the simplest solar technology, solar heating, is not yet here for the masses. As for other sources of energy, windmills are still losing their blades in high winds, and it is not clear whether large-scale biomass conversion is practical, or even a net energy producer.

The argument on solar goes much deeper. If you look closely, you will find that those who advocate immediate conversion to a solar-energy economy, coupled with the abandonment of currently available energy sources, are in fact proposing to change American society without explicitly indicating their intent.

It is not possible to characterize en masse the various no-nukes groups, but there appear to be three major recurring themes in their energy discussions.

The first is a general distrust of a society with abundant energy supplies. We find Stanford biology professor Paul Ehrlich, an anti-nuclear environmental spokesman, stating: "In fact, giving society cheap abundant energy at this point would be the equivalent of giving an idiot child a machine gun." Amory Lovins of Friends of the Earth puts it this way: "If you ask me, it'd be a little short of disastrous for us to discover a source of clean, cheap, abundant energy because of what we would do with it. We ought to be looking for energy sources that are adequate for our needs, but that won't give us the excesses of concentrated energy with which we could do mischief to the earth or to each other."

A second theme is that society should be forced to alter and reorient itself to minimize energy use. Higher energy prices through resource severance taxes, onerous financial penalties to those deemed to use too much energy, the requirements that more expensive but more energy-efficient appliances be utilized, the elimination of free work-place parking, mandatory indoor summer and winter temperature limits, the control of household appliances from remote switching stations, a change by part of the population to night time living activities through imposed time-of-day utility rates and the expanded use of manual labor are some of the vehicles proposed to help achieve this goal.

A third theme is a general dissatisfaction with the present social and economic structure of society and the suggestion that energy should be used as a means of societal change not directly connected with energy.

Environmentalist Barry Commoner proposes to move away from capitalism; Ralph Nader advocates a consumer-controlled economy; the Friends of the Earth argue for a steady-state economy of a form hardly recognizable from present-day America, and Jane Fonda and Tom Hayden in the California Campaign for Economic Democracy tell us that "the stink in our midst is called 'corporate capitalism'" and that the answer is a new economic system of public planning and public control called "economic democracy."

And with the no nukes, it is not possible to categorize all of the nuclear advocates under one banner. But, philosophically, most nuclear advocates believe that abundant energy is a key element of a productive and stable society.

Although the increasing affluence of the United States has not been without its problems, the pro-energy advocates claim that accompanying this affluence has been beneficial societal effects. Discrimination against Jews, Asians and other minorities has greatly diminished. Blacks and women have started to emerge from economic serfdom.

Nuclear advocates believe that to accomplish such goals as further improving the living conditions of the disadvantaged and cleaning up the cities, additional energy supplies will be required.

Fundamentally, pro-energy groups argue that, as world petroleum supplies diminish, the expanded use of nuclear energy and other energy sources will help prevent forced changes in our society and will provide a means for worldwide improvement in living conditions. They note that, with increasing affluence and accompanying energy consumption, birth rates voluntarily decline. Pro-energy groups argue tha there is little hope of improving the lot of humanity without the energy supplies central to improved standards of living, and thus believe it is appropriate that some risk and inconvenience be accepted to obtain these supplies.

All of this is not intended to suggest that the energy dilemma is devoid of significant technical, economic and environmental issues. It is misleading, for example, to gloss over difficulties in the areas of nuclear wastes, nuclear proliferation, reactor safety analysis and reactor economics on the basis that nuclear power is needed, whatever its failings. But public discussions of such difficulties can also be misleading when they start from the philosophical presumsption—as do Ehrlich and Lovins—that nuclear power would still be unacceptable even if all its technical, social and economic problems were solved.

One must differentiate between the identification of a technical difficulty and the suggested conclusion that may result more from philosophical desires than from technical considerations. For example, the permanent disposal of high-level nuclear waste can by law only be handled by the federal government. Does it follow that because the government has not yet built a nuclear-waste repository, nuclear waste is unmanageable and that nuclear power should be abandoned? Or does it follow instead that the government program should be strengthened, and impediments removed, so as to speed up the construction of a waste repository?

If nuclear power is abandoned in favor of coal, for example, will the wastes from coal present a lesser problem? And, if it is concluded that coal is not satisfacory, or that coal cannot make up the deficit from the abandonment of nuclear power, will it be easier to deal with lack of energy than with nuclear wastes? As with most problems in life, one must deal with alternatives, and balance the risks and benefits of each.

The alternative to our imperfect energy sources is not a perfect source; there is none available. If we continue to place impediments in the way of development of available energy sources, the alternative we will have chosen is a changed society, limited by energy-supply constraints.

OPPOSING NUCLEAR ENERGY

The article "What Opponents of Nuclear Energy Forget" [Viewpoints, Feb. 15] by Bertram Wolfe, vice president and general manager of the nuclear fuel and services division of the General Electric Co., was indicative of an alarming shift in the tactics of the nuclear industries spokesmen.

In the past, the industry tried to deny that problems with radiation leaks, fuel disposal and cost effectiveness existed. Now that the facts are known and the "technical issues" weigh against their case, the nuclear industry is trying to defend itself with philosophy.

What Wolfe says is that the economic status quo depends on an ever-increasing energy supply and that any attempt to curb skyrocketing consumption is an attack on the American system. In my view, General Electric does not represent the American system and I am not willing to accept a contaminated planet in order to preserve it.

Wolfe credits the progress of minorities—specifically blacks, Asians, Jews and women—to America's expanding energy-intensive economy. It is an utterly absurd attempt to recruit the disadvantaged and formerly disadvantaged into the ranks of those who have held them back so long. It has been those of us committed to changing society who have brought about, through political action, the improved status of minorities in America. GE executives did not compose a high percentage of those involved in the civil rights movement.

Furthermore, Wolfe's attempt to characterize antinuclear groups as part of a radical fringe, instead of people genuinely concerned with their safety and the future of our planet, is extremely dishonest and self-serving.

Douglass C. McCrae
Baldwin

* * *

Regarding Robert Slomovitz' letter praising nuclear energy [Feb. 14]: He says that "nuclear energy" has been proved safe and efficient." The truth is, a way to dispose of nuclear waste safely hasn't yet been developed. Plutonium-239, one of the many dangerous by-products of nuclear reactors, may be the most toxic substance known to man. Its half-life is 24,400 years. What can be done with a substance like that? Bury it so rainfall will wash it into our underground water supply? Put it in metal drums and drop it in the ocean? How long could those drums stand up to the ocean's corrosive salt water—100 years, 200 years? What then?

If nuclear power is so safe, then why did American insurance companies provide only limited liability insurance coverage from the beginning? This is why we have the Price-Anderson Act, renewed by Congress every 10 years since 1957, which lays the bulk of the liability for a nuclear accident on the "government" (the taxpayers).

How can Slomovitz say Three Mile Island was a "media event blown out of proportion by the no-nukes crowd whose ultimate aim is the destruction of our economic and political systems"? First of all, Three Mile Island was not a media event. It was a near meltdown of a nuclear reactor. The wedding of Prince Charles and Lady Diana was a media event. Second of all, because I want this world safe for my children and future generations, it doesn't mean that my aim is "the destruction of our political and economic systems,"

There are plenty of alternatives to nuclear energy. Wind and solar power have both been proved effective. Brazil runs its automobiles on methyl alcohol. Methyl alcohol can be easily produced from garbage, plant matter and many other sources; in addition, it burns cleaner than gasoline. The only reason nuclear energy is still being used is because the government and big business have invested too much to turn back now. I think nuclear energy is like a pact with the devil. You might enjoy it now, but you'll pay for it later.

Bill Frey
East Northport

TEACHER.   Now that you've had a chance to get more information, perhaps you could tell me what the nuclear energy problem is all about?

FRED.   The more I read, the worse this thing gets. One side of me says, "Our scientists have this all under control," but then the other side says, "Wait a minute, we better check this out carefully!"

SUE.   I think all the scientific mumbo-jumbo is what gets me, what the scientist calls technical questions.

RICHARD.   But let's get to the point! What worries people most about nuclear energy is the danger of radiation.

TEACHER.   Why?

RICHARD.   All of the stuff I read made it very clear that radiation is a powerful force and fission a process that has to be carefully controlled. They fear an explosion!

SARAH.   But the books I looked at don't seem to say that explosions are really likely. The reactors are not bombs and can't really explode.

TIM.   Now wait, wait, wait! The book I read was really worried about the future because some forms of radiation last a long time. There are dangers now and in the future and anyway we have our own senses about things. What about Three Mile Island?

JOH.   Well, no one was really hurt!

TOM.   But they could be! That's it, they could be! The question is really whether we want to chance it for the power we receive, the power we maybe don't need!

CHRIS.   My father works at the Shoreham plant and he says there are problems everywhere, just like the news article stated. You could electrocute yourself in your own bathroom. A nuclear power plant is probably safer because everyone knows there are dangers and they give it extra care.

MELISSA.   I don't believe that! You have a stake in it because your father works there.

TEACHER.   Whoa! No personal comments. Make your point.

MELISSA.   I mean people want these power plants because they have jobs there. Lots of money has been poured into developing nuclear power. First, we had only destructive uses but now we're trying to sell it as a peaceful thing. I think that's great, but it still doesn't mean you're not playing with a very dangerous source of energy.

BOB.   I think we are getting into philosophy. It's not all technical.

	What means more to us, the risk and the power, or the future costs and the safety from harm.
TEACHER.	Explain that, please.
BOB.	You know, it's all a trade-off. If we don't develop nuclear energy as a power source, then we may get caught short later or have to depend on outside sources we don't like for energy. Or we can try to control the problems created by nuclear energy, and have a great source of energy for the future. It's not clear which will cost more in the future, nuclear or other, but we need controls. Is that it?
TEACHER.	What do you think? You have to decide and you seem to be doing fine so far!
PAT.	But it's still a mess. That news article by the scientist sounds so-o-o careful and considerate, but the people who answered him are not convinced anyway? Why? Who can we believe?
NED.	Yeah, what are the facts?
TEACHER.	What do you think? Are there really facts in this case? Or is it all opinion?
NED.	I say it's all opinion!
JIM.	No, no, there are facts, but it depends a lot on how they are interpreted. The book I read gave a history of nuclear theory and practice and there's a lot to know about it, but a lot we don't know too!
TEACHER.	What do we know? Really know?
JEFF.	For one thing, nuclear radiation *is* dangerous, and it's dangers are worse, or at least scarier than those from our usual sources, oil, coal, gas, and water power. And certainly scarier than wind or solar energy which haven't really been given a good try yet.
SARAH.	I guess we'd all agree on that.
JOHN.	Sure, it's dangerous, but isn't the issue how much more it is a problem than the others? Is the risk worth it? From my reading, I would say that accidents are possible but not likely, especially since so many people are so worried.
KEN.	This is really the power people and pro-industry group versus the environmentalists. I think that's who is represented by the scientists and the letter writers. The environmentalists want a lot of assurance about safety and prevention of pollution.
TEACHER.	What do you think is the better view?
KEN.	Environmentalists.

TEACHER.   Why?

KEN.   Because so far we only have our one world to use and if we pollute it too terribly, all of us will be miserable, even with all our great power.

JOHN.   I think that's *too* sympathetic to the nature freaks. People all over wreck their environments in a lot of ways, garbage, chemicals, poisons, weapons, and, we can clean it up if we want to. I think that will be true of nuclear power problems too. They'll fix the leaks and contain the wastes.

CHRIS.   I agree, we have to move forward, not backward, and this is one way to go.

TOM.   I don't think a lot of us here want to throw our science away, but we have a right to caring and to ask that care be taken— extreme care. Radiation is like a poison and, once loose, can cause tremendous damage.

MIKE.   So there we have it—care of the environment versus cheap and easily available power. Where do we stand? How can we decide?

TEACHER.   Yes, how and where. You really summed it up, Mike, and I'd like to know where you and everyone else here stand.

TIM.   We need to know more, much more. More opinions, experts, more info!

(*Bell rings.*)

FLORA.   I'm still not sure who or what to believe on this problem. It makes my head hurt. . . .

(*Laughter*)

TEACHER.   Well, let's compromise. We'll do more research for our next round, but we can't go on forever. New items will turn up, new problems. So let me ask you to take a stand at our next meeting even if you are not satisfied with your facts or your understanding of all points in the nuclear energy question. OK?

The second day of discussion produced much greater interest in the debate, and many more sharply focussed expressions of opinion. While several participants were still reluctant to be drawn in too deeply or to express their own views in support of, or in opposition to, nuclear power, a large number worked to clarify and understand both the data and social issues involved in the total problem. It should also be noted that students developed ideas at greater length than on the first day of discussion, probably as a result of greater knowledge and self-confidence in dealing with a complex issue. They were more comfortable dealing with controversy and some members of the class spoke directly with their peers in an exchange of views and ideas that signal greater depth and heightened self-confidence.

The teacher supported inquiry by offering evidence of both sides to the argument and by challenging students to give reasons for their interpretations. Encouragement was offered to those bold enough to venture an opinion of their own, however tentative or unsure. As observed in the response pattern, student participation was fairly well distributed in the class, and responses tend to grow in length as ideas developed and grounding was sought to support interpretations.

The discussion as a whole grew less and less exploratory in nature, and more analytical as many students attempted to fit data with viewpoints in the controversy in order to arrive at a decision about what to do or which position to favor. Examination of values in the sense of understanding, analyzing, and adopting a defensible position in a controversy takes time and, in this case, grows slowly from an acquaintance with the data and contrasting philosophies surrounding the problem. Very little in the way of snap judgments were exhibited by the students and the teacher remained neutral on the issues, preferring to probe for student meaning and interpretation as the exchange of ideas expanded and sharpened. Since there were positions expressed toward the conclusion of the second day, the instructor asked that each student prepare a position for the next phase of the inquiry.

Third Day

Given two days worth of discussion and free reading time outside of class, students came to class better informed on the issues and the background to the nuclear energy development question. The teacher asked each student to make a judgment and be ready to defend it against other views. After concluding the roll call and completing a few administrative matters, the group jumped right into the problem.

TEACHER. So then, today is our day for a decision, one way or the other on nuclear energy!

MARGE. I'm not sure I can give an opinion of what I've read so far. The scientific writing gets me very confused, even though most of what I've seen so far seems to say that nuclear power can be handled. But how am I supposed to decide?

TEACHER. Can't you give me an opinion anyway? *Your* opinion. How would you personally vote if you could on a nuclear power moratorium, a stop to all new development?

MARG. I just don't know.

JOHN.   We're all entitled to an opinion, but in this case it's really rough to know what to do. We need advice.

SARAH.   But if you listen to the advice, then you'll have to just take someone on faith or still make up your own mind anyway.

MIKE.   I've made mine up! I think we need all power sources, and nothing so bad has happened that we should stop *all* development. I think we have to be careful, just as you do with anything dangerous, but that doesn't mean no nuclear research at all or no power at all.

PAT.   Hey now, your decision sounds too easy for me. Nuclear power is much worse than the other types because of the radiation possibility and because any damage or leakage would last a *long* time.

MELISSA. Yes, it seems OK to say the risks are low, but what if *you* are caught up in the accident? What if it's your town that has been poisoned? What if. . . .

JEFF,
MIKE.   No, no. I think. . . .

JOHN,
OTHERS.   No . . . Yes . . . Quiet.

TEACHER. Jeff.

JEFF.   This is much too dramatic! Let's get off the big worry. Let's be reasonable. There are lots of dangers. Mining is dangerous and lousy from what I've read and heard. Oil drilling can kill you. I remember reading about a sea platform that went under. People have to try anyway to overcome the odds.

FLORA.   Odds! Odds! We're talking about lives and babies and living things maybe being contaminated. I don't think anyone should take chances if there isn't any need for it. Do we really need the nuclear power? I don't think so. I'm not convinced that it is so terribly needed. I might not want to see those places already built torn down, but no more, I say.

SUE.   The oil prices have been going down. Articles I read say there is enough coal for hundreds of years, but it is polluting, usually, of the air.

CHRIS.   Nuclear power is clean, if there are no mistakes or leaks.

MELISSA. If, if!

SUE.   Yes, if is a big word . . . too big and I'm not convinced either by the scientists. They can make anything sound good. If science is exact, then why are some of the scientists, like Conmoner and Ehrlich against nuclear power. The facts, if they are facts, should convince them, too. I think nuclear

	power is too new for anyone to say that they really know what will happen.
BOB.	We still must come to a decision.
KEN.	Excuse me, but I think that decision should be one against all nuclear development because of the problems surrounding its use. What about the limited insurance mentioned by the letters written? Three-Mile-Island was no joke, a meltdown is not a joke and boy, is it expensive.

(*Laughter*)

BOB.	Yes, and I. . . .
CHRIS.	That's just not fair! We need power, jobs, machinery, science. We'd still be in the Dark Ages without science.
BOB.	But maybe this is a Frankenstein!
SUE.	Let's not get crazy . . . Frankenstein and all. What are the facts? Let's stick to the facts!
BOB.	Yes.
TEACHER.	Why don't you review the facts?
BOB.	The facts are heavy. There are a lot of them, but I think it's fair to say that there are dangers of radiation, leakage, pollution, melt down, and maybe, maybe an explosion. But, there are also advantages including power for our electrical appliances, power we can control and count on (hopefully), and the possibility that experience and new research will show us how to clean up the nuclear power process, fission, so many of the problems will be avoided.
NED.	I read that fusion may replace fission in the future and that it is not dangerous at all!
SARAH.	But why are so many worried? I see more to worry over. I don't trust government. My parents don't have much good to say about government lately, so how can we know if safety standards have really been met, if the nuclear stations are really not polluting, if wastes are properly stored? How can we be sure? I'm not in favor of anything that knowingly can harm human life.
TEACHER.	Why?
SARAH.	Because I think life is sacred.
TOM.	What about the miners then?
SARAH.	I guess I'd like to see that stopped if we could. I think coal mining is awful, disease producing, and all.
SUE.	I agree, that's really the point of all this. Why take on new problems when we have enough of the old ones?
JIM.	Yes, Sue and Sarah, but why do people take terrible jobs

and risk their lives looking for gold, oil, copper, coal, and so forth. Because people want and need these things and are willing to pay with money and life and sweat.

NED.   I read, for example, that there seems to be no problem getting people to work in nuclear power stations, no more than any other kind of energy job. It's probably no more dangerous, maybe less since they're sure it's harmful if mistakes are made.

TOM.   And mistakes of some sort will always be made, but I think people have to go on anyway, otherwise all progress will come to an end.

PAT.   You make it sound like we have only two choices, nuclear power or nothing, but that's not so. The material I read mentions maybe a dozen or more power sources, some of which have barely been tapped so far. It's just that we have already put a lot into nuclear, what with the bomb and all. Why not put as much into solar? I know it isn't workable yet! But nuclear doesn't seem so workable either!

MIKE.   So where are we then. A draw?

SUE.   That's it, a draw on facts and on views.

FRED.   Well, I feel a little better anyway because I know a lot more than before and still need to know more, and some science, too.

TOM.   Me, too, I agree with you! And I know that right now I wouldn't go completely with either side. We can't really tear apart what has already been built in nuclear power and we shouldn't. We need it, even if it can cause problems. So far it seems most can at least be patched up. But we should be very careful too, as though handling poison. Slow and careful, I say, but forward.

FRED.   Yes, slow and careful, so I don't think we should quit.

TEACHER.   What about the moratorium on development, on new plants?

FRED.   Slow, but sure, I think. Keep going but take great care. Invite in the public to see the places and the papers to report on them.

FLORA.   But slow can be too fast. Maybe very slow is best with no new development until we have more and better research on how to prevent meltdown, get rid of radioactive wastes, and make sure there are *no* disasters!

MIKE.   More? No disasters can't be guaranteed by anyone. Everything new has to be given a chance and to learn from experience.

MELISSA.   But what if the experience is fatal?

TOM.   Here we go again!

MARGE.   I think this is one of the most complicated problems we've ever discussed in this class.

TEACHER.   Why do you think so?

MARGE.   Because there is so much to it.

TEACHER.   Explain.

MARGE.   There are really two, maybe four areas for argument. One is over the science behind nuclear energy, you know, how atomic energy was discovered and put to use, why radiation occurs, and the pros and cons of fission power. Then there's the whole moral side to the argument, like how much risk is involved; whether it's worth it; how much need there is and whether it is worth meeting. So you see, I think this really *is* complicated.

RICHARD.   I don't know about the rest of the class, but I feel very much as Marge does. Maybe a lot of the kids who remained quiet in this discussion did because they were confused by the whole thing.

TOM.   I feel for you, but somewhere along the line each person has to make a decision on this or avoid it.

CHRIS.   Maybe most like to avoid what is unpleasant or a problem or an issue.

RICHARD.   Maybe so.

JIM.   Maybe so, but I think it's a lot braver to make your decision and take your chances. The decision doesn't have to be final, does it? New news always comes up and we can change our minds.

NED.   Yes, we can always change our minds if they're open to information and argument.

MELISSA.   If they're open!

NED.   If they're not, then you might make a big mistake.

MELISSA.   If it's too open, then you might just go whichever way the wind blows.

SUE.   I think we need still more reading and debate on this.

TOM.   A debate sounds like fun.

TEACHER.   How does everyone feel about a debate and more study? Why not organize pro and con teams for a debate? That would give all of us a chance to sharpen our views, collect more information, and maybe make a more intelligent decision. Let's continue this.

While many students did not take a position or expressed confusion with respect to adopting a view of their own, many did give voice to strong arguments for or against the development of nuclear energy as a large-scale power source. Positions varied widely, ranging from nearly total abandonment of development to pushing for continued research and expansion of nuclear power stations. These views echoed and reflected the opinions, philosophies, and materials students had absorbed in and out of the classroom, but were often expressed in a way which indicated an identification with a position rather than simply its recounting. Several students engaged in sharp and heated argument, which helped others to clarify their own ideas and feelings as they moved, toward a decision. Many student arguments were quite lengthy, taking the form almost of a soliloquy or debate abstract. Efforts were made to organize and support a stand or to justify why continued indecision or fence-sitting was a choice.

The teacher pressed for decisiveness, but did not force anyone to decide in favor or against nuclear development, particularly if they had reasons for avoiding a firm commitment. After all, it seemed clear to everyone in this classroom that value problems in general, and this case in particular, are far from simple and should be open to the challenge of new ideas and evidence. However, the point was also made that most issues demand some sort of decision—a vote, for example—and that moral and civic responsibility calls for a choice if at all possible. Thus, both abstention and decisions were invited by the teacher in this phase of the inquiring, but with requests for grounding in evidence or logical argument. Students were encouraged to defend or explain their feelings and ideas, and, in fact, most did just that while very few expressed snap judgments, Comments were thoughtful and often insightful rather than brief and exploratory. Sharp disagreements erupted often showing that students were much more familiar with each other, the issue, and the process of carrying on a discussion of a controversy which is value-laden.

Even three class sessions, however, did not settle the debate nor resolve everyone's confusion. Indeed, at a number of points in the discussion, students expressed a desire for more information, especially of an objective nature, if possible. Awareness of bias and distortion in data and in presentations of views was clearly exhibited throughout the third session in a way that was more deeply felt and more carefully thought out than on previous days.

Two additional class sessions were devoted to the nuclear energy issue, with most of the effort going into a formal debate, in teams, for or against nuclear development in the future. Debate teams presented the opposing sides, cross-examined evidence and arguments, and concluded with a summation of the problem. Finally, a vote was held in class on the issue and on the persuasiveness of each debating team's presentations. The vote was fourteen against new development, eight for continued technological advancement in this field, seven abstentions, and three who expressed a view of total antipathy toward any nuclear development including a dismantling of what has already been built.

Students felt pleasure in the debate and nearly all expressed greater self-confidence in dealing with this particular issue, as well as handling controversy in general. Many felt that their respect had grown for classmates even where views differed. Some argued that most important of all for them was the realization that nearly all information, especially on problems which involve a value component, must be critically analyzed for bias, distortion, or underlying philosophy. As one student put it after the debate, "Watch out. Everyone seems to have some sort of ax to grind!"

No consensus or complete resolution was reached by students or demanded by the teacher, (although the teacher strongly encouraged decision making as a spark to thinking) and none is probably possible on an issue of this nature in which both data and viewpoint are open to argument and discussion. This openness, with its complexity, mystery and drama, are precisely the elements that make a controversy so frustrating and yet so exciting to students of any age.

INTERGROUP RELATIONS IN BRAZIL: AN ISSUE OF DISCUSSION IN A BIOLOGY CLASS

Excerpts from an article in *Ebony* magazine which described racial intermarriage in Brazil were presented to a group of sophomores. This group was studying biology in a summer session at a high school in Chicago's South side. This discussion, an isolated experience for this class, was used as a "break" from ordinary classroom activity. The students were a mixed group of widely varied abilities, but the majority could be called "average." The instructor wished to determine in this study how his students would apply some of the biology they had learned to a complex social issue. This episode could be taken as an example of the integration of biology and social studies.

The article reproduced here describes Brazilian racial attitudes, but it seems to imply that whenever two or more different races live together in the same country the amalgamation of the races will be beneficial to all concerned.

DOES AMALGAMATION WORK IN BRAZIL?[6]
by Ern Bell Thompson

The marriage of Portuguese men to colored women and the marriage of white women to colored men, is Brazil's way of solving a race

[6]Excerpted from *Ebony* magazine, July, 1965, pp. 27–41. Reproduced with permission.

problem before it begins. As the processes of amalgamation advance, the darker elements of the nation's population continue to disappear. With no Negro, there can be no Negro problem. Most Brazilians believe they have no problem now, therefore there can be no racial prejudice or discrimination. . . .

Historically the Portuguese have always mixed with darker races. Themselves infused with the blood of Moors and Berbers, they freely mixed with and married first native Indians, then African slaves in Brazil. Today, Brazil is heralded as a model democracy where a drop of black blood and a drop of red, makes a white man a Brazilian. . . . With so many conflicting opinions and so much racial prejudice in our own country, *Ebony* sent me to Brazil to find out if racial prejudice and discrimination do exist and to see how amalgamation works. I wanted to know why, in a country with almost four times as many (37%) colored people as the USA, where slavery began earlier (1532) and lasted 111 years longer (1888), there are no sit-in demonstrations or little Selmas; why a nation which granted the Negro full civil rights along with abolition passed an anti-discrimination law 13 years before we did; why there are disproportionately more dark people sweeping office floors than sitting behind office desks.

The darker a man is the greater his problems. Poet Gregorio de Mates was conscious of this back in the 17th century when he wrote:

"Brazil is the hell of the Negro,
The purgatory of the white
And the paradise of the mulatto."

The Brazil I saw was neither the Negro haven it is reputed to be, nor is it the Negro's hell of Gregorio's pen, but the Negro still finds more social acceptance there than in any other 'white' country. They say that wealth and education can "make a black man white," and marriage to a white women further enhances his social status. But with two out of three poor Brazilians illiterate, and the masses of the black people poor, 'white black' men remain relatively scarce. Social mobility being faster at the low end of the color spectrum, a black man of means and education can move into the pardo (mixed) group without difficulty. A few become upper class 'whites' but elite, never. They may marry white women of the same level or lower, but they seldom marry 'up.'

When a colored man passes over into white society, he does so openly, for in Brazil the Negro . . . has no need to hide. Fashionable ladies and distinguished gentlemen speak matter-of-factly of black forebears and are socially none the worse for the relationship. "We are a mulatto country, the only one in the world," author Jorge Amado told me. "None of us can say we do not have colored blood, that we are 100% white.

. . . I saw no "Negro neighborhoods" in the cities I visited. It is true that the favelas (slums) are largely Negro, but so are the poor. Dark people of means told me they have had no difficulty in renting or buying in the neighborhood of their choice. White people have never demonstrated against a Negro neighbor. . . .

The biggest stumbling block to advancement for all Brazilians, are poverty and inadequate educational facilities. Solve the economic problem, they told me, and the Negro problem disappears.

The median intelligence level of the group may be termed "average"; that is, the majority of the students have IQ ratings that fall into the 90–100 range. The class was composed of "Caucasian" students drawn from many different ethnic groups.

After giving each member of the class a copy of the article to read, the biology instructor assumed a nondirective role throughout the course of the ensuing discussion. The instructor encouraged the students to express freely their own reactions to and feelings about the excerpts they had read. The conversation, which lasted for about an hour, is given on the following pages.

TEACHER.	What are some reactions to that article?
LINDA.	Sounds good, but it won't happen here.
SARAH.	I think it will, but not for about 500 years.
MARGIE.	But look—they still have problems in Brazil—it is stated in the article that there aren't any upper-class intermarriages in that country yet.
JOE.	They might get some someday, though.
CONNIE.	It sounds as though it will happen soon in Brazil. They are already mixing at all the other levels of society.
LINDA.	It's too late for America now—maybe in a few cases it might work.
CHAD.	Why is it too late? Do you think we'll always have prejudice?
LINDA.	I think we will!
BARRY.	I think prejudice and discrimination will have to disappear here eventually.
MARGIE.	But why? That's very optimistic.
BARRY.	Because no one here is 100 per cent of anything. You know that all people are at least a little bit mixed genetically. No discrimination can exist because it would be self-discrimi-

	nation. We would all hate ourselves as well as each other.

JERRY.   The more illiterates you have the easier it is to have inter-marriages.

HANK.   Some places have different morality. The middle and upper classes will have what you say is a lower-class morality. It will change because there'll be more and more Negroes with money and high positions, even more and more Negro millionaires. I think money and advancement will make them more acceptable to the rest of the people.

CINDY.   It won't happen—I can't see it, and if it comes I'm glad I won't be here to see it.

CHAD.   I think there will be a great deal of intermarriages. It has happened before to religious and nationality groups. Next it will be the race barrier. But not *all* differences will fade away. There will probably always be *some* differences.

HANK.   College education, if you must look around, makes it easier for different races to mix and accept one another. We won't see it, but maybe in three or four hundred years we'll all intermarry freely and not think anything of it.

FRANK.   Race problems may disappear, but you'll always have class differences. They won't disappear. They will tell in inter-racial marriages. The article on Brazil points out that, free as they are, Negroes there still don't marry into the highest circle.

PENNY.   Maybe the colored people won't want to marry with us.

BARRY.   That's the way you think now because you *feel* the difference between you and the colored people. It means something to you. That's why people tell you that it is bad to intermarry, but they never really explain why you shouldn't or why it's bad. They just feel it. If everything changed overnight and it became acceptable to intermarry racially, I bet you'd change too.

FRANK.   Did you ever notice that mixed couples usually live in Negro or changing neighborhoods?

BARRY.   That's because they are considered outcasts by the white people, but if standards changed there'd be no trouble and they could live anywhere.

CONNIE.   In Africa whites aren't accepted.

CHAD.   How do you know that?

CONNIE.   I read it.

CHAD.   Where?

CONNIE.   Well, I don't remember, but I know it was about the Congo.

CHAD.   Well, maybe there whites are hated and killed and not accepted, but I'm sure that in other places whites are accepted, for instance, Nigeria, or Kenya. Maybe it's just certain whites who are disliked. Anyway, what does that prove? That Negroes can be prejudiced too?

CONNIE. Well, all I'm trying to say I guess is that all the trouble isn't just one-sided.

BARRY. Are mulattoes accepted or are they outcasts? I don't think there are too many of them.

JERRY. Who said mulattoes aren't very numerous? At least 75 per cent of all Negroes in America are mulattoes. Just look around the next time you meet some of them.

FRANK. Whites here identify the class of mulattoes and the class of Negroes, but then they seem to lump both groups together as Negroes when they feel like discriminating against them. The economic situation makes things doubly confusing.

CHAD. Some Negroes are so mulatto that they are actually white.

SARAH Huh? That sounds almost like a joke.

FRANK. It is a kind of nasty joke. That's because race doesn't really mean anything and the majority of American Negroes are already mixed racially.

HANK. Society uses the convenience of skin color today to separate people. Soon it'll be something else.

PENNY. Society always wants a difference between the top and the bottom. It doesn't matter what it is—skin pigment, money— it will always be the same.

ROBERT. People will talk but they won't do anything about it when it comes down to a choice. It's the children who change things if they want to.

CINDY. Since there are already so many marriages like that, the children won't matter.

ROBERT. There aren't *that* many, and the point is that they are not accepted as a natural part of life.

SHIRLEY. Maybe they shouldn't be accepted. Even if you intermarry, you don't know what the child is going to come out looking like. You won't be able to avoid his color. Whites won't like the child and the Negroes probably won't like you.

SARAH. They won't be accepted because of attitudes like yours. Mulattoes are Negroes because people want them to be Negro. If everyone, or almost everyone, didn't want them to be thought of in that way, they wouldn't be. They'd just be themselves.

HANK. I wonder about the Negro point of view. Do Negroes view mulattoes as whites?

JOE.	But won't Negroes eventually be eliminated entirely if intermarriage keeps up for a long time?
JERRY.	You'll remain with whites and mulattoes and the nigg— oops!!—Negroes will be eliminated.
BARRY.	If there are already so many mulattoes, then there are already very few true Negroes left. They are vanishing rapidly.
FRANK.	Where do you draw the line between white and mulatto and Negro anyway? It's unrealistic to do so because there are so many shades in existence already that it is hard to make clear distinctions.
MARGIE.	A white-Negro couple would not be able to adopt a child because they're not allowed to make things tough for a child from having parents of two different races.
FRANK.	I read that only 5 per cent of colored babies are adopted, while 80 per cent of white babies are adopted.
HANK.	That may be true because there are many more well-to-do whites than well-to-do Negroes.
PENNY.	Negroes have more illegitimate births than whites, so more Negro babies are up for adoption than white, and more are in orphanages.
CONNIE.	Coloreds seem more uncivilized than whites—why is that?
CHAD.	Coloreds live in the slums because they have had no education or they have no money. Many of them are bad off and are disturbed and come from bad homes. There are just as many smart Negroes as there are white kids who are smart, but the Negroes have had much less of a chance to show their talents. Poor slum whites are in the same spot as the poor Negroes. Mostly, they've all had less of a chance than we have had.
CONNIE.	What about Africa—why don't they get ahead? Maybe because it's hot and hard to work there. Maybe they were too isolated. Hey! I'm answering my own question. I guess it's because of the environment.
HAROLD.	Crime is high in Negro neighborhoods.
FRANK.	Maybe it's high in all poor neighborhoods, white or colored. Ever consider that problem?
JERRY.	I'll bet if there were 50 per cent colored in this class, we wouldn't be having this conversation.
SARAH.	We did it in our English class. There were more than enough Negroes in it.
CINDY.	In C.V.S. (Chicago Vocational High School) the whites and Negroes were each arguing for their own side so the teacher

had to stop it. I think lots of colored are bad because they have nothing to gain or lose anyway.

CHAD.   That's exactly it. They feel downtrodden and degraded, with no stake in our society. That's the problem.

MARGIE.   Of course, isn't it still wrong to take the law into your own hands and become violent rather than try to help yourself in a constructive way—in all the constructive ways possible? I think so.

HANK.   In the past hundred years Negroes in Africa have gone from cannibalism to sending their sons to Oxford. In America after the Emancipation Proclamation, the Negroes had nowhere to go—they couldn't get represented or protected legally in the South so they stayed just about the same for a hundred years.

FRANK.   The Italians had it bad and so did the Poles, and the Negroes will too. It will take a long time, and it will be hard. But they will do it, if everyone is willing to let them have the chance, and if they continue to organize and march for what they want.

HANK.   They didn't have the training or organization before. Now that they are getting it, they will advance. You can see it already.

JERRY.   Other people should march and complain, too. Many, many people are poor and don't have it so good. Of course, the Negroes have it worse because they are colored—easier to look down upon after being identified.

SARAH.   People still feel prejudiced toward colored people.

BARRY.   But there really isn't anything to that biologically. It's all social.

CINDY.   Even so, it's still a tremendous problem, and it seems to me that some of them act much too much like savages.

HAROLD.   But the problem is why they act that way, isn't it?

CHAD.   If the problem is social—and I think it is, then social advancement for these persons called Negro or mulatto will bring about more acceptance and finally more intermixture and integration. It would be pretty much like Brazil then, except that it might take longer for much intermarriage to take place here than it will in Brazil.

HANK.   We might even become exactly like Brazil in this respect. The last part of our society to give in to social pressures in favor of intermarriages would be our "high society," too.

CINDY.   It makes me feel funny to think of it in that way.

FRANK.   That's the way it is now, but I don't think it will be that way in the future. When things loosen up in the future, we will probably all be better off for it and get along with each other much more easily.

BARRY.   Really, does intermarriage matter? I think we really need to see a change in everyone's attitude toward Negroes. If we think of them as real people, we won't be upset over intermarriage. It won't really matter who marries whom; any combination will be OK. Negroes or whites won't have to disappear or mix because they will all be getting along with each other just being the way they are.

The students' comments appear to have passed through five discernible, though cumulative, stages which may be characterized by the following general summary:

STAGE 1. A brief introductory comparison of racial amalgamation in Brazil and the United States.

STAGE 2. A discussion of racial attitudes and their probable correlation with socio-economic class.

STAGE 3. Testing the validity of race concepts through an investigation of the relationship between mulattoes, whites, and blacks.

STAGE 4. A capsule analysis of the current status, characteristics, and problems of the American black.

STAGE 5. A summation, bringing together and further developing previously mentioned economic, social, historical, and attitudinal factors that bear upon the problem of racial amalgamation.

It should be observed that the magazine article, though describing Brazil, sparked a discussion of race relations in the United States. Immediate comparisons were made between the two countries; for example, Linda's remark, "It's too late for America now—maybe in a few cases it might work." The article itself is almost ignored throughout the discussion that followed, as are the specific problems of Brazil. The class tends to discuss racial intermarriage in general or with reference to the United States, and it avoids cross-cultural comparisons of racial attitudes. It appears that race relations in the United States are very crucial and vivid for the participants, particularly the relationship between whites and blacks.

The students may be placed into two different position groups according to the type of statements they usually made. The members of one group, including Cindy, Linda, Jerry, Connie, Shirley, and Penny, tend to make statements that are personal, emotional, and demonstrative of hostility toward blacks; for example, Cindy's remark, "It won't happen—I can't see it, and if it comes I'm glad I won't be here to see it," or Connie's idea that, "Coloreds seem more un-civilized than white. . . ." The members of the other group, consisting of Hank, Barry, Frank, Sarah, and Chad, usually argue in favor of attitudinal change to improve race relations, stating their ideas in the form of explanations or analyses of the causes of current poor condi-tions; for instance, Chad's discourse, "Coloreds live in the slums be-cause they have had no education or they have no money. . . . There are just as many smart Negroes as there are white kids . . . but Negroes have had less of a chance. . . . Poor slum whites are in the same spot as the poor Negroes." From the course of the discussion, it appears that the members of the group in favor of attitudinal changes conducive to racial harmony are attempting to change their fellow classmates' out-looks concerning this problem. Chad, Frank, Hank, and Barry seem to reinforce one another's arguments but direct their comments to the class rather than to each other. A conscious effort to modify the racial beliefs of the class, particularly about blacks, is evident throughout the conversation.

Sensitivity to and awareness of the controversial and possibly emo-tive nature of the topic was demonstrated when several of the partici-pants discussed the issue. It was pointed out that such a discussion involves deep personal feelings and beliefs. The composition of the group was brought up by Jerry's comment, 'I'll bet if there were 50 per cent colored in this class, we wouldn't be having this conversation," which was immediately countered by Sarah's remark, "We did it in our English class. There were more than enough Negroes in it." It may be inferred from this that some of the discussants were frightened or upset by the trend of the conversation, whereas others wished to bring the whole problem into the open, even to the extent of having participation of black students in class.

Even though the students demonstrated an awareness of the deli-cacy of the topic, or perhaps because of this, their comments were rather restrained, without sharp disagreements or emotional expres-sions of opinion. Based upon their predilections and limited knowl-edge, the discussants were attempting to reason with one another concerning the attitudes one should hold toward other races. While some clashes of opinion did occur, these were rapidly smoothed over by greatly expanded analyses of the American blacks' specific pres-ent-day difficulties and of the race concept, in general.

Three factors strongly influenced the pattern and outcome of this discussion: the impromptu offering of the article about Brazilian inter-marriage, the class's interest in the current racial problems of Ameri-can society, and the setting of the conversation in a biology class. The participants did not seek outside data to support their claims and assertions. They used whatever they could remember in the way of relevant statistical or historical information, but tended to rely primarily upon their own experiences and observations. This was probably caused by the impromptu quality of the episode, and by the digressive nature of the topic in relation to the regular work of the class.

The focal point of class interest was upon the race problems presently encountered by American society. This interest relegated the "springboard" article to the background of the discussion. The majority of the speakers stated their views in terms of social consequence rather than personal behavior; that is their comments reflected a general concern for what is best for our society as a whole rather than a specific concern for each person's individual psychological prejudices. Considering what is best for society, it was argued that certain attitudes should or should not be adopted or changed. Personal commitments for or against racial intermarriage were generally absent from the discussion; however, there were many remarks made in favor of attitudinal change covering all race relations. In other words, the arguments presented in favor of improved race relations in the United States were based upon the assumption that, if the society generally adopts an open-minded and equilitarian attitude toward blacks, then the problem of racial intermarriage will be of little importance since amalgamation will not be necessary to bring about a race harmony that would already exist, and such mixing as might occur would not engender any social stigma.

Several members of the class displayed a sophisticated understanding of the complexities of the race concept in their discussion of the relationship between white, mulatto, and black. This understanding was probably fostered by the students' accumulated experience as members of a biology class. There appeared to be a prompt acceptance of the idea that "no one here is 100 per cent of anything." Since the biological components of the race problem were quickly agreed upon and eliminated from conversation, the discussants move strongly emphasized the social and psychological factors relevant to the subject of discourse. The social problems created by disharmonious black-white relations thus became the center of the discussion, and, indirectly, the psychological attitudes of each individual were called into question. Though the restrained style of discussion continued throughout the episode, personal values were definitely being challenged whenever attitudes were investigated or analyzed. Rather than couching comments directly in personal terms which might cause emotional outbursts or hurt feelings, the participants chose to use an impersonal vocabulary with which to carry on their discourse.

Beginning with an article on racial intermarriage in Brazil, the participants developed this into a discussion concerning black-white relations in the United States. In a sense, the group set a new task for itself by emphasizing American racial attitudes rather than studying Brazilian race problems. The students evolved a conversation relevant to their own needs out of the original printed material. They also developed their own mode of discussion, suitably adapted to the topic, restrained and rather impersonal, yet indirectly betraying deep individual values. The members of the class were thus almost completely responsible for structuring the situation, setting their own tasks, and managing the discussion by themselves without outside interference or guidance.

SUMMARY

As may have been observed in the discussion pertaining to racial amalgamation, students are sometimes rather reserved about expressing their personal feelings on many subjects. Discussants may also display considerable unwillingness to debate or argue their viewpoint with either peers or teachers. Therefore, in conversations involving the expression of sentiment, values, ethics, beliefs, or personal judgments, and in discussions conducive to conflict, controversy, and argument, the teacher must, above all, create a classroom atmosphere that legitimizes the free and orderly exchange of such ideas and views. To do this, it would appear to be useful to allow the process of group interaction—the give-and-take of thoughts among people—to carry inquiry forward. Statements of logic and evidence drawn from material previously studied or immediately available should be encouraged to function as the counterbalance to the flow of personal opinion that occurs when values are being openly discussed and examined. Teacher involvement in such situations must be limited if a frank and honest exchange of views is to take place. The teacher may, however, safely and effectively play the role of participant within a group engaged in the expression, analysis, and formation of ethical positions. The instructor may continue to umpire the discussion of a controversial issue; however, with respect to the expression of personal value judgments, all participants ought to be on equal terms. Strong interference in a classroom argument by someone in a position of authority will result in the repression of statements of personal feeling and in the imposition of an outside value judgment upon the discussions. This does not, however, imply that the teacher should remain "value-less" throughout a debate or argument. The teacher may indeed offer views, as well as play devil's advocate from time to

time, but not until the students' positions have been clearly formulated and some evidence bearing on the issue has been analyzed by
the class as a whole. When offering an opinion, reasons and grounds
should accompany each position taken.

When examining moral and ethical principles or matters of deep
personal concern, the arbitrary imposition of ideas must be eliminated, or the values expressed will represent or reflect those of the
authority rather than what might be arrived at through open argument
and debate among all the participants in a group, including the instructor. Although the teacher ought to challenge ideas or ask questions, the students themselves should search for new evidence with
which to defend their various viewpoints. The motivation and desire
to defend and support a particular hypothesis or philosophy should
develop from personal interest and the process of group interaction.
This process would likely entail many challenges, questions, or even
taunts from various participants directed at their peers, who would
then be required to support their contention with evidence or logical
argument. The teacher by use of reward and redirection should support student argument and diminish personal invective as much as is
practical.

Controversy sparks the interest of most people, adults or students,
and arouses the emotions. For teachers, this has both advantages and
disadvantages. On the one hand, controversial issues and ethical problems are usually inherently fascinating and people are motivated to
involve themselves in debate. Yet on the other hand, many people
fear to express strong views because of lack of knowledge, fear of
conflict, a desire not to hurt another's feelings, or ambivalence toward
the problem itself. Wariness and interest seem to go hand in hand
when issues are discussed. In addition, while problems containing
ethical and judgmental questions can really get a discusion going
there is often more heat than light produced which can lead to personal remarks and opinionizing and eventually dissatisfaction with
the discussion. Therefore, ethical and policy problems, even where
scientifically based, must be handled carefully in the classroom so as
to develop both interpersonal skills and increase understanding of the
data and philosophies upon which views are based.

In each example in this chapter, groups of students demonstrated
considerable excitement in the process of investigating personal beliefs and often developed new positions or reformulated and rede-
fined old ones. While often wary of probing too deeply into value
preferences, students exhibited a strong interest in and commitment
to the positions they had taken on a variety of problems ranging from
politics and race relations to the development of nuclear energy. The

examination of values was enhanced and encouraged by the availability of data to promote and direct thinking, and by a classroom atmosphere in which opinions could be expressed without fear of disapproval. Conformity to specific standards of right and wrong was not required by the teacher; rather students were encouraged—through positive remarks and approval redirection and questioning—to seek, compare, and analyze alternatives with a goal of adopting a position of their own. This process of identification and decision making was at the heart of each example, and forms the basis for responsible discussion of morality and values based on publicly defensible propositions.

CHAPTER FIVE

The Stimulating Classroom

THE PURPOSES AND PROCEDURES OF THIS BOOK

As stated in the opening chapter, our work sought to explore ways in which students of high school age may be stimulated to order their own learning experiences and to engage in serious scholarship with regard to social and natural phenomena. To put it in different words, we tried (a) to identify and describe the kinds of classroom strategies and techniques that would motivate the participants to locate problems in their environment and to seek solutions, and (b) to provide an appropriate intellectual climate which would enable the participants to perform logical operations necessary to the conduct of inquiry.

The initial springboard for the study was given to us by Jerome Bruner in his *The Process of Education* and in subsequent publications dealing with intuitive or creative thinking and with the method of discovery. Brunner contended that the soundest way to optimize human capability for learning is to create the classroom conditions under which children or adolescents, through the process of discovery and through their own efforts, locate the fundamental ideas of a discipline (the "guts" of a discipline) and understand how these ideas are related to each other. For Bruner, each scholarly subject or discipline (e.g., physics, geography, biology) has a structure and the task of the learner is to figure out that structure independently.

In part, then, our efforts were directed to putting Bruner's ideas to the test. In order to do so, we experimented with some thirty classes in two different public high schools in Chicago over a period of three years. Subsequent testing took place in schools in other parts of the country. Several teachers provided direct assistance by preparing materials relevant to inquiry and discovery, by testing these materials and the ideas to which they applied in their own classes, and by providing tapes and subjective evaluations of classroom discussion.

In the process of trying out Bruner's ideas we were able to accomplish several additional tasks, which, in turn, enlarged our perspective on curriculum, teaching, and learning. For example, we have been able to collect a number of recorded classroom transactions which described different learning environments. This repertory of actual classroom discourse in our possession generated additional hypotheses and allowed us to make comparisons of different ability groups and school subjects. We have incorporated some of the transcriptions of these tape-recorded sessions in this book, hoping that this approach to curriculum research will prompt other investigators to gather illustrations of what actually does happen in the classroom rather than what ought to happen. In other words, our work with tapes and direct observations of student interaction pointed to the need for description rather than prescription of the teaching act. Although prescriptions might follow from descriptions, the two tasks of the curriculum maker and researcher need to be separated.

As we proceeded with our work, we began to observe that changes in one of the aspects of the educative process caused a chain reaction and brought about changes in other areas as well. For example, the introduction of "discovery episodes" in the classroom effected a change in the role of the teacher, in the organization and sequence of the curriculum, in the self-image of the student, and in the nature of knowledge itself. In observing the changes taking place, we became conscious of the need to develop a broad framework of teaching and learning within which to examine individual and class behavior. Thus our framework gradually incorporated the affective or values area, an area that Bruner and his associates did not consider, but later authors, such as Lawrence Kohlberg, did. In cases such as these we tried to incorporate in the material ideas from other sources so that gaps in Bruner's theories could be somewhat reduced. Our work has stressed the concepts and generalizations that can be discovered in a field of knowledge as well as the problems of society that confront young people. In dealing with social problems in the classroom, although we recorded the dialogue faithfully, we also realized that the classification and analysis of issue-centered discussion is quite difficult for several reasons. First of all, most curriculum and instruction models in education have either neglected the value dimensions altogether or they dealt with values in an intellectually "dishonest" way. For example, schools have traditionally dealt only with "safe" value dilemmas. Thus there were no readily available models to give us useful clues and guidelines. Second, controversial issues and value judgments pose peculiar problems in that they are ineluctably entailed in the character and the personality of the individual; each person's views of social policy, of justice, and of the good life are different and these differences certainly reflect each personality and cultural background. Third, we do now know enough about values and their root bases to make defensible generalizations about ways in which they are and should be negotiated or adjudicated in a group situation. The perennial question of determining how one value judgment is better than another is still with us and poses serious problems to those who are committed to the rational examination of social issues and cleavages. For these main reasons, we have used our work on the examination of values in an exploratory way—to generate hypotheses and new methods of analysis which will be employed in future work.

As we have mentioned repeatedly, our observations and findings should be considered tentative and subject to further experimentation and testing. We do not offer any foolproof instructional formulas, nor do we guarantee that, given the initial creative encounter, classroom discussion will take the same course as that taken in our illustrations. Many other situational factors may very well adversely influence the motivation of the students and the tempo and direction of the dialogue. Bearing these qualifications in mind, the reader should keep our findings and observations in the same flexible frame in which they are presented.

THE EMERGING ROLE OF THE TEACHERS

Although it is difficult to generalize and predict the posture that classroom teachers who value and emphasize creative learning and inquiry will take, it is possible to identify some teacher tasks that are vital to inquiry and can be abstracted with a degree of confidence. Actually we started out with an "ideal-type" and we made some changes in our conception of the role of the teachers as we went along. The following list summarizes the multifarious roles and tasks that the inquiry-centered teachers performed in our study.

1. *Teachers as Planners.* In this role, they carefully plan a sequence of learning activities covering a period of time, usually a semester. Planning involves collection of documents and other objects, and preparation of materials for classroom use. When maps, diagrams, pictures, statistical tables, and objects of art are involved, the teachers use their ingenuity to make accurate reproductions of the material for use in their class. One teacher reported that the preparation of a geography problem consumed between ten and fifteen hours of hard work.

Media are selected always with the idea of fostering self-generated activities and independent thinking.

2. *Teachers as Introducers.* After the material has been prepared, the teachers decide on a propitious time to introduce it to their class. The material, be it a short poem or a physics problem, becomes what we called the "discovery episode" and generally serves as a springboard to initiate inquiry. To be effective the material needs to have an element of surprise or mystery. Several examples of such materials have been supplied in this volume. These materials, mostly free or inexpensive, are always within the grasp of teachers and can be used much like the manner illustrated in the previous pages.

3. *Teachers as Questioners and Inquiry Sustainers.* The initial confrontation with the problematic material or discovery episode and the perplexity caused by it is sustained and reinforced by the teachers. Their general attitude is that of fellow-inquirers who have no final and absolute answers to give out. They make it clear in the very beginning that statements or claims to knowledge are accepted in the open forum of ideas and that no person including the teacher or the author of the textbook is immune from questioning and detailed probing. Regardless of the age, sex, personality, and ethnic and cultural background of the discussant, their assertions are considered in the light of the grounds that support them. No knowledge-claim is ever better than the data on which it stands. Teachers seek to get everyone involved in the discussion by constantly raising questions and personalizing the topic at hand. Teachers try to minimize to the extent possible their own talk in class. They believe that students not teachers should monopolize discussion. As a matter of strategy, the teachers usually redirect questions addressed to them. If the students demand of them information about the cultural origin of an object or the location of the object in a geographic region, the teachers, however tempted they are to supply the answer, pose the same question to the students adding, perhaps, something like this, "I don't see why you can't provide your own answers." In general, the teachers play the role of the devil's advocate, constantly prodding the students and asking the students to explore, explain, support, and evaluate their ideas. Their posture in class vis-a-vis knowledge and learning is dialectical rather than didactic.

4. *Teachers as Managers.* Although the teachers' main task is to initiate and sustain the process of inquiry, they perform some managerial functions which are necessary for the conduct of an orderly discussion. When there is an issue, they may introduce new ways of looking at the issue or raise additional questions. Furthermore, they execute several routine tasks such as recognizing students, keeping

order, and maintaining a record of attendance. Students are encouraged to be actively involved in the planning and maintenance of the total classroom environment. The idea is to transform the classroom, to the extent possible, into a laboratory where there is genuine concern for finding out, creatively, how things work—in human societies as well as in the physical world.

5. *Teachers as Rewarders.* The teachers involved in our classroom illustrations made a conscious effort to reward students for imaginative and creative work and for participation in the dialogue of inquiry. The notion that legitimizing and rewarding the free exchange and testing of ideas in class leads to higher levels of motivation is borne out by our research. We have produced some evidence here to show that when internal rather than external rewards are applied, there is more participation in discussion, there is more enthusiasm for learning and the exploration of new areas of knowledge, and there is more flexibility and freedom in debating important ideas about people and nature. On the other hand, it should be realized that it is extremely difficult to change the overall student orientation toward learning in one class over a relatively short period of time. It appears that most of the conditions prevailing in our schools operate against creativity, free discussion of issues, and the genuine motivation to learn. The prevailing grading system, the promotion policies, the subject-by-subject division of knowledge, the standardized and college entrance examinations, and the general organization and structure of the school usually put severe restraints on a discovery- or inquiry-centered program. While at the abstract level we find general consensus that student motivation for learning should come from within, in actual practice we do just the opposite and we superimpose external rewards and punishments on the student. As rewarders, teachers avoid criticizing students' ideas; rather they accept each student's contribution as legitimate, meriting consideration and review by all class members. In the end students learn that creative participation in dealing with ideas provides its own reward.

6. *Teachers as Value Investigators.* With regard to the treatment of values, the teachers generally subscribe to the position of defensible partiality, i.e., they place emphasis on the process of inquiry, the public defensibility of all value judgments, and the democratic classroom climate. They operate under the major assumption that values are not taught but critically examined. Again, as with analytical problems, the teachers probe and raise quesions regarding problems of an ethical or value nature. They may take a grounded position on a particular issue, but they refrain from doing so in the introductory phases of discussion. Actually our case studies in this area are too limited to

allow us to give a clearer image of the teacher when they introduce controversial issues which are, by definition, emotionally charged. Our work in the future will focus on the role of the teacher in a class debating crucial problems of society and on the way participants in such debate support their judgments and directives for action. As value investigators teachers encourage students to express their own feelings and explain these feelings to others. They also try to have students examine the personal and social bases for diversity in attitudes, values, and policies. Students are prompted to explore the implication of holding certain value positions. Grounded value positions prompt students to act judiciously as needed.

7. *Teachers as Formative Evaluators.* The teachers who stress creativity use evaluation methods which depart significantly from the traditional. First of all, evaluation measures are used not for grading students but for ascertaining whether or not teachers have attained their instructional objectives. Second, the results of evaluation are used not for punishing students but for sharing with them strengths and areas in which both teachers and students need to improve.

In sum, teachers who perform the roles above serve as models in the classroom. They demonstrate behaviors that reflect their interest, curiosity, critical thinking, active involvement, creativity, empathy, fairness, and willingness to probe the evidence. It should be remembered that it does not take long for students to understand if teachers don't practice what they preach!

STUDENTS AS INVESTIGATORS

Our observations about student roles and performance in the creative inquiry classroom are based on transcribed dialogues, some of which have been reproduced in this book, and on informal chats and exchanges with participating students and their teachers. Generally speaking, our work indicates that when students are encouraged to engage in the conduct of inquiry on their own, they are quite capable of doing so. However, let us be more specific and take each observation separately.

1. Some educators have questioned the practice of providing an open climate of discussion (i.e., a situation in which the teacher does not give directions or "right" answers). These educators aver that under such conditions students become apprehensive and feel threatened—they do not know how to behave autonomously. While it is true that students become frustrated and insecure when they are prompted

to provide their own answers to problems and issues, for the majority of them this initial frustration and insecurity does not go beyond the opening phases of inquiry. As indicated elsewhere, given the opportunity, the students begin to value open discussion of ideas and issues and they develop or further sharpen certain human capabilities that remained dormant before. Some frustration and disappointments will exist not only in school but in society. The approach and its underlying philosophy that we have explored do not offer panaceas for all problems of learning, but do suggest that the persons who are capable of solving social and intellectual problems on their own will be better prepared to solve their own emotional problems if and when they arise.

2. What we consider to be the most important outcome of trying out the various inquiry methods we have described in this study is a change in student attitude toward knowledge. Our tapes and observations indicate that as the students participate in inquiry they begin to view knowledge as tentative rather than absolute and they consider all knowledge-claims as being subject to continuous revision and confirmation. This attitude toward knowledge is reinforced by the teacher who encourages the students to examine critically statements made by authors of printed materials or claims made by the students themselves. As members of the class engage in providing their own answers to difficult questions about people and their environment, they internalize the complexity of verifying knowledge and of determining what is involved in the process.

3. There is much to be said about the opportunity to learn how to learn, or what Bruner calls the heuristics of learning. In our work we found out that most high school students are capable of organizing and systematizing their classroom experiences for learning. For example, given the initial stimulus or springboard, students were able to perform such logical tasks as identifying and delimiting a problem, suggesting intellectual strategies in dealing with the problem, and developing explanatory hypotheses which guided them in their search for reliable and relevant data. In other words, we found our students possessing all of the skills that are needed in exploring a scientific problem or an aesthetic experience; given the creative encounter the students proceeded to make logical deductions of concepts and of operations and procedures. Our observation and analysis of transcripts generally confirm our initial hypotheses that (a) students of high school age are quite logical and they can perform complicated intellectual tasks (often better than their teachers) and (b) not only are students capable of discovering or rediscovering concepts about human and natural phenomena but they are capable of devising new

strategies of investigation which are quite ingenious and which lead to further knowledge and exploration. More than anything else, students need to have understanding teachers who provide a permissive climate in the classroom, conducive to exploration and discovery.

4. Within limits, we were able to vary the student population in terms of intelligence as measured by IQ tests and observe the outcomes. Our observations confirm the initial hypothesis that methods of inquiry and discovery can be used profitably not only with high IQ students but with students whose IQ is below average. The low IQ students (i.e., students whose IQ was in the 80 to 90 range) were capable of performing such intellectual tasks as defining the problem, hypothesizing, drawing logical inferences, gathering relevant data, and generalizing. In addition to being able to perform high level mental processes, the low IQ students were as motivated as the high IQ students who were in the 110–130 range. As we look at our data, we may infer that (a) high intelligence as measured by IQ tests is not a precondition to logical performance and the quest for knowledge and (b) our intellectual exercises can motivate equally students who are below and above average intelligence.

In view of our findings, we would join Getzels and Jackson in saying that creativity and intelligence are not synonymous. As shown in the case of the Sumerian statuette, the low IQ students were extremely creative and original in their initial response to the problem. As they hypothesized about the origin of the object, they drew from their personal experiences and immediate environment. They thought of the problem in terms of their daily life. The high IQ students, on the other hand, dealt with the problem in a more abstract and sophisticated manner. Generally speaking, they were more restrained in providing hypotheses regarding the object. Much more than the low IQ group, they were constantly considering the grounds upon which their proposition rested and the consequences to which they led. They were afraid to take too much of a chance in supplying an answer, whereas this was not the case with the low IQ group. In sum, the low IQ group was more creative in its response but it did not persist in following through its hunches. The high IQ group had fewer and less original explanations but it was more persistent in systematically following its explanations through to a logical conclusion, even if it had to conclude that a particular proposition led to a dead end road. Perhaps the reluctance of the high IQ student to engage indiscriminately in conjecture and speculation is in part due to the highly competitive climate in the class—students are trying to show who is smarter. Mistakes or faux pas are often the subject of ridicule. This high competitive spirit is not prevalent in the low IQ class. Here, however, the students seek from the teacher more positive reinforcement in their quest to solve the problem. Much more research needs to be done in differentiating groups in their ability to proceed logically to solve a problem.

5. We have already mentioned the high level of class motivation that was prompted by the discovery episode or by the material used as springboard. We have observed that students seem to be more interested in learning when (a) they are confronted with a puzzle, a problem, or a game in the way of an object, a map, a written passage, or a tape, (b) the teacher makes them understand that the game is not a game of chance, that there are explanations or imterpretations which are more or less plausible and that there are no "right" or "wrong" answers in every question or every procedure, (c) the exchange of ideas in a dialectical form does not take place between teacher and student but between student and student, (d) the teacher casually asks for the defensibility of all claims, and (e) the class is not plagued by the "ground-covering" idea but enjoys a thorough examination of selected human or environmental events or phenomena. Also, it is important to note that while a springboard provides the initial student interest and excitement, this interest is sustained by the attempt to explore and find general principles which explain the world and humans' place in it. Student exploration soon escapes the particular instance and moves into the examination of a general class of phenomena; the exploratory principles and hypotheses apply to class of events at all times and places rather than to a unique event in a unique culture.

The more quantitative measure of motivation was furnished by the tapes and the count of the number of students participating in classroom discussion. In general terms, we found that under the new conditions student participation doubled. Participation was spontaneous and uncoerced. Also, testimony given by librarians and other teachers supported the notion that given the stimulus, student motivation and quest for knowledge will go beyond the confines of the classroom. Students looked into library material, newspapers, and sometimes into sources which are usually thought to be outside the reach of secondary school students—museums, scholarly conferences and seminars, curators, and other experts; they questioned and probed unmercifully other teachers and librarians, trying to find additional clues or new strategies to approach their problem.

6. Our study indicated that it is realistic to expect students to investigate rationally controversial social issues. In our case studies which involved value-permeated topics such as "city bossism" and "good Samaritanism" as well as other controversial subjects such as

nuclear energy policy and "interracial marriages in Brazil" the students examined the issues, and they acted very responsibly in pointing out the magnitude of each problem. If nothing else, our transcribed dialogues indicate that controversy can be a legitimate subject of discussion and that it can be studied dispassionately.

In more concrete terms, we found that controversial issues elicited a great deal of discussion and the introduction of a variety of views. In the consideration of different judgments and value positions, the students drew from their own personal experience and from data that were available at school. As they presented their ideas which were continuously challenged by their peers, they began to see that usually judgments cannot be accepted on faith, that judgments stand or fall on the nature of the grounds which support them and on the implications to which they tend. From our records, it is quite clear that students did see the need and the justification for public communicability and defensibility of values; that is, the need to clarify normative ambiguities in our language and to express value judgments and their justification publicly rather than keep these judgments personal and private. Although solutions to some serious social problems were not forthcoming, it was the experience of critically debating such problems that was important rather than the solutions themselves. In this work we cannot really say much about the causes for certain students' beliefs nor how socioeconomic factors influence students to make certain judgments. All we can do here is to report the discussion and begin to devise means for its analysis.

Our analysis and assessment of student outcomes are based on the transcripts of the dialogue, our own classroom observations, and the testimony of other teachers and of librarians and school administrators. We did not use any standardized instruments largely because they do not measure exactly what we wanted them to measure—student ability to engage in inquiry and to order their own learning experiences and their level of motivation while they are confronted with perplexing situations. From our experience, we can say that, by and large, the students participating in the study showed great enthusiasm with the inquiry methods that were applied. We are including here three statements of student assessment of their learning experience.

STEPHEN. This semester in U.S. history, I have progressed further than I ever thought possible. In the mere time of twenty weeks, I have begun to become a questioner and not just a believer. This is the greatest asset of this style of teaching. In the future, all my reading will be done with thoughtful, constructive questioning. I will determine for myself what is true and what is not.

Our teacher distributes among the students a series of statements spoken by the people of the period you are studying—the actual accounts, no historian or textbook's opinions at all. By analyzing each document, you will get a cross-section of the views on a certain topic. This is the point. By getting several people who disagree on a certain issue and not knowing which one is correct (if any) you must logically decide by yourself what the truth or the closest to the truth is. Too many of the other teachers have been indoctrinated in the idea that memory work that you throw back at the teacher on a test is soon forgotten (unless reviewed, or built on). In other words, you learn to forget. This is true with most memory work, especially cramming before a test. Learn the rules and learn how to apply them. Once you understand this concept you can apply it to almost anything you study or endeavor.

ANONYMOUS. I think the teaching methods employed in this course were very effective. They have stimulated most of the students to think rather than to memorize.

The students have acquired a knowledge much more valuable than a list of facts. They have learned the way to think logically and apply this thinking to the practical world. As well, they have learned to judge the "truth" or at least to judge which are the most logical answers to a given question.

KARYN. This course is successful in its primary aims, mainly because there is no pressure put on the students. They can read and discuss the material presented in class, and really learn, with the aid of the opinions of the other students. They can easily and intelligently express their own opinions or views which will be accepted and pondered upon by the class, in turn. They do not have to worry about which facts are most important, or when the next test is, or what the homework assignment is—at the time allotted for class work. During this time, they can just be freely concerned with the documents being discussed.

The test of grouping for facts out of basically nothing, as the encounter with the statue, is difficult for an individual, but is very successful and interesting when a group works at it. This experiment makes the student aware of what difficulties are encountered by people who probe into the past. It is interesting to note the different guesses that can be made and then disregarded for one reason or another.

All in all, I feel that this is a very "relaxing" course. Not relaxing in view of laziness, but relaxing in that the mind has a chance to loosen its muscles and widen its scope for a further, different type of learning.

THE NATURE OF KNOWLEDGE

As mentioned earlier, teaching through discovery or induction is closely associated with the idea of the structure of knowledge. It is generally assumed that each learned discipline has a distinct structure—a folklore, a body of concepts, and peculiar methods of investigation—which the learners are expected to figure out on their own. Hence, the emphasis in recent years on teaching and learning through discovery to find the structure of history, or of math, or whatever the subject that a person is studying.

It is not the intention here to unearth deep-seated epistemological controversies regarding the organization, syntax, and substantive structure of knowledge. To answer questions such as "What is knowledge?" "What is a discipline?" or "Can autonomous disciplines be integrated or synthesized in a school program without losing their intellectual rigor and integrity?" is certainly beyond the scope of the volume. On the other hand, some relevant observations based on our work may indeed give us some useful clues.

1. Whatever the logical bases for distinguishing between disciplines and types of knowledge, the psychological bases for distinction do not emerge in a clear-cut way; at least they are not readily observable. On the contrary, we have some evidence to suggest that what the students see in a given problem is for the most part a function of their interest and creativity. Generally speaking, students do not label concepts and methods as historical or anthropological; they just proceed to finish the task at hand without any concern for associating it with any of the traditional disciplines. This was evident in the exercises which asked students to locate cities on a map or the exercises that

asked for the cultural origin of an artifact, document, or demographic trends. In some cases, the students employed their own concepts and tools of analysis as well as ideas and investigative techniques that may be attributed to several of the social and behavioral sciences, to history and to other fields of study. In other words, the persons who engaged in the solution of a problem were able to synthesize ideas and procedures from their readings, from their experiences, and from their school background and to apply them to the particular situation. When there are gaps in knowledge or in experience, the students devise their own strategies to reach their goal. Thus, while the subject matter, be it biology or English, may set some boundaries and may somewhat color the perception of the student, ideas about natural and social phenomena are, to a large degree, human transformations of what the person considers important and real. To suggest that organized knowledge exists out there and humans just acquire it (they either have it or do not have it) denies the importance of individuals in forming their own claims about reality, making their own judgments about society and nature, and being able to order their own learning experiences. Also, group process and group consensus have something to do with the way we perceive knowledge and truth-claims. This conception of knowledge may also assume that knowledge which is out there is static rather than changeable and emergent.

The following notions are generally supported by our work: (a) It is extremely difficult to attribute a distinct structure to a given field of knowledge, especially in such closely related fields as sociology, political science, anthropology, and history; (b) Although logically we may make a case for unique fields of knowledge, psychologically we are inclined to make a case for synthesis, to emphasize the similarities and complementarities of the disciplines. Although all of our classroom exercises point to the validity of these notions, the value cases provide more direct and explicit grounds for their acceptance. As students got involved in discussions of graft, bad Samaritanism, racial intermarriage, and foreign policy, they employed knowledge and analytical methods from social science, psychology, art, history, law, jurisprudence, philosophy, and science, and they capitalized on their own experiences and views of society and the prevailing ethical code. Had the class remained within the traditional confines of subject matter specialization and differentiation, it would never have explored the foregoing value-permeated and controversial topics.

2. The second major concern in this area, which follows from our discussion, is curriculum development. Our experience generally indicates that the method of inquiry, as we have defined it and in all of its dimensions, implies a curriculum that is organized around key

concepts and problems rather than discrete items of information put together on the basis of vague criteria. A program built around such concepts as "culture," "power," "legitimacy," "modernization," and "authors" may provide the foci around which ideas, generalizations, and data may be grouped. The same type of organization may be conceived in mathematics, physical science, art, or English. The main goal for grouping ideas and data together would be to illustrate and emphasize the need to employ analytical concepts and procedures in understanding the forces of society and nature. The curriculum notwithstanding, the instructor still needs to escape from what Joseph Schwab calls a "rhetoric of conclusions," a state of mind that accepts knowledge in the books as given and in turn seeks to impart it uncritically to the younger generations.

The curriculum that emerges from our research is concept-centered and student-centered. It is concept-centered to the extent that broad ideas or recurring problems of mankind form the basic principle in selecting the relevant from irrelevant data and materials. It is student-centered to the extent that students, not teachers, are given the opportunity to select ideas and problems and examine them carefully. As we have seen, curriculum topics may be drawn from the body of concepts of any established discipline (e.g., physics, mathematics, social studies) or from life experiences. A dynamic curriculum (i.e., a curriculum that is in a continuous process of emerging and that provides the basis to maximize inquiry learning) focuses on human and natural issues and problems and on reliable concepts and generalizations. These concepts are developed and refined by the inquiring students themselves.

IMPLICATIONS

We have stressed over and over in this book that our work is exploratory and that it merely attempts to open up new areas for careful study. We generally hoped that our observations and tentative findings would motivate more researchers and teachers to work together in testing and reformulating some of our ideas on teaching and learning. We would like to emphasize that it is important for the educator and the classroom teacher to form a team and conduct their work together. The educators may have the necessary theoretical constructs, experimental designs, and a special vocabulary for studying a particular education phenomenon, but they need the help of the classroom practitioner to understand the intricate relationships that exist among students and to see the human context in which teaching and learning take place. The teachers, however well they know their subject, their school, and their students, need the help of the educator in order to design appropriate methods to try our ideas experimentally. The moral of all this is that the partnership of teacher and educator is both necessary and fruitful in the conduct of inquiry into classroom inquiry.

The more specific implications of our work are as follows:

1. There is a need to develop systematically a category system to analyze classroom discourse. This category system may include logical operations (e.g., hypothesizing, inferring, and generalizing) or psychological elements (e.g., degree of motivation, image of self, participation in discussion, and relationship with teacher). Furthermore, the category system may apply to discourse which is issue-centered and value-centered (e.g., degree of bias, ability to present conflicting points of view, and defending a value position on logical grounds). Some of this work has already begun, but more needs to be done. See for example the "Michigan Social Issues Cognitive Category System" which was developed for the purpose of analyzing classroom discussion which centers on social issues and controversy; in B. G. Massialas, N. F. Sprague, J. B. Hurst, *Social Issues Through Inquiry: Coping in an Age of Crises*, Englewood Cliffs, N.J.: Prentice-Hall, 1975.

2. Although we may or may not develop a highly elaborate category system to analyze classroom interaction, we need more and more reproductions of classroom discussions. Actually, at this stage of educational research, we know very little about what teachers and students do in classroom situations. There is a great deal in the educational literature about what teachers "ought" to do but very little of what they are actually doing. We need to have many descriptive accounts, through observations, tapes, and videotapes, of classroom transactions in order to talk meaningfully about teaching and learning. The armchair theorizing, in many cases indistinguishable from wishful thinking, will have to give way to empirical research.

3. Some of the ideas and materials that have been explored here need to be replicated in other classes, in a variety of geographic locations, and with teachers representing different backgrounds and personalities. In this connection, we would recommend that the characteristics of the experimental classes, the locations, and the teachers be fully described and carefully recorded—perhaps more elaborately than we have done in this work.

4. It would be desirable to conduct longitudinal studies of students who have been exposed to the process of inquiry and discovery. The main questions here would be to see how their personality is affected

by a nondirective, inquiry-centered approach, and what transfer value this approach may have if applied consistently over a period of years. Also, we need to explore further student motivation in terms of the Hawthorne effect, to see whether the novelty of the approach accounts for the difference in the degree of interest and participation.

5. There is a need to get more data (e.g., personality, intelligence, socioeconomic background, and ethnicity) on students who participate in studies of inquiry. We need to establish the relationships between personal and social variables of the subjects and intellectual performance and motivation to learn.

6. Future works should focus more directly on the structure of knowledge in the different fields. The work should try to explore the similarities as well as the differenes between the learned disciplines as they apply to inquiry patterns in the classroom. For example, the work may move in the direction of carefully differentiating between concepts and methods of investigation in English and in history, to name but two school subjects which have several overlapping elements. We need to be able to see both the logical and the psychological elements in curriculum and instruction and to see ways in which the two can be harmonized.

7. In connection with item 6, we need to experiment with different types of curriculum organization and sequence. We may, for example, develop a completely nongraded school in which students have several options in pursuing their ideas without a rigid system of grades and rewards and punishments. In the 60s and 70s, the nongraded school was tried with varying degrees of success. It is currently somewhat out of favor as an educational panacea.

We may, in a school such as this, regroup subjects or experiences on bases other than the traditional subject-matter differentiation.

8. From the practical standpoint we need to have more springboards and discovery episodes distributed to teachers throughout the United States so that they may, in turn, try out some of these ideas on inquiry and discovery in their own classrooms. These materials should be worked out carefully and should include the range of discovery items—experiences from life, documents, artifacts, music, paintings, archaeological findings, newspaper articles, and so on. We need to have a larger repertory of discovery episodes beyond the ones we mentioned in our opening chapter which can be used fruitfully in the classroom.

In closing, we hope that this report of our experiences will motivate teachers to try out and apply some of our intellectual experiences. Let this study be a challenge to the profession to refute or validate the ideas contained in it.

Glossary of Terms

Affective objectives. Educational goals that emphasize emotions, attitudes, appreciations, or values.

Analytical skills. Skills and abilities such as formulating hypotheses, defining terms, testing the logical consequences of propositions, and generalizing. Analytic thinking normally involves step-by-step deductive and inductive procedures and operations.

Cognitive objectives. Educational goals that involve the undertaking of an intellectual task—from simple recognition of material to application and synthesis of highly complex ideas.

Concept. A category of attributes that clearly discriminates a cluster of factors from that of another. At times "concept" has been used interchangeably with "idea"; for example, the idea or concept of power or the concept of feudalism.

Controversial social issue. Identifiable components of larger social problems in which alternatives are proposed for critical decision. Initially the issue must elicit some kind of emotional reaction from the discussant.

Discovery episode. Material prepared and introduced by the teacher which serves as the springboard or creative encounter in the discovery process.

Discovery process. As used in this study, the process of drawing plausible inferences from given data. The process of discovery operates as a strong motivational device and leads to the identification of concepts and relationships.

Generalization. Invariable associations or relations between two or more events or phenomena that have been tested or validated.

Hypothesis. A propositional statement about relation between variables or events. The hypothesis has a provisional status; when it is tested and confirmed, it becomes a generalization.

Inquiry process. Generally the process of identifying, exploring, and validating alternatives. Involves both deductive and inductive processes as they apply to questions of fact and of value.

Intuitive thinking. The process that involves hunches, conjectures, and "intuitive leaps." Given limited information, the student goes beyond the data to solve a problem. In contrast to analytical thinking, intuitive thinking does not proceed in orderly and sequential steps. In our work we have used "intuitive thinking" interchangeably with "creative thinking."

Normative judgments. Judgments about the merit or worthiness of a policy or action based on certain evaluative norms. We engage in normative judgment when we assess an action or a process as being good, bad, desirable, or undesirable. We use interchangeably with "value judgments."

Problem solving. The process of exploring and testing alternative hypotheses to solve an indeterminate situation or problem.

Reflective thinking. Used interchangeably with the process of inquiry.

Value judgments. Used interchangeably with normative judgments; the evaluation of actions or policies as good or bad on the basis of certain norms.

A Selected Bibliography

Bruner, Jerome S., *The Process of Education*. Cambridge, Mass.: University Press, 1960. Reports the meeting at Woods Hole in 1959 which prompted thinking and research in such areas as the structure of knowledge, intuitive and analytic thinking, learning through discovery, and the spiral curriculum.

Bruner, Jerome S., *Toward a Theory of Instruction*. Cambridge, Mass.: Harvard University Press, 1966. Makes a good case for the need of developing instructional theory as distinguishable from psychological theory or theory of learning.

Carin, Arthur, and Robert B. Sund. *Creative Questioning and Sensitive Listening Techniques*. Columbus Ohio: Charles Merrill & Co., 1982. An excellent nuts-and-bolts source of questions and lessons for all subjects aimed at teachers of kindergarten through ninth grade.

Dewey, John, *How We Think*. Boston: D. C. Heath and Company, 1933. A classic statement on the complete act of thought.

Elam, Stanley, ed., *Education and the Structure of Knowledge*, Chicago: Rand McNally & Company, 1964. Reports a conference that explores the organization, and the substantive and syntactical structure of each of the learned disciplines. Relates in a direct way to Bruner's concept of structure discussed in this book.

Engel, S. Morris, *With Good Reason*. New York: St. Martin's Press, 1982. A witty and provocative introduction to the kinds of explanations and arguments people employ in both formal and informal situations.

Getzels, Jacob W., and Philip W. Jackson, *Creativity and Intelligence*. New York: John Wiley and Sons, 1962. Reports a study that attempted to see if there are meaningful ways in which intelligence may be distinguished from creativity. The findings suggest that the highly intelligent students are not necessarily highly creative and vice versa.

Green, Maxine. *Teacher As Stranger*. Belmont, CA.: Wadsworth Publishing Co., 1978. A thought-provoking philosophical inquiry into the role of the teacher in and out of classrooms.

Hullfish, H. Gordon, and Philip G. Smith, *Reflective Thinking: The Method of Education*. New York: Dodd, Mead & Company, 1961. Makes a good case for controlled inquiry to provide the focus in education. Examines the various operations performed in thinking.

Joyce, Bruce, and Marsha Weil, *Models of Teaching, Second Edition*. Englewood Cliffs, N.J.: Prentice-Hall, 1980. Provides some twenty-five models of teaching divided into four general categories: information processing models; personal models; social interaction models; and behavioral models.

Kaplan, Abraham, *The Conduct of Inquiry*. San Francisco: Chandler Publishing Company, 1964. An excellent analysis of the purposes, concepts, and methods of the behavioral and social sciences. Should be required reading of all teachers in training.

Kneller, George F., *The Art and Science of Creativity*. New York: Holt, Rinehart and Winston, 1965. A good and insightful summary and synthesis of theories in the area of creativity.

Larrabee, Harold A., *Reliable Knowledge: Scientific Methods in the Social Studies*. Boston: Houghton Mifflin Company, 1964. A very good analysis of the approaches of the behavioral and social sciences. The earlier edition (1945) includes a chapter on the role of values in the social sciences.

Lipman, Mathew, and Ann M. Sharp (Eds.), *Growing Up With Philosophy*. Philadelphia, Pa.: Temple University Press, 1978. An anthology of essays and analyses by well-known educators and philosophers who share a common interest in how children think and develop.

Massialas, Byron G., and C. Benjamin Cox, *Inquiry in Social Studies*. New York: McGraw-Hill Book Company, 1966. Attempts to show how classroom inquiry relates to problems of society, the school curriculum, textbooks and materials, evaluation instruments, research, and the preparation of the social studies teacher. Several chapters are devoted to the process of inquiry in the cognitive as well as in the affective domains.

Massialas, Byron G., and Joseph B. Hurst, *Social Studies in a New Era: The Elementary School as a Laboratory*. New York: Longman, 1978. Discusses how a school can be used as a laboratory providing for real-life experiences and the role that teachers can perform in the cognitive, affective, and participatory domains.

Massialas, Byron G., Nancy F. Sprague, and Joseph B. Hurst, *Social Issues through Inquiry: Coping in an Age of Crises*. Englewood Cliffs, N.J.: Prentice-Hall, 1975. Provides research data to illustrate different approaches for promoting critical investigation of pressing social issues. Compares three types of teaching: expository, opining, and inquiry teaching. Applies a new system for making systematic observations in the classroom.

Organ, Troy Wilson, *The Art of Critical Thinking*. Boston: Houghton Mifflin Company, 1965. A practical guide for developing and refining critical thinking skills, such as identifying problems, recognizing assumptions, drawing logical inferences, and making and interpreting observations.

Parnes, Sidney J., and Harold F. Harding, eds., *A Source Book for Creative Thinking*. New York: Charles Scribner's Sons, 1962. A very useful guide and source book with interesting problems and exercises for the classroom.

Presno, Vincent, and Carl Presno, *The Value Realms: Activities for Helping Students Develop Values*. New York: Teachers College Press, 1980. Provides specific activities for teachers to encourage examination of values in such realms as economic, technological, esthetic, and legal.

Purpel, David, and Kevin Ryan, eds., *Moral Education . . . It Comes with the Territory*. Berkeley, Calif.: McCutchan, 1976. Deals with instructional issues in moral education; with value clarification; and provides a critique of Kohlberg's stages of moral development.

Schwab, Joseph, *Biology Teacher's Handbook*. New York: John Wiley and Sons, 1963. A handbook which incorporates developments in the biology curriculum, with special emphasis on an inquiry approach. Special exercises for students are offered in the form of "invitations to enquiry."

Schwab, Joseph J., and Paul E. Brandwein, *The Teaching of Science*. Cambridge, Mass.: Harvard University Press, 1962. Contains two thought-provoking lectures: "The Teaching of Science as Enquiry" by Joseph J. Schwab and "Elements in a Strategy for Teaching Science in the Elementary School" by Paul E. Brandwein.

Scriven, Michael, *Reasoning*. New York: McGraw-Hill, 1976. A strong, philosohically-grounded discussion of the art of thinking, with special attention to logical and fallacious reasoning.

Taylor, Calvin W., ed., *Creativity: Progress and Potential* New York: McGraw-Hill Book Company, 1964. Presents papers given at a conference which emphasized training and education for creativity.

Taylor, Calvin W., *Scientific Creativity*. Malabar, Florida: Krieger Publishing Co., Inc., 1975. Stimulates the individual and public interest in the area of scientific creativity, and brings together selected and revised research reports by leading figures in the field of psychology and creativity.

Torrance, E. Paul, *Creativity*. Washington: Department of Classroom Teachers, American Educational Research Association of the National Education Association, 1963. ("What Research Says to the Teacher" Series No. 28). Provides a summary of research on creativity with suggestions for classroom application.

Torrance, E. Paul, *Guiding Creative Talent*. Malabar, Florida: Krieger Publishing Co., Inc., 1976. Gives useful insight in defining, assessing and developing creative talents in creative children, and counselor, teacher and administrator qualifications, and problems in maintaining or repressing creativity, are described.

Torrance, E. Paul, *Rewarding Creative Behavior*. Englewood Cliffs, N.J.: Prentice-Hall, 1965. Reports studies in creativity and suggests ways in which teachers may maximize creative thinking in the classroom.

Vivian, Frederick, *Thinking Philosophically*. New York: Basic Books, 1969. Examines the role of philosophical thinking in the use of language. Discusses difference between knowledge and belief.

Wadsworth, Barry J., *Piaget for the Classroom Teacher*. New York: Longman, 1978. An excellent discussion of the theoretical foundations of Piaget and their direct application to the classroom. Of special interest are the chapters on reading instruction and the learning of mathematics and science concepts.

Zevin, Jack, *Cities: A Discovery Unit for the Middle School*. The Queens College Curriculum Project Series. New York: Trillium Press, 1983. One part of a multidisciplinary program of problem-solving booklets specifically designed to foster student imagination and creative growth in many learning areas.

Index